중학 영작 + 서술형 대비

내공

중학
영작문 2

저자 약력

전지원

미국 오리건 주립대 석사
한국 외국어대학교 외국어연수 평가원 영어 전임강사(현)

〈Grammar's Cool〉(YBM), 〈빠르게 잡는 영문법〉(천재교육),
〈Grammar plus Writing〉(다락원), 〈Grammar plus Writing Start〉(다락원),
〈It's NEAT Speaking Basic / Listening Basic〉(에듀조선) 등 다수의 교재 공저

박혜영

미국 하와이 주립대 석사
한국 외국어대학교 외국어연수 평가원 영어 전임강사(현)

〈Grammar's Cool〉(YBM), 〈빠르게 잡는 영문법〉(천재교육),
〈Grammar plus Writing〉(다락원), 〈Grammar plus Writing Start〉(다락원),
〈It's NEAT Speaking Basic / Listening Basic〉(에듀조선) 등 다수의 교재 공저

지은이 전지원, 박혜영
펴낸이 정규도
펴낸곳 (주)다락원

초판 1쇄 발행 2017년 12월 18일
초판 8쇄 발행 2024년 11월 5일

편집 서정아, 김미경
디자인 박나래
삽화 JUNO
영문 감수 Michael A. Putlack

대락원 경기도 파주시 문발로 211
내용문의 (02)736-2031 내선 503
구입문의 (02)736-2031 내선 250~252
Fax (02)732-2037
출판등록 1977년 9월 16일 제406-2008-000007호

ISBN 978-89-277-0815-5 54740
         978-89-277-0813-1 54740 (set)

http://www.darakwon.co.kr
다락원 홈페이지를 방문하시면 상세한 출판정보와 함께
동영상강좌, MP3자료 등 다양한 어학 정보를 얻으실 수 있습니다.

중학 영작 + 서술형 대비

내공

중학
영작문 2

＊ 전지원, 박혜영

다락원

HOW TO STUDY THIS BOOK

STEP 1 　 LEARN

문법 학습

영작에 필요한 핵심 문법을
알기 쉬운 표와 예문을
통해 학습

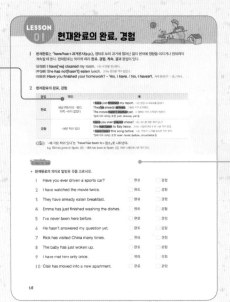

CHECK UP

학습한 문법 사항을 간단한
문제를 통해 바로바로 체크

STEP 2 　 PRACTICE

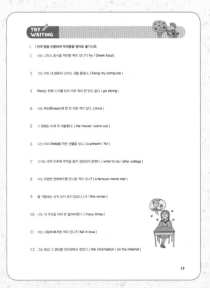

| SENTENCE PRACTICE 1 | ▶ | SENTENCE PRACTICE 2 | ▶ | TRY WRITING |

SENTENCE PRACTICE 1
학습한 문법을 포인트별로 하나씩
문장에 적용해보는 기초 연습

SENTENCE PRACTICE 2
학습한 문법을 포인트별로 다양한
문장에 적용해보는 연습

TRY WRITING
학습한 문법을 이용해 최종적으로
완전한 문장을 써보는 연습

미리 보는 서술형 SCHOOL TEST

학교 시험에 대비할 수 있도록 실제 기출
문제를 응용한 서술형 문제로 단원 마무리

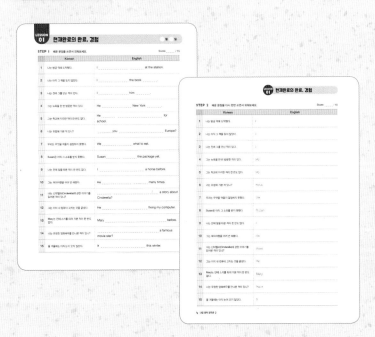

문장 암기 WORKBOOK

각 Lesson의 핵심 문장을 쓰고
읽으면서 암기할 수 있는
Workbook 제공

CONTENTS

UNIT
01

현재완료

현재완료의 완료, 경험

I 현재완료는 「have/has＋과거분사(p.p.)」 형태로 쓰여 과거에 일어난 일이 현재에 영향을 미치거나 현재까지 계속될 때 쓴다. 현재완료는 의미에 따라 **완료, 경험, 계속, 결과** 용법이 있다.

(긍정문) I **have['ve] cleaned** my room. 나는 내 방을 청소했다.
(부정문) She **has not[hasn't] eaten** lunch. 그녀는 점심을 먹지 않았다.
(의문문) **Have** you **finished** your homework? – Yes, I **have**. / No, I **haven't**. 숙제 끝냈니? – 응. / 아니.

2 현재완료의 완료, 경험

용법	의미	예
완료	방금 (막)/이미 ~했다, 아직 ~하지 않았다	I have *just* finished my report. 나는 방금 내 리포트를 끝냈다. They've *already* arrived. 그들은 이미 도착했다. The movie hasn't started *yet*. 그 영화는 아직 시작하지 않았다. *함께 자주 쓰이는 표현: just, already, yet 등
경험	~해본 적이 있다	Have you *ever* played chess? 너는 체스를 해본 적이 있니? She has been to Italy *twice*. 그녀는 이탈리아에 두 번 가본 적이 있다. I have heard this song *before*. 나는 전에 이 노래를 들어본 적이 있다. *함께 자주 쓰이는 표현: ever, never, before, once/twice 등

NOTE '~에 가본 적이 있다'는 「have/has been to＋장소」로 나타낸다.
e.g. Bill *has gone to* Spain. (X) → Bill *has been to* Spain. (O) Bill은 스페인에 가본 적이 있다.

CHECK UP

● 현재완료의 의미로 알맞은 것을 고르시오.

I Have you ever driven a sports car? ☐ 완료 ☐ 경험

2 I have watched the movie twice. ☐ 완료 ☐ 경험

3 They have already eaten breakfast. ☐ 완료 ☐ 경험

4 Emma has just finished washing the dishes. ☐ 완료 ☐ 경험

5 I've never been here before. ☐ 완료 ☐ 경험

6 He hasn't answered my question yet. ☐ 완료 ☐ 경험

7 Rick has visited China many times. ☐ 완료 ☐ 경험

8 The baby has just woken up. ☐ 완료 ☐ 경험

9 I have met him only once. ☐ 완료 ☐ 경험

10 Clair has moved into a new apartment. ☐ 완료 ☐ 경험

box 안의 예문을 참고하여 우리말과 일치하도록 문장을 완성하시오.

WRITING POINT ❶

· The plane **has** just **landed** at the airport. 그 비행기는 / 방금 착륙했다 / 공항에

1 나는 방금 역에 도착했다. I _____ just _____ at the station.

2 그들은 방금 저녁식사를 끝냈다. They _____ just _____ their dinner.

3 그녀는 이제 막 새 직장을 찾았다. She _____ just _____ a new job.

4 나는 이미 그 영화를 봤다. I _____ already _____ the movie.

5 그는 이미 그 셔츠를 샀다. He _____ already _____ the shirt.

6 그들은 이미 잠자리에 들었다. They _____ already _____ to bed.

7 나는 아직 그 책을 읽지 않았다. I _____ _____ the book yet.

8 그는 아직 집에 오지 않았다. He _____ _____ home yet.

9 비는 아직 그치지 않았다. The rain _____ _____ yet.

WRITING POINT ❷

· I **have seen** a koala before. 나는 / 본 적이 있다 / 코알라를 / 전에

1 나는 전에 그를 만난 적이 있다. I _____ _____ him before.

2 나는 전에 그 이름을 들은 적이 있다. I _____ _____ the name before.

3 그는 뉴욕을 한 번 방문한 적이 있다. He _____ _____ New York once.

4 그녀는 그 책을 두 번 읽었다. She _____ _____ the book twice.

5 그들은 월드컵에서 네 번 우승했다. They _____ _____ the World Cup four times.

6 나는 그와 말해본 적이 한 번도 없다. I _____ never _____ to him.

7 그는 학교에 지각한 적이 한 번도 없다. He _____ never _____ late for school.

8 너는 유럽에 가본 적 있니? _____ you ever _____ to Europe?

9 너는 배로 여행해본 적 있니? _____ you ever _____ by ship?

우리말과 일치하도록 빈칸에 알맞은 말을 넣으시오.

• 현재완료의 완료 •

1 그 콘서트는 방금 시작했다. (start)

→ The concert _____ _____ _____.

2 Jack과 Paul은 벌써 나갔다. (go out)

→ Jack and Paul _____ _____ _____ _____.

3 우리는 무엇을 먹을지 결정하지 못했다. (decide)

→ We _____ _____ what to eat.

4 Susan은 아직 그 소포를 받지 못했다. (receive)

→ Susan _____ _____ the package yet.

5 너는 벌써 바이올린 연습을 끝냈니? (finish)

→ _____ _____ _____ _____ practicing the violin?

• 현재완료의 경험 •

6 너는 아프리카에 가본 적이 있니? (ever)

→ _____ _____ _____ _____ to Africa?

7 나는 아버지와 낚시하러 가본 적이 있다. (go fishing)

→ I _____ _____ _____ with my father.

8 나는 전에 말을 타본 적이 한 번도 없다. (never / ride)

→ I _____ _____ _____ a horse before.

9 그는 해외여행을 여러 번 해봤다. (travel abroad)

→ He _____ _____ _____ many times.

10 너는 신데렐라(Cinderella)에 관한 이야기를 읽어본 적이 있니? (ever)

→ _____ _____ _____ _____ a story about Cinderella?

( ) 안의 말을 이용하여 우리말을 영어로 옮기시오.

1 너는 그리스 음식을 먹어본 적이 있니? (try / Greek food)

2 그는 이미 내 컴퓨터 고치는 것을 끝냈다. (fixing my computer)

3 Mary는 전에 스키를 타러 가본 적이 한 번도 없다. (go skiing)

4 나는 부산(Busan)에 한 번 가본 적이 있다. (once)

5 그 영화는 이제 막 개봉했다. (the movie / come out)

6 나는 이미 Stella를 위한 선물을 샀다. (a present / for)

7 그녀는 대학 이후에 무엇을 할지 결정하지 못했다. (what to do / after college)

8 너는 유명한 영화배우를 만나본 적이 있니? (a famous movie star)

9 올 겨울에는 아직 눈이 오지 않았다. (it / this winter)

10 나는 내 우산을 여러 번 잃어버렸다. (many times)

11 너는 사랑에 빠져본 적이 있니? (fall in love)

12 그는 방금 그 정보를 인터넷에서 찾았다. (the information / on the Internet)

LESSON 02 현재완료의 계속, 결과

현재완료의 계속, 결과

용법	의미	예
계속	(계속) ~해왔다	My parents **have lived** in Busan *for 10 years*. 나의 부모님은 10년 동안 부산에 살고 계신다. He **has worked** at a bank *since 2015*. 그는 2015년부터 은행에서 일해오고 있다. *How long* **have** you **played** soccer? 너는 축구를 한 지 얼마나 되었니? *함께 자주 쓰이는 표현: for+기간, since+과거시점, How long ~? 등
결과	~해버렸다 (그래서 지금 ~하다)	Emily **has lost** her car keys. Emily는 그녀의 차 열쇠를 잃어버렸다. (지금도 잃어버린 상태) My friend **has gone** to Japan. 내 친구는 일본에 가버렸다. (가버리고 지금 여기에 없는 상태) *함께 자주 쓰이는 표현: 동사 lose, go, leave 등

NOTE have been to vs. have gone to
have been to는 '~에 가본 적이 있다'란 경험의 의미를, have gone to는 '~에 가버렸다(그래서 지금 여기에 없다)'란 결과의 의미를 나타낸다.

2 현재완료 vs. 단순과거

현재완료는 과거 발생 시점이 중요하지 않으므로 명확한 과거 시점을 나타내는 표현(yesterday, last week, two years ago, in 1999, when 등)과 함께 쓸 수 없다.

I **have eaten** lunch *an hour ago*. (X)
I **ate** lunch *an hour ago*. (O)

CHECK UP

● 현재완료의 의미로 알맞은 것을 고르시오.

1 Bella has lived in that house since 2011. ☐ 계속 ☐ 결과

2 Paul has left for Spain. ☐ 계속 ☐ 결과

3 James has lost his job again. ☐ 계속 ☐ 결과

4 I haven't seen you for a long time. ☐ 계속 ☐ 결과

5 Mike has had his dog since he was young. ☐ 계속 ☐ 결과

6 He and his family have gone to Australia. ☐ 계속 ☐ 결과

7 They have been married for 30 years. ☐ 계속 ☐ 결과

8 How long have you lived in this city? ☐ 계속 ☐ 결과

9 David has gained 7 kilograms. ☐ 계속 ☐ 결과

SENTENCE PRACTICE 1

box 안의 예문을 참고하여 우리말과 일치하도록 문장을 완성하시오.

WRITING POINT ①

· He **has taught** English for 10 years. 그는 / 가르쳐왔다 / 영어를 / 10년 동안

---

1 나는 일주일 동안 아팠다.　　　　　I _____ _____ sick for a week.

2 그는 10년 동안 영어를 공부해왔다.　　He _____ _____ English for 10 years.

3 우리는 오랫동안 여기에 살아왔다.　　We _____ _____ here for a long time.

4 그들은 2014년부터 서로 알아왔다.　　They _____ _____ each other since 2014.

5 그는 월요일부터 이 호텔에 묵었다.　　He _____ _____ at this hotel since Monday.

6 그는 어렸을 때부터 안경을 써왔다.　　He _____ _____ glasses since he was young.

7 너는 피아노를 친 지 얼마나 되었니?　　How long _____ _____ _____ the piano?

8 그는 여기서 일한 지 얼마나 되었니?　　How long _____ _____ _____ here?

9 그녀는 감기에 걸린 지 얼마나 되었니?　How long _____ _____ _____ a cold?

WRITING POINT ②

· I **have lost** my cell phone. 나는 / 잃어버렸다 / 내 휴대전화를

---

1 나는 내 시계를 잃어버렸다.　　　　　I _____ _____ my watch.

2 나는 그의 이름을 잊어버렸다.　　　　I _____ _____ his name.

3 누군가 창문을 깨뜨렸다.　　　　　　Someone _____ _____ the window.

4 그는 살이 많이 쪘다.　　　　　　　He _____ _____ a lot of weight.

5 그녀는 해외로 가버렸다.　　　　　　She _____ _____ abroad.

6 그 기차는 역을 떠났다.　　　　　　The train _____ _____ the station.

7 그 책은 내 인생을 바꿔놓았다.　　　The book _____ _____ my life.

8 그들은 실종된 아이를 찾았다.　　　　They _____ _____ the missing child.

9 봄이 왔다.　　　　　　　　　　　Spring _____ _____ .

SENTENCE PRACTICE 2

우리말과 일치하도록 빈칸에 알맞은 말을 넣으시오.

• 현재완료의 계속 •

1 나는 1월부터 불어를 공부해왔다. (study)

→ I _____ _____ French _____ January.

2 그 집은 석 달째 비어있다. (empty)

→ The house _____ _____ _____ _____ three months.

3 나의 부모님은 결혼한 지 20년이 되었다. (married)

→ My parents _____ _____ _____ _____ 20 years.

4 Greg은 2010년부터 자신의 차를 갖고 있었다. (have)

→ Greg _____ _____ his car _____ 2010.

5 너는 이 아파트에 산 지 얼마나 되었니? (live)

→ _____ _____ _____ _____ _____ in this apartment?

• 현재완료의 결과 •

6 Mark는 체육관에 가버렸다. (go)

→ Mark _____ _____ to the gym.

7 James는 복사기를 망가뜨렸다. (break)

→ James _____ _____ the copy machine.

8 내 친구는 독일로 떠나버렸다. (leave for)

→ My friend _____ _____ _____ Germany.

9 Adel은 유명한 가수가 되었다. (become)

→ Adel _____ _____ a famous singer.

10 많이 컸구나! (grow up)

→ You _____ _____ _____!

( ) 안의 말을 이용하여 우리말을 영어로 옮기시오.

1 그는 5년 동안 수의사로 일했다. (as a vet)

2 우리는 그때부터 절친이었다. (best friends / then)

3 나는 집 열쇠를 잃어버렸다. (my house key)

4 그는 5살 때부터 피아노를 쳤다. (he was 5 years old)

5 영어를 공부한 지 얼마나 되었니? (study English)

6 그녀는 한 달 동안 병원에 입원해있다. (be in the hospital)

7 Tim과 Susan은 쇼핑하러 갔다. (go shopping)

8 Amy는 집에 숙제를 놓고 왔다. (leave / at home)

9 Angela는 그녀의 개를 오랫동안 키웠다. (have / a long time)

10 그들은 오늘 아침부터 아무것도 먹지 않았다. (not / eat anything)

11 너는 두통이 있은 지 얼마나 되었니? (have a headache)

12 그는 살이 많이 빠졌다. (lose / a lot of)

1 주어진 단어를 이용하여 다음 대화의 밑줄 친 우리말을 영작하시오.

> **A** Tom, are you still doing your homework?
> **B** No, Mom. <u>방금 제 숙제를 끝냈어요.</u> (just)

→ _____

2 우리말과 같은 뜻이 되도록 주어진 단어를 바르게 배열하시오.

> 그 기차는 아직 역을 떠나지 않았다.
> (yet / the train / left / hasn't / the station)

→ _____

3 주어진 단어를 이용하여 우리말을 영작하시오.

(1) 그는 태국 음식을 먹어본 적이 한 번도 없다.
 (never, eat, Thai food)

→ _____

(2) 너는 기린을 본적이 있니? (ever, a giraffe)

→ _____

4 주어진 우리말을 참고하여 대화를 완성하시오.

> **A** _____ _____ _____
> _____ Australia?
> (너는 호주에 가본 적이 있니?)
> **B** Yes, I have. I _____ _____
> _____ last year.
> (응, 있어. 나는 작년에 호주에 갔었어.)

5 다음 두 문장을 같은 의미의 한 문장으로 바꾸어 쓰시오. (단, 현재완료를 사용할 것)

(1) I lost my camera. So I don't have it now.

→ _____

(2) Emily went to Paris. So she is not here.

→ _____

6 두 문장이 같은 의미가 되도록 빈칸에 알맞은 말을 쓰시오.

(1) I started to learn Chinese five years ago, and I still learn it.

→ I _____ _____ Chinese
 _____ five years.

(2) Aron was sick last week, and he is still sick.

→ Aron _____ _____ sick
 _____ last week.

7 다음 중 어법상 틀린 문장 3개를 찾아 바르게 고쳐 쓰시오.

> **A** ① Have you been to Busan?
> **B** ② Yes, I have. ③ Actually, I have lived there 3 years ago.
> **A** I see. ④ Then, where do you live now?
> **B** ⑤ I live in Daejeon.
> **A** ⑥ How long do you live there?
> **B** ⑦ I've lived there for March.

_____

_____

_____

UNIT
02

5형식 문장

동사 + 목적어 + 형용사 / 명사

1 5형식은 「주어＋동사＋목적어＋목적격보어」로 이루어진 문장이다. 목적격보어는 동사만으로 뜻이 불충분한 문장에서 목적어를 보충 설명해주는 역할을 하며, 동사에 따라 형태가 달라지므로 주의하도록 한다.

Exercising regularly **makes** your body **healthy**. 규칙적으로 운동하는 것은 네 몸을 건강하게 만든다.
  주어   동사   목적어   목적격보어

2 형용사를 목적격보어로 취하는 동사

make	~을 …하게 만들다	He always makes me happy. 그는 항상 나를 행복하게 만든다.
keep	~을 …하게 유지하다	You should keep it clean. 너는 그것을 깨끗하게 유지해야 한다.
leave	~을 …인 채로 두다	Please leave the door open. 문을 열어두세요.
find	~이 …인 것을 알게 되다	I found the class fun. 나는 그 수업이 재미있다는 것을 알게 되었다.

3 명사를 목적격보어로 취하는 동사

make	~을 …로 만들다	She made me a fool. 그녀는 나를 바보로 만들었다.
call / name	~을 …라고 부르다 / 이름 짓다	Don't call me a liar. 나를 거짓말쟁이라고 부르지 마.
keep	~을 …로 유지하다	Can you keep it a secret? 그것을 비밀로 해줄 수 있니?
find	~이 …인 것을 알게 되다	We found him a great teacher. 우리는 그가 훌륭한 선생님인 것을 알게 되었다.

CHECK UP

● 목적어에는 동그라미를 하고, 목적격보어에는 밑줄을 치시오.

1 I found her advice helpful.

2 Please leave me alone.

3 Always keep your desk clean.

4 The game made people excited.

5 The noise kept him awake all night.

6 They left the problem unsolved.

7 The red dress made her lovely.

8 The girl calls the doll Barbie.

9 They kept the party a secret.

10 The movie made him a world-famous star.

box 안의 예문을 참고하여 우리말과 일치하도록 문장을 완성하시오.

> **WRITING POINT ①**
>
> • The story made me **happy**. 그 이야기는 / 만들었다 / 나를 / 행복하게

I	그 소식은 우리를 슬프게 만들었다.	The news made us _____.
2	그 숙제는 그를 바쁘게 만들었다.	The homework made him _____.
3	그녀를 화나게 하지 마.	Don't make her _____.
4	이 코트는 너를 따뜻하게 해줄 거야.	This coat will keep you _____.
5	그는 항상 그의 방을 어둡게 유지한다.	He always keeps his room _____.
6	그들은 그 소녀를 혼자 두었다.	They left the girl _____.
7	냉장고를 열어두지 마라.	Don't leave the refrigerator _____.
8	나는 그 책이 흥미롭다는 것을 알게 되었다.	I found the book _____.
9	나는 그 시험이 쉽다는 것을 알게 되었다.	I found the exam _____.

> **WRITING POINT ②**
>
> • His invention made him **a rich man**. 그의 발명품은 / 만들었다 / 그를 / 부자로

I	그 코치는 그를 훌륭한 선수로 만들었다.	The coach made him _____.
2	그 노래는 그를 유명한 가수로 만들었다.	The song made him _____.
3	사람들은 그를 영웅이라고 부른다.	People call him _____.
4	그의 친구들은 그를 천재라고 부른다.	His friends call him _____.
5	그들은 그녀를 Julie라고 이름 지었다.	They named her _____.
6	내 가족은 우리 개를 Roy라고 이름 지었다.	My family named our dog _____.
7	너는 이것을 비밀로 유지해야 한다.	You should keep this _____.
8	그들은 그가 의사인 것을 알게 되었다.	They found him _____.
9	그는 그것이 좋은 운동인 것을 알게 되었다.	He found it _____.

우리말과 일치하도록 빈칸에 알맞은 말을 넣으시오.

• 5형식: 주어 + 동사 + 목적어 + 형용사 •

I   그 영화는 나를 졸리게 만들었다. (sleepy)

→ The movie _____ _____ _____.

2   교통 체증은 그를 회사에 늦게 만들었다. (late)

→ The traffic jam _____ _____ _____ for work.

3   누가 그 문을 열어뒀니? (the door)

→ Who _____ _____ _____ _____?

4   커피를 너무 많이 마시는 것은 당신을 밤에 깨어있게 할 것이다. (awake)

→ Drinking too much coffee will _____ _____ _____ at night.

5   경찰은 그 아이가 살아있다는 것을 알게 되었다. (the child / alive)

→ The police _____ _____ _____ _____.

• 5형식: 주어 + 동사 + 목적어 + 명사 •

6   사람들은 바흐(Bach)를 음악의 아버지라고 부른다. (the father of music)

→ People _____ Bach "_____ _____ _____ _____."

7   나는 그것이 유용한 도구인 것을 알게 되었다. (a useful tool)

→ I _____ it _____ _____ _____.

8   그 부부는 그들의 딸을 Eva라고 이름 지었다. (daughter)

→ The couple _____ _____ _____ _____.

9   그녀의 노력은 그녀를 훌륭한 피아니스트로 만들었다. (great)

→ Her effort _____ _____ _____ _____ _____.

10 나는 네 결정을 비밀로 할게. (decision)

→ I'll keep _____ _____ _____ _____.

( ) 안의 말을 이용하여 우리말을 영어로 옮기시오.

1 너는 그 상자를 안전하게 보관해야 한다. (should / safe)

2 그 TV 쇼는 그를 스타로 만들었다. (a star)

3 그 커튼이 너의 방을 어둡게 유지해줄 것이다. (the curtains / will)

4 그녀는 그 일이 매우 지루하다는 것을 알게 되었다. (very boring)

5 그의 공연은 그의 팬들을 흥분하게 만들었다. (his performance / his fans / excited)

6 그들은 그것을 비밀로 유지하기로 약속했다. (promise to)

7 문을 열어두지 마라. (leave)

8 우리는 그것이 좋은 기회인 것을 알게 되었다. (a good opportunity)

9 에어컨은 그 방을 시원하게 유지시켜준다. (the air conditioner)

10 너무 늦게까지 일하는 것은 너를 피곤하게 만들 것이다. (working too late)

11 그의 반 친구들은 그를 '리틀 지성'이라고 부른다. (Little Jiseong)

12 무엇이 그녀를 그렇게 화나게 만들었니? (what / so upset)

LESSON 04 동사 + 목적어 + to부정사

1 5형식은 목적격보어로 형용사, 명사뿐만 아니라 **to부정사**를 취할 수 있다.

My parents **want** me **to study** harder. 나의 부모님은 내가 더 열심히 공부하기를 원하신다.
　주어　　　　동사　목적어　목적격보어

2 to부정사를 목적격보어로 취하는 동사

want	~가 …하는 것을 원하다	I **want** you **to go** with me. 나는 네가 나와 함께 가기를 원한다.
tell	~에게 …하라고 말하다	He **told** us **to come** in. 그는 우리에게 들어오라고 말했다.
ask	~에게 …하라고 요청하다	We **asked** them **to be** quiet. 우리는 그들에게 조용히 해달라고 부탁했다.
advise	~에게 …하라고 조언하다	The doctor **advised** her **to rest**. 의사는 그녀에게 휴식을 취하라고 조언했다.
expect	~가 …할 거라고 기대하다	I **expect** him **to pass** the exam. 나는 그가 그 시험에 합격할 거라고 기대한다.

3 동사 **help**는 뒤에 **목적격보어**가 오면 '~가 …하는 것을 돕다'라는 뜻이다. help의 목적격보어는 **동사원형**과 **to부정사기** 모두 올 수 있다.

I **helped** him **(to) do** his homework. 나는 그가 숙제 하는 것을 도와주었다.

> **PLUS**　동사 help는 같은 뜻으로 「help+목적어+with+명사」 형식으로 쓸 수도 있다.
> e.g. I helped him *with his homework*.

- 목적어에는 동그라미를 하고, 목적격보어에는 밑줄을 치시오.

1 I want the rain to stop soon.

2 Do you want me to take you home?

3 The police officer told the driver to stop.

4 Cindy asked me to join her club.

5 I advised Rick to go to the dentist.

6 We expect him to arrive before dinner.

7 The boy is helping the old woman to carry her bag.

8 Can you help me to find this book?

9 I don't want my parents to know about it.

10 Please tell him to call me as soon as possible.

box 안의 예문을 참고하여 우리말과 일치하도록 문장을 완성하시오.

WRITING POINT ①

· I want you **to go** with us. 나는 / 원한다 / 네가 / 우리와 함께 가기를

1 나는 네가 더 오래 머무르길 원한다.   I want you _____ longer.

2 나는 네가 파티에 오길 원한다.   I want you _____ to the party.

3 너는 내가 저녁을 요리하기를 원하니?   Do you want me _____ dinner?

4 Jin은 나에게 자신을 기다리라고 말했다.   Jin told me _____ for her.

5 김 선생님은 우리에게 앉으라고 말했다.   Mr. Kim told us _____ down.

6 나는 그에게 창문을 열어달라고 부탁했다.   I asked him _____ the window.

7 나는 그에게 의자를 옮겨달라고 부탁했다.   I asked him _____ the chair.

8 그는 John에게 담배를 끊으라고 조언했다.   He advised John _____ smoking.

9 우리는 그가 가수가 될 거라고 기대한다.   We expect him _____ a singer.

WRITING POINT ②

· I helped my mom **(to) prepare** lunch. 나는 / 도왔다 / 엄마가 / 점심식사 준비하는 것을

1 그는 내가 내 컴퓨터 고치는 것을 도왔다.   He helped me _____ my computer.

2 그는 내가 숙제 하는 것을 도왔다.   He helped me _____ my homework.

3 나는 아버지가 세차하시는 것을 도왔다.   I helped my father _____ his car.

4 나는 그녀가 집을 청소하는 것을 도왔다.   I helped her _____ the house.

5 내가 나무 심는 것을 도와줄 수 있니?   Can you help me _____ a tree?

6 내가 케이크 만드는 것을 도와줄 수 있니?   Can you help me _____ a cake?

7 이 책은 내가 영어 배우는 것을 돕는다.   This book helps me _____ English.

8 이 차는 당신이 잘 자도록 돕는다.   This tea helps you _____ well.

9 이 도구는 당신이 일을 빨리 하도록 돕는다.   This tool helps you _____ fast.

우리말과 일치하도록 빈칸에 알맞은 말을 넣으시오.

• 5형식: 주어 + 동사 + 목적어 + to부정사 •

1 나는 그에게 음악 소리를 줄여달라고 부탁했다. (turn down)

→ I _____ _____ _____ _____ _____ the music.

2 그는 나에게 다음 정거장에서 내리라고 말했다. (get off)

→ He _____ _____ _____ _____ _____ at the next stop.

3 나는 나의 할머니가 건강하시길 원한다. (healthy)

→ I _____ my grandmother _____ _____ _____ .

4 우리는 네 꿈이 이뤄질 거라고 기대한다. (come true)

→ We _____ your dream _____ _____ _____ .

5 선생님이 너에게 무엇을 하라고 조언하셨니? (do)

→ What did the teacher _____ _____ _____ _____ ?

• 5형식: 주어 + help + 목적어 + (to) 동사원형 •

6 이 앱은 내가 영어 배우는 것을 돕는다. (learn)

→ This app _____ _____ _____ English.

7 그들은 그녀가 그녀의 가족을 찾는 것을 도왔다. (find)

→ They _____ _____ _____ her family.

8 쓰레기 내다버리는 것 좀 도와줄래? (take out)

→ Can you _____ _____ _____ _____ the trash?

9 요가를 하는 것은 당신이 긴장을 푸는데 도움이 될 수 있다. (relax)

→ Doing yoga can _____ _____ _____ .

10 미안하지만, 나는 네가 설거지하는 것을 도와줄 수가 없어. (wash)

→ I'm sorry, but I can't _____ _____ _____ the dishes.

( ) 안의 말을 이용하여 우리말을 영어로 옮기시오.

I 나는 네가 주의 깊게 듣기를 원한다. (listen carefully)

2 엄마는 나에게 내 침대를 정돈하라고 말했다. (make my bed)

3 그 의사는 나에게 규칙적으로 운동하라고 조언했다. (exercise regularly)

4 이 탁자 옮기는 것 좀 도와줄래? (can / move)

5 나는 그에게 더 크게 말해달라고 부탁했다. (speak louder)

6 내가 너에게 조심하라고 말했지. (careful)

7 Dave는 내가 그 문제 푸는 것을 도와주었다. (solve)

8 우리는 그가 시험을 잘 볼거라고 기대한다. (do well on the exam)

9 윤 선생님(Ms. Yoon)은 우리에게 제시간에 오라고 말했다. (be on time)

10 나는 그녀에게 7시에 깨워달라고 부탁했다. (wake me up)

II 그 드라마는 Mike가 한국어 배우는 것을 돕는다. (the drama / Korean)

I2 그 소년은 그 노인이 길을 건너는 것을 돕고 있다. (the old man / cross the street)

LESSON 05 지각동사, 사역동사

l 5형식 문장에 **지각동사(see, hear, smell, feel 등)**가 쓰일 경우, 목적격보어는 **동사원형** 또는 현재분사(동사+-ing)가 온다.

see	~가 …하는 것을 보다	I saw my sister jump/jumping rope. 나는 내 여동생이 줄넘기하는 것을 보았다.
hear	~가 …하는 것을 듣다	We heard him sing/singing. 우리는 그가 노래 부르는 것을 들었다.
smell	~가 …하는 냄새를 맡다	She smelled something burn/burning. 그녀는 뭔가 타는 냄새를 맡았다.
feel	~가 …하는 것을 느끼다	He felt someone touch/touching his arm. 그는 누군가가 그의 팔을 만지는 것을 느꼈다.

NOTE 지각동사의 목적격보어가 현재분사일 경우에는 동작이 진행중임을 나타낸다.

e.g. I saw him *eat* lunch at a restaurant. (점심 먹는 것을 처음부터 끝까지 다 보았다는 의미)
I saw him *eating* lunch at a restaurant. (보았을 때 점심을 먹고 있는 중이었다는 의미)

2 사역동사(make, have, let)는 주어가 목적어에게 어떤 동작을 하거나 시키는 동사이다. 5형식 문장에 사역동사가 쓰일 경우, 목적격보어는 **동사원형**이 온다.

make	~가 …하게 하다	He always makes me laugh. 그는 항상 나를 웃게 만든다.
have	(지시·요청) ~에게 …하 라고 하다/시키다	I had him mail a letter. 나는 그에게 편지를 부치라고 시켰다.
let	(허락) ~가 …하게 해주다	She let me use her computer. 그녀는 내가 그녀의 컴퓨터를 쓰게 해주었다.

CHECK UP

● 빈칸에 알맞은 말을 고르시오.

l I saw the thief _____ away. ☐ run ☐ ran

2 I had the repairman _____ my car. ☐ fix ☐ to fix

3 Your smile always makes me _____ good. ☐ feel ☐ to feel

4 Her father won't let her _____ alone. ☐ go ☐ going

5 She heard birds _____ outside her window. ☐ sang ☐ singing

6 I felt my dog _____ my hand. ☐ licking ☐ to lick

7 He _____ us wait for two hours. ☐ asked ☐ made

8 Mom _____ me set the table. ☐ told ☐ had

9 His boss _____ him leave early. ☐ let ☐ wanted

10 I _____ Dave washing his car. ☐ saw ☐ helped

box 안의 예문을 참고하여 우리말과 일치하도록 문장을 완성하시오.

WRITING POINT ①

· I saw a boy **dance/dancing** on the stage. 나는 보았다 / 한 소년이 / 춤추는 것을 / 무대에서

1 나는 그가 길을 건너는 것을 보았다.　　　　I saw him _____ the street.

2 나는 그가 집을 나서는 것을 보았다.　　　　I saw him _____ the house.

3 나는 그들이 웃는 것을 들었다.　　　　　　I heard them _____ .

4 나는 그들이 통화하는 것을 들었다.　　　　I heard them _____ on the phone.

5 부엌에서 밥 짓는 냄새가 난다.　　　　　　I can smell the rice _____ in the kitchen.

6 오븐에서 빵 굽는 냄새가 난다.　　　　　　I can smell the bread _____ in the oven.

7 나는 누군가 나를 보는 것을 느꼈다.　　　　I felt someone _____ at me.

8 나는 누군가 나를 따라오는 것을 느꼈다.　　I felt someone _____ me.

WRITING POINT ②

· She makes me **feel** happy. 그녀는 / 만든다 / 나를 / 기분 좋게

1 아빠는 내가 숙제를 끝내게 했다.　　　　　My dad made me _____ my homework.

2 엄마는 내가 피아노를 연습하게 했다.　　　My mom made me _____ the piano.

3 우리 선생님은 우리가 줄을 서게 했다.　　　Our teacher made us _____ in line.

4 나는 그에게 편지를 쓰라고 시켰다.　　　　I had him _____ a letter.

5 나는 그에게 호텔을 예약하라고 시켰다.　　I had him _____ a hotel.

6 나는 그에게 전화를 받으라고 시켰다.　　　I had him _____ the phone.

7 그녀는 내가 그 케이크를 먹게 해주었다.　　She let me _____ the cake.

8 그녀는 내가 그녀의 책을 빌리게 해주었다.　She let me _____ her book.

9 그녀는 내가 그 콘서트에 가게 해주었다.　　She let me _____ to the concert.

우리말과 일치하도록 빈칸에 알맞은 말을 넣으시오.

• 5형식: 지각동사 + 목적어 + 동사원형/현재분사 •

1 우리는 그가 벤치에 앉아있는 것을 보았다. (sit)

→ We ＿＿＿＿＿＿ ＿＿＿＿＿＿ ＿＿＿＿＿＿ on the bench.

2 나는 그가 내 이름을 부르는 것을 들었다. (call)

→ I ＿＿＿＿＿＿ ＿＿＿＿＿＿ ＿＿＿＿＿＿ my name.

3 그녀는 누군가 자신의 어깨를 만지는 것을 느꼈다. (touch)

→ She ＿＿＿＿＿＿ ＿＿＿＿＿＿ ＿＿＿＿＿＿ her shoulder.

4 뭔가 타는 냄새 안 나니? (burn)

→ Can you ＿＿＿＿＿＿ ＿＿＿＿＿＿ ＿＿＿＿＿＿?

5 너는 사람들이 크게 환호하는 소리가 들리니? (cheer)

→ Can you ＿＿＿＿＿＿ ＿＿＿＿＿＿ ＿＿＿＿＿＿ loudly?

• 5형식: 사역동사 + 목적어 + 동사원형 •

6 그 영화는 나를 울게 만들었다. (make)

→ The movie ＿＿＿＿＿＿ ＿＿＿＿＿＿ ＿＿＿＿＿＿.

7 나는 그에게 슈퍼마켓에서 우유를 사오도록 시켰다. (have)

→ I ＿＿＿＿＿＿ ＿＿＿＿＿＿ ＿＿＿＿＿＿ some milk at the supermarket.

8 메뉴 좀 볼게요. (let)

→ ＿＿＿＿＿＿ ＿＿＿＿＿＿ ＿＿＿＿＿＿ at the menu.

9 그녀의 남자친구는 그녀를 웃게 하려고 애썼다. (make)

→ Her boyfriend tried to ＿＿＿＿＿＿ ＿＿＿＿＿＿ ＿＿＿＿＿＿.

10 엄마는 내가 친구 집에서 하룻밤 묵는 걸 허락하시지 않을 것이다. (let / stay overnight)

→ My mom won't ＿＿＿＿＿＿ ＿＿＿＿＿＿ ＿＿＿＿＿＿ ＿＿＿＿＿＿ at my friend's house.

( ) 안의 말을 이용하여 우리말을 영어로 옮기시오.

1 음악을 듣는 것은 나를 기분 좋게 만든다. (feel good)

2 그는 누군가 노크하는 소리를 들었다. (knock on the door)

3 우리 선생님은 우리에게 한 달에 책 두 권을 읽게 하신다. (make / a month)

4 나는 그녀가 버스 정류장에서 버스를 기다리는 것을 보았다. (wait for / at the bus stop)

5 그 남자는 나에게 그의 사진을 찍게 했다. (have / take a picture of him)

6 그 코치는 그의 팀이 휴식을 취하게 해주었다. (let / take a break)

7 내가 그 축구경기에서 득점하는 거 봤니? (score a goal / in the soccer game)

8 나는 누군가 내 머리를 잡아당기는 것을 느꼈다. (pull my hair)

9 나는 옆방에서 누군가 코를 고는 소리를 들었다. (snore / in the next room)

10 너는 봄이 오는 걸 느낄 수 있니? (can / the spring)

11 Kate는 그녀의 남편에게 장을 보라고 시켰다. (have / do the grocery shopping)

12 나의 언니는 내가 그녀의 옷을 입지 못하게 한다. (let / her clothes)

1 주어진 단어를 바르게 배열하여 문장을 완성하시오.

(1) (his speech / very / found / I / impressive)

→ _____

(2) (warm / keeping / the chicken / the eggs / is)

→ _____

2 〈보기〉에서 적절한 말을 골라 우리말을 영작하시오.

그 소식은 그들을 행복하게 해줄 것이다.

보기 happy / happily / the news / they / them / will / make / makes

→ _____

3 주어진 우리말을 참고하여 대화를 완성하시오.

A Who _____ the door _____?
(누가 문을 열어두었니?)
B I don't know. I guess Brad did.

4 그림을 보고 주어진 단어를 이용하여 문장을 완성하시오.

→ Yuna's mom told _____
_____. (Yuna, the dishes)

5 다음 중 어법상 틀린 곳을 찾아 바르게 고쳐 쓰시오.

(1) Mary wants Paul clean the house.
(2) He advised me telling the truth.

(1) _____ → _____
(2) _____ → _____

6 대화의 내용과 일치하도록 ( ) 안에 주어진 단어를 이용하여 문장을 완성하시오.

Jinsu Mom, can I play outside?
Mom Sorry, you can't. You have to do your homework.

→ Jinsu's mom doesn't _____ him
_____ _____. (let)
She _____ him _____
_____ _____. (make)

7 주어진 단어를 이용하여 우리말을 영작하시오.

(1) 나는 그가 그 건물로 들어가는 것을 보았다. (see, enter)

→ _____

(2) 그는 누군가 그의 등을 만지는 것을 느꼈다. (feel, back)

→ _____

UNIT
03

조동사

LESSON 06 추측을 나타내는 조동사

1 조동사 may는 '~일지도 모른다'란 뜻으로 불확실한 사실을 추측할 때 쓴다. '~이 아닐지도 모른다'는 **may not**을 쓴다.

| may | ~일지도 모른다 | A: Where is Sally? Sally는 어디 있니?
B: I'm not sure. She may be in the library. 글쎄. 도서관에 있을지도 몰라. |
| may not | ~이 아닐지도 모른다 | They may not know the truth. 그들은 진실을 알지 못할지도 모른다. |

PLUS may는 약한 추측 이외에 '~해도 좋다, ~해도 되나요?'라는 허락의 의미를 나타내기도 한다.

e.g. You *may* leave now. 이제 가도 좋다.
May I ask a question? 질문 하나 해도 될까요?

2 조동사 must는 '~임에 틀림없다'란 뜻으로, may보다 더 **강한 추측**이나 **확신**을 나타낼 때 쓴다. '~일 리가 없다'는 **cannot**을 쓴다.

| must | ~임이 틀림없다 | A: Alex can speak five languages. Alex는 5개 국어를 할 수 있어.
B: Wow! He must be very smart. 와! 그는 매우 똑똑함에 틀림없어 |
| cannot | ~일 리가 없다 | Jane cannot be sick. I just saw her at the gym.
Jane은 아플 리가 없어. 그녀를 방금 체육관에서 봤거든. |

CHECK UP

● 빈칸에 알맞은 조동사를 고르시오.

1 Be careful! You _____ slip on the floor. ☐ may ☐ may not

2 It's -10°C outside. It _____ be very cold. ☐ must ☐ cannot

3 He _____ be Jerry. He is much taller. ☐ must ☐ cannot

4 The baby is crying. He _____ be sick. ☐ may ☐ may not

5 Emily keeps yawning. She _____ be sleepy. ☐ must ☐ cannot

6 It _____ be a mouse. It's too big! ☐ must ☐ cannot

7 It's too late. You _____ get lost in the dark. ☐ may ☐ may not

8 They are late. They _____ know the way here. ☐ may ☐ may not

9 He lives in a big house. He _____ be rich. ☐ must ☐ cannot

10 He's just eaten lunch. He _____ be hungry. ☐ must ☐ cannot

box 안의 예문을 참고하여 우리말과 일치하도록 문장을 완성하시오.

WRITING POINT ①

· He **may know** my name. 그는 / 알지도 모른다 / 내 이름을
· He **may not know** my name. 그는 / 알지 못할지도 모른다 / 내 이름을

---

1 그는 회의에 올지도 모른다.   He _____ to the meeting.

2 그는 회의에 못 올지도 모른다.   He _____ to the meeting.

3 그녀는 그 선물을 좋아할지도 모른다.   She _____ the present.

4 그녀는 그 선물을 좋아하지 않을지도 모른다.   She _____ the present.

5 내일은 비가 올지도 모른다.   It _____ tomorrow.

6 내일은 비가 안 올지도 모른다.   It _____ tomorrow.

7 너에게 또 다른 기회가 있을지도 모른다.   There _____ another chance for you.

8 너에게 또 다른 기회가 없을지도 모른다.   There _____ another chance for you.

WRITING POINT ②

· She **must be** in her room now. 그녀는 / 있음이 틀림없다 / 자기 방에 / 지금
· She **cannot be** in her room now. 그녀는 / 있을 리가 없다 / 자기 방에 / 지금

---

1 그녀는 오늘 아픈 것이 틀림없다.   She _____ sick today.

2 그녀는 오늘 아플 리가 없다.   She _____ sick today.

3 그는 너보다 나이가 많음에 틀림없다.   He _____ older than you.

4 그는 너보다 나이가 많을 리가 없다.   He _____ older than you.

5 그들은 자매임에 틀림없다.   They _____ sisters.

6 그들은 자매일 리가 없다.   They _____ sisters.

7 그 아기는 배가 고픈 것이 틀림없다.   The baby _____ hungry.

8 그 아기는 배가 고플 리가 없다.   The baby _____ hungry.

우리말과 일치하도록 빈칸에 알맞은 말을 넣으시오.

• 약한 추측: may •

1 나의 부모님은 오늘 저녁에 외출하실지도 모른다. (go out)

→ My parents _____ _____ _____ this evening.

2 믿지 않을지도 모르지만, 그것은 사실이다. (believe)

→ You _____ _____ _____ it, but that's true.

3 네 휴대전화는 차 안에 있을지도 모른다. (be)

→ Your cell phone _____ _____ in the car.

4 이번 주말에는 비가 안 올지도 모른다. (it)

→ _____ _____ _____ _____ this weekend.

5 화성에는 생명체가 있을지도 모른다. (there)

→ _____ _____ _____ life on Mars.

• 강한 추측: must / cannot •

6 그녀는 당신을 좋아하는 것이 틀림없다. (like)

→ She _____ _____ _____.

7 그 소문은 사실일 리가 없다. (true)

→ The rumor _____ _____ _____.

8 전화 잘못 거신 것 같아요. (have)

→ You _____ _____ the wrong number.

9 그들은 서로 알고 있을 리가 없다.

→ They _____ _____ each other.

10 와! 너 정말 신나겠다. (excited)

→ Wow! You _____ _____ very _____.

( ) 안의 말을 이용하여 우리말을 영어로 옮기시오.

1 우리는 이번 여름에 태국에 갈지도 모른다. (Thailand)

2 그는 의사일 리가 없다. (a doctor)

3 그들은 틀림없이 매우 피곤할 것이다. (tired)

4 너는 이 영화를 좋아하지 않을지도 모른다. (this movie)

5 너희 부모님은 틀림없이 너를 자랑스러워하실 것이다. (be proud of)

6 그는 언젠가 유명한 가수가 될지도 모른다. (one day)

7 이번 크리스마스에는 눈이 올지도 모른다. (it / this Christmas)

8 그는 내 전화번호를 알지 못할지도 모른다. (phone number)

9 저기 있는 남자는 James임이 틀림없다. (the man over there)

10 그녀는 나에게 화가 났음에 틀림없다. (be angry with)

11 이것은 실수임에 틀림없다. (a mistake)

12 그 문제를 해결할 방법이 있을지도 모른다. (there / a way to solve the problem)

의무, 필요를 나타내는 조동사

1 조동사 **must**는 '~해야 한다'라는 뜻으로 **강한 의무**를 나타낸다. 부정형인 **must not**은 '~해서는 안 된다'라는 **금지**의 의미이다.

| must | ~해야 한다 | Drivers must wear seat belts. 운전자들은 안전벨트를 메야 한다. |
| must not | ~해서는 안 된다 | People must not break the law. 사람들은 법을 어겨서는 안 된다. |

2 조동사 **have/has to**는 must처럼 '~해야 한다'라는 **의무**나 **필요**를 나타낸다. 부정형인 **don't/doesn't have to**는 '~할 필요가 없다'라는 **불필요**의 의미이다.

have/has to	~해야 한다	We have to eat a balanced diet. 우리는 균형 잡힌 식사를 해야 한다. She has to feed her dog. 그녀는 그녀의 개에게 먹이를 줘야 한다.
don't/doesn't have to	~할 필요가 없다	You don't have to wait for me. 너는 나를 기다릴 필요 없다.
had to	~해야 했다	He had to run to catch the train. 그는 그 기차를 타기 위해 뛰어야 했다.
Do/Does + 주어 + have to ~?	~해야 하나요?	Do I have to pay for the entrance fee? 제가 입장료를 내야 하나요?

PLUS '~해야 한다'라는 의미는 must와 have to 모두 쓸 수 있지만, 강한 추측(~임에 틀림없다)을 나타내는 must는 have to로 바꾸어 쓸 수 없다.

CHECK UP

● 빈칸에 알맞은 조동사를 고르시오.

1 You _____ drive carefully at night. ☐ must   ☐ must not

2 Kevin, you _____ play in the street. ☐ have to   ☐ must not

3 We _____ keep water clean. ☐ have to   ☐ must not

4 You _____ eat if you're full. ☐ must   ☐ don't have to

5 All students _____ take an entrance exam. ☐ must   ☐ must not

6 You _____ take medicine for your cold. ☐ have to   ☐ must not

7 _____ get off at the next stop? ☐ Have I to   ☐ Do I have to

8 The children _____ play with fire. ☐ must not   ☐ don't have to

9 She _____ finish her report by Friday. ☐ has to   ☐ have to

10 Sam _____ take a taxi last night. ☐ must   ☐ had to

box 안의 예문을 참고하여 우리말과 일치하도록 문장을 완성하시오.

WRITING POINT ①

- They **must work** late. 그들은 / 일해야 한다 / 늦게까지
- They **must not work** late. 그들은 / 일하면 안 된다 / 늦게까지

---

1 너는 이곳을 떠나야 한다. You ＿＿＿＿＿＿ here.

2 너는 이곳을 떠나면 안 된다. You ＿＿＿＿＿＿ here.

3 그녀는 지금 그에게 전화해야 한다. She ＿＿＿＿＿＿ him now.

4 그녀는 지금 그에게 전화하면 안 된다. She ＿＿＿＿＿＿ him now.

5 그들은 자기 음식을 가져와야 한다. They ＿＿＿＿＿＿ their food.

6 그들은 자기 음식을 가져오면 안 된다. They ＿＿＿＿＿＿ their food.

7 나는 그에게 그 비밀을 말해야 한다. I ＿＿＿＿＿＿ him the secret.

8 나는 그에게 그 비밀을 말하면 안 된다. I ＿＿＿＿＿＿ him the secret.

WRITING POINT ②

- I **(don't) have to** meet her. 나는 / 만나야 한다 (만날 필요가 없다) / 그녀를
- **Do I have to meet** her? 제가 만나야 하나요 / 그녀를?

---

1 그는 그곳에 가야 한다. He ＿＿＿＿＿＿ there.

2 그는 그곳에 갈 필요가 없다. He ＿＿＿＿＿＿ there.

3 그가 그곳에 가야 하나요? ＿＿＿＿＿＿ there?

4 그들은 교복을 입어야 한다. They ＿＿＿＿＿＿ school uniforms.

5 그들은 교복을 입을 필요가 없다. They ＿＿＿＿＿＿ school uniforms.

6 그들은 교복을 입어야 하니? ＿＿＿＿＿＿ school uniforms?

7 나는 다음주에 시험을 봐야 한다. I ＿＿＿＿＿＿ a test next week.

8 나는 다음주에 시험을 볼 필요가 없다. I ＿＿＿＿＿＿ a test next week.

9 제가 다음주에 시험을 봐야 하나요? ＿＿＿＿＿＿ a test next week?

우리말과 일치하도록 빈칸에 알맞은 말을 넣으시오.

• 강한 의무: must •

1 당신은 이 양식을 먼저 작성하셔야 합니다. (fill out)

→ You _____ _____ _____ this form first.

2 너는 부모님 말씀을 잘 들어야 한다. (listen to)

→ You _____ _____ _____ your parents.

3 학생들은 학교에 지각하면 안 된다. (late)

→ Students _____ _____ _____ _____ for school.

4 방문객들은 동물원의 동물들에게 먹이를 주면 안 된다. (feed)

→ Visitors _____ _____ _____ the animals in the zoo.

5 너는 종이컵들을 사용하는 대신 네 컵을 가져와야 한다. (bring)

→ You _____ _____ your cup instead of using paper cups.

• 의무/필요: have/has to •

6 나는 내 개를 수의사에게 데리고 가야 한다. (take)

→ I _____ _____ _____ my dog to the vet.

7 Jane은 그녀의 남동생을 돌봐야 한다. (take care of)

→ Jane _____ _____ _____ _____ _____ her little brother.

8 우리는 그를 30분 동안 기다려야 했다.

→ We _____ _____ _____ for him for 30 minutes.

9 그들은 토요일에 일해야 하니?

→ _____ _____ _____ _____ _____ on Saturday?

10 Tom은 정장을 입고 출근할 필요가 없다. (wear)

→ Tom _____ _____ _____ _____ a suit to work.

( ) 안의 말을 이용하여 우리말을 영어로 옮기시오.

1   우리는 교통법규를 지켜야 한다. (follow / the traffic rules)

2   우리는 그 기차를 놓쳐서는 안 돼. (miss)

3   학생들은 시험에서 커닝하면 안 된다. (cheat on a test)

4   너는 수영장에서 수영모를 써야 한다. (a swimming cap / in the pool)

5   제가 얼마나 기다려야 하나요? (how long / wait)

6   너는 모든 것을 외울 필요는 없다. (memorize / everything)

7   나는 이 책을 도서관에 반납해야 한다. (return / to the library)

8   너는 수업시간에 집중해야 한다. (pay attention / in class)

9   미안하지만, 지금 가야겠어. (go)

10   너는 반 친구들을 괴롭혀서는 안 된다. (bully)

11   그녀는 다이어트를 할 필요가 없다. (go on a diet)

12   너는 운전면허를 따려면 18세가 되어야 한다. (to get a driver's license)

LESSON 08 조언, 권고를 나타내는 조동사

1 조동사 should는 '~해야 한다'란 뜻이다. 주로 **조언**할 때 많이 쓰이기 때문에 좀 더 부드럽게 '~하는 것이 좋다' 정도로 해석해도 지연스럽다.

should	~해야 한다	You should read more books. 너는 더 많은 책을 읽어야 한다.
should not (= shouldn't)	~해서는 안 된다	You should not[shouldn't] eat too many sweets. 너는 단것을 너무 많이 먹으면 안 된다.
should의 의문문	~해야 하나요?	Should I wear a jacket today? 오늘 재킷을 입어야 할까? What should I do for you? 너를 위해 내가 무엇을 해야 할까?

PLUS must와 have to는 강한 의무나 필요를 나타내는 반면, should는 좀 더 부드러운 충고나 조언을 나타낸다.
e.g. You *must/have to* do your homework. (= It is necessary to do your homework.)
You *should* do your homework. (= It is a good idea to do your homework.)

2 조동사 had better는 '~하는 게 낫다'라는 **권고**의 뜻을 나타낸다. 과거형으로 혼동할 수 있지만 현재형이며, 주어에 따라 형태가 변하지 않는다.

had better (= 'd better)	~하는 게 낫다	We had better meet early. 우리는 일찍 만나는 게 낫다.
had better not (= 'd better not)	~하지 않는 게 낫다	He had better not say anything. 그는 아무 말도 하지 않는 게 낫다.

PLUS had better는 should와 비슷한 의미이지만 어떤 행동을 하지 않으면 좋지 않은 결과가 예상될 때 주로 쓴다.
e.g. She'd better leave now, or she'll be late. 그녀는 지금 떠나는 게 낫다. 그렇지 않으면 늦을 것이다.

CHECK UP

● 빈칸에 알맞은 조동사를 고르시오.

l You _____ make noise at night. ☐ should ☐ should not

2 We _____ spend money wisely. ☐ should ☐ should not

3 People _____ throw litter on the street. ☐ should ☐ should not

4 You _____ wear a hat in the sun. ☐ should ☐ should not

5 The kids _____ sit so close to the TV. ☐ should ☐ should not

6 We _____ take a taxi. The buses are so slow. ☐ had better ☐ had better not

7 I _____ sleep now. I'm too tired. ☐ had better ☐ had better not

8 It's the last train. We _____ miss it. ☐ had better ☐ had better not

9 Ali _____ eat more ice cream. He'll be sick. ☐ had better ☐ had better not

box 안의 예문을 참고하여 우리말과 일치하도록 문장을 완성하시오.

WRITING POINT ①

- We **should (not) take** a picture here. 우리는 / 찍어야 (찍지 말아야) 한다 / 사진을 / 여기서
- **Should we take** a picture here? 우리가 찍어야 할까요 / 사진을 / 여기서?

1 우리는 그를 파티에 초대해야 한다.   We _____ him to the party.

2 우리는 그를 파티에 초대하면 안 된다.   We _____ him to the party.

3 우리가 그를 파티에 초대해야 할까?   _____ him to the party?

4 나는 그 재킷을 사야 한다.   I _____ the jacket.

5 나는 그 재킷을 사면 안 된다.   I _____ the jacket.

6 내가 그 재킷을 사야 할까?   _____ the jacket?

7 Erin은 살을 빼야 한다.   Erin _____ weight.

8 Erin은 살을 빼면 안 된다.   Erin _____ weight.

9 Erin이 살을 빼야 할까?   _____ weight?

WRITING POINT ②

- She **had better (not) listen** to him. 그녀는 / 듣는 게 (듣지 않는 게) 낫다 / 그의 말을

1 너는 그를 다시 보는 게 낫다.   You _____ him again.

2 너는 그를 다시 보지 않는 게 낫다.   You _____ him again.

3 우리는 여기 머무는 게 낫다.   We _____ here.

4 우리는 여기 머물지 않는 게 낫다.   We _____ here.

5 그는 그곳에 차로 가는 게 낫다.   He _____ there.

6 그는 그곳에 차로 가지 않는 게 낫다.   He _____ there.

7 그들은 그 계획을 변경하는 게 낫다.   They _____ the plan.

8 그들은 그 계획을 변경하지 않는 게 낫다.   They _____ the plan.

우리말과 일치하도록 빈칸에 알맞은 말을 넣으시오.

• 조언: should •

I 우리는 오늘 호텔을 예약해야 한다. (book)

→ We _____ _____ a _____ today.

2 너는 좀 더 조심해야 한다. (careful)

→ You _____ _____ more _____.

3 너는 Jane의 생일을 잊으면 안 돼. (forget)

→ You _____ _____ _____ Jane's birthday.

4 제 신발을 벗어야 하나요? (take off)

→ _____ _____ _____ _____ my shoes?

5 언니 결혼식에 뭘 입고 가야 할까?

→ _____ _____ _____ _____ to my sister's wedding?

• 권고: had better •

6 너는 집에 가서 누워 쉬는 게 낫다. (go / stay)

→ You _____ _____ _____ home and _____ in bed.

7 너는 네 가방을 여기에 두지 않는 게 낫다. (leave)

→ You _____ _____ _____ _____ your bag here.

8 너는 그 전선을 만지지 않는 게 낫다. (touch)

→ You _____ _____ _____ _____ the wire.

9 우리는 그 여행을 취소하는 게 나을 거 같아. (cancel)

→ I think we _____ _____ _____ the trip.

10 그녀는 그의 조언을 받아들이는 게 낫다. (take)

→ She _____ _____ _____ his advice.

( ) 안의 말을 이용하여 우리말을 영어로 옮기시오.

I 우리는 어려움에 처한 사람들을 도와야 한다. (in need)

2 우리는 공항에서 차를 빌리는 게 낫다. (rent a car)

3 그녀는 옷에 너무 많은 돈을 쓰면 안 된다. (spend / on clothes)

4 너는 그 우유를 마시지 않는 게 낫다. (the milk)

5 제가 그에게 도움을 청해야 할까요? (ask him for help)

6 내가 너를 몇 시에 데리러 갈까? (pick you up)

7 너는 잠자리에 들기 전에 창문 닫는 걸 잊으면 안 된다. (forget to / the window / go to bed)

8 너는 만일에 대비해 돈을 저축해야 한다. (for a rainy day)

9 영어를 향상시키기 위해 제가 뭘 해야 할까요? (to improve my English)

10 그는 다시는 늦지 않는 게 낫다. (late)

11 우리는 눈이 얼어붙기 전에 치우는 게 낫다. (clear / freeze)

12 사람들은 그들의 애완동물들에 대해 책임을 져야 한다. (be responsible for)

1 우리말과 같은 뜻이 되도록 빈칸에 알맞은 말을 쓰시오.

(1) 그는 내일 올지도 모른다.

→ He _____ _____ tomorrow.

(2) 그 아기는 배고픈 게 틀림없다.

→ The baby _____ _____ hungry.

(3) 그들은 여기에 살 리가 없다.

→ They _____ _____ here.

2 주어진 단어를 바르게 배열하여 문장을 완성하시오.

(1) (may / in this book / wrong / the answer / be)

→ _____

(2) (a problem / be / there / must)

→ _____

3 두 문장이 같은 의미가 되도록 빈칸에 알맞은 말을 쓰시오.

You must wear a helmet for your safety.
= You _____ _____ wear a helmet for your safety.

4 우리말과 같은 뜻이 되도록 주어진 단어를 바르게 배열하시오.

너는 그 식물에 매일 물을 줄 필요는 없다.
(don't / you / water / every day / to / the / have / plant)

→ _____

5 그림을 보고 주어진 단어와 조동사 should를 이용하여 문장을 완성하시오.

(1)   (2)

(1) You _____ _____ _____ paper cups and plates. (use)

(2) You _____ _____ _____ the water when you brush your teeth. (turn off)

6 주어진 우리말을 참고하여 대화를 완성하시오.

A I have a toothache.
B Well, you _____ _____ _____ _____ _____ _____. (너는 치과에 가는 게 낫겠다.)

7 다음 문장을 어법에 맞도록 바르게 고쳐 다시 쓰시오.

(1) He had better to take the subway.

→ _____

(2) You had not better touch the dog.

→ _____

UNIT
04

수동태

수동태의 시제

I **능동태**는 '누가 무엇을 하는가'를 나타내는 문장이고, **수동태**는 '무엇이 누구에 의해 어떻게 되는가'를 나타내는 문장이다. 수동태는 「be동사＋과거분사(p.p.)」 형태로 나타내고, 행위자는 문장 맨 뒤에 「by＋목적격」을 써서 나타낸다.

| (능동태) | Tom | broke | the window. | Tom이 그 창문을 깼다. |

| (수동태) | The window | was broken | by Tom. | 그 창문은 Tom에 의해 깨졌다. |

NOTE 행위자가 일반인이거나 중요하지 않은 경우는 「by＋목적격」을 생략할 수 있다.
e.g. English *is spoken* in many countries. 영어는 많은 나라에서 쓰인다.

2 수동태의 시제

현재	am/are/is p.p.	The farmers grow the rice. 농부들은 그 쌀을 재배한다. → The rice is grown by the farmers. 그 쌀은 농부들에 의해 재배된다.
과거	was/were p.p.	The cat caught the mouse. 그 고양이는 그 생쥐를 잡았다. → The mouse was caught by the cat. 그 생쥐는 그 고양이에게 잡혔다.
미래	will be p.p.	Mr. Lee will teach the class next year. 이 선생님은 내년에 그 반을 가르칠 것이다. → The class will be taught by Mr. Lee next year. 그 반은 내년에 이 선생님에게 배울 것이다.

CHECK UP

● 빈칸에 알맞은 말을 고르시오.

1 Our classroom _____ by us.   ☐ cleans   ☐ is cleaned

2 Alice _____ the flowers.   ☐ planted   ☐ was planted

3 Koalas _____ by many people.   ☐ love   ☐ are loved

4 I _____ some books tomorrow.   ☐ will buy   ☐ will be bought

5 Your bike _____ by next week.   ☐ will fix   ☐ will be fixed

6 *Romeo and Juliet* _____ by Shakespeare.   ☐ wrote   ☐ was written

7 They _____ their homework.   ☐ finished   ☐ were finished

8 The World Cup _____ every four years.   ☐ holds   ☐ is held

9 Everyone _____ to the party.   ☐ will invite   ☐ will be invited

10 Who _____ the telephone?   ☐ invented   ☐ was invented

box 안의 예문을 참고하여 우리말과 일치하도록 문장을 완성하시오.

WRITING POINT ①

• The movie **is loved** by children. 그 영화는 / 사랑 받는다 / 아이들에게

1 그 택시는 나의 삼촌이 운전한다. The taxi _____ by my uncle.

2 수학은 Allen 선생님이 가르친다. Math _____ by Mr. Allen.

3 멕시코에서는 스페인어를 말한다. Spanish _____ in Mexico.

4 내 옷들은 엄마가 세탁한다. My clothes _____ by my mom.

5 그 차들은 로봇들에 의해 만들어진다. The cars _____ by robots.

WRITING POINT ②

• The cookies **were baked** by my mom. 그 쿠키들은 / 구워졌다 / 엄마에 의해

1 그 시는 내 친구가 썼다. The poem _____ by my friend.

2 그 꽃병은 내 개가 깼다. The vase _____ by my dog.

3 그 벌레는 그 새에게 먹혔다. The worm _____ by the bird.

4 이 사진들은 Tom이 찍었다. These pictures _____ by Tom.

5 그 나무들은 나의 아버지가 심었다. The trees _____ by my father.

WRITING POINT ③

• The work **will be finished** by me tomorrow. 그 일은 / 끝날 것이다 / 나에 의해 / 내일

1 Jack은 그 차를 팔 것이다. The car _____ by Jack.

2 그 축제는 다음달에 열릴 것이다. The festival _____ next month.

3 그 집은 Mike가 칠할 것이다. The house _____ by Mike.

4 그 음악은 그 밴드가 연주할 것이다. The music _____ by the band.

5 그 질문은 곧 답변될 것이다. The question _____ soon.

우리말과 일치하도록 빈칸에 알맞은 말을 넣으시오.

• 현재 수동태 •

1 그 궁전은 많은 관광객들이 방문한다. (visit)

→ The palace _____ _____ _____ many tourists.

2 Robin 선생님은 그의 학생들에게 존경 받는다. (respect)

→ Mr. Robin _____ _____ _____ his students.

3 그 아이들은 자원봉사자들에 의해 도움을 받는다. (help)

→ The children _____ _____ _____ volunteers.

• 과거 수동태 •

4 내 자전거는 누군가에 의해 도난당했다. (steal)

→ My bike _____ _____ _____ someone.

5 고양이 한 마리가 차에 치였다. (hit)

→ A cat _____ _____ _____ a car.

6 파피루스는 고대 이집트에서 사용되었다. (use)

→ Papyrus _____ _____ in ancient Egypt.

7 그 집들은 지진으로 인해 피해를 입었다. (damage)

→ The houses _____ _____ _____ the earthquake.

• 미래 수동태 •

8 저녁식사는 7시에 제공될 것이다. (serve)

→ Dinner _____ _____ _____ at 7 o'clock.

9 그 역할은 레오나르도 디카프리오(Leonardo Dicaprio)가 연기할 것이다. (play)

→ The role _____ _____ _____ _____ Leonardo DiCaprio.

10 새로운 도서관이 그 회사에 의해 지어질 것이다. (build)

→ A new library _____ _____ _____ the company.

( ) 안의 말을 이용하여 우리말을 영어로 옮기시오.

1 그 TV 쇼는 많은 사람들이 시청한다. (watch / many)

2 Frank는 그의 선생님께 칭찬을 받았다. (praise)

3 그 와인은 프랑스에서 생산되었다. (the wine / produce)

4 이 그림들은 피카소(Picasso)가 그렸다. (these pictures / paint)

5 오늘날, 한국 음식은 많은 사람들이 즐긴다. (these days / Korean food / many)

6 한글(Hangeul)은 세종대왕(King Sejong)이 창제했다. (invent)

7 그 도둑은 한 젊은이에 의해 잡혔다. (the thief / catch / a young man)

8 우천 시, 그 콘서트는 취소될 것이다. (in case of rain / the concert / cancel)

9 차와 커피가 식후에 제공될 것이다. (serve / after the meal)

10 그 건물 안의 사람들은 곧 구조될 것이다. (rescue / soon)

11 그 박물관은 유명 건축가가 설계했다. (design / a famous architect)

12 그 개들은 동물보호소에서 보살핌을 받고 있다. (take care of / at an animal shelter)

LESSON 10 주의해야 할 수동태

1 수동태의 부정문은 be동사 뒤에 **not**을 붙여 만든다. **수동태의 의문문은 be동사를 주어 앞으로 보내서 만든다.**

부정문	be동사+not+p.p.	The picture was drawn by me. → The picture was not drawn by me. 그 그림은 내가 그리지 않았다.
의문문	Be동사+주어+p.p. ~?	They were invited to the party. → Were they invited to the party? 그들은 파티에 초대받았니?

2 수동태의 행위자는 「by+목적격」으로 나타내지만, by 대신 다른 전치사를 쓰는 경우도 있다.

be filled with	~로 가득 차다	be tired of	~에 싫증나다
be covered with	~로 덮여 있다	be made of/from	~로 만들어지다 (물리적/화학적 변화)
be crowded with	~로 붐비다	be known as	~로 알려지다
be satisfied with	~에 만족하다	be known for	~로 유명하다
be disappointed with/at	~에 실망하다	be known to	~에게 알려지다
be interested in	~에 관심이 있다	be worried about	~에 대해 걱정하다

CHECK UP

● 빈칸에 알맞은 말을 고르시오.

1 The book _____ used in the class. ☐ doesn't ☐ isn't

2 He _____ deliver the letters. ☐ didn't ☐ wasn't

3 The football match _____ canceled. ☐ didn't ☐ wasn't

4 _____ they wash the dishes? ☐ Did ☐ Were

5 When _____ the house built? ☐ did ☐ was

6 Are you tired _____ studying? ☐ at ☐ of

7 I am not interested _____ sports. ☐ in ☐ about

8 The box is filled _____ toys. ☐ in ☐ with

9 This shelf is made _____ wood. ☐ of ☐ in

10 Jeju is known _____ its beautiful beaches. ☐ for ☐ to

box 안의 예문을 참고하여 우리말과 일치하도록 문장을 완성하시오.

WRITING POINT ①

- She **was not shocked** by the news. 그녀는 / 충격 받지 않았다 / 그 소식에
- **Was she shocked** by the news? 그녀는 / 충격 받았니 / 그 소식에?

1 그 축제는 해마다 열리지는 않는다. The festival _____ every year.

2 그 축제는 해마다 열리니? _____ the festival _____ every year?

3 그 책들은 수업에 쓰이지 않는다. The books _____ in class.

4 그 책들은 수업에 쓰이니? _____ the books _____ in class?

5 그 반지는 Clair가 발견하지 않았다. The ring _____ by Clair.

6 그 반지는 Clair가 발견했니? _____ the ring _____ by Clair?

7 그 편지들은 James가 쓰지 않았다. The letters _____ by James.

8 그 편지들은 James가 썼니? _____ the letters _____ by James?

WRITING POINT ②

- The bus **is crowded with** people. 그 버스는 / 붐빈다 / 사람들로

1 그 방은 사람들로 가득 차 있다. The room is filled _____ people.

2 그 산은 눈으로 덮여 있다. The mountain is covered _____ snow.

3 그는 그 시험 결과에 만족했다. He was satisfied _____ the test result.

4 그는 그 시험 결과에 실망했다. He was disappointed _____ the test result.

5 그 집은 벽돌로 만들어졌다. The house is made _____ bricks.

6 그 와인은 포도로 만들어졌다. The wine is made _____ grapes.

7 그 섬은 아름다운 경치로 유명하다. The island is known _____ its beautiful scenery.

8 그 섬은 많은 관광객들에게 알려져 있다. The island is known _____ many tourists.

9 그는 그 발표에 대해 걱정했다. He was worried _____ the presentation.

우리말과 일치하도록 빈칸에 알맞은 말을 넣으시오.

• 수동태의 부정문, 의문문 •

1 그 문은 잠겨 있지 않다. (lock)

→ The door _____ _____ _____.

2 그 소포는 제때 배달되지 않았다. (deliver)

→ The package _____ _____ _____ in time.

3 그 꽃들은 내가 심지 않았다. (plant)

→ The flowers _____ _____ _____ _____ me.

4 그 남자는 경찰에게 잡혔니? (catch)

→ _____ the man _____ _____ the police?

5 그들은 병원에 보내졌니? (take)

→ _____ _____ _____ to the hospital?

• by 이외의 전치사를 쓰는 수동태 •

6 그 서랍은 먼지로 뒤덮여 있다. (cover)

→ The drawer _____ _____ _____ dust.

7 그들은 그 소식에 실망했다. (disappoint)

→ They _____ _____ _____ the news.

8 Carol은 유럽 역사에 관심이 있다. (interest)

→ Carol _____ _____ _____ European history.

9 하와이는 최고의 휴양지로 알려져 있다. (know)

→ Hawaii _____ _____ _____ the best vacation spot.

10 사람들은 지구 온난화에 대해 걱정한다. (worry)

→ People _____ _____ _____ the global warming.

( ) 안의 말을 이용하여 우리말을 영어로 옮기시오.

1 그 사무실은 매일 청소되지는 않는다. (the office / every day)

2 그 다리는 강철로 만들어졌다. (the bridge / make / steel)

3 그 아기는 그 소음에 깨지 않았다. (wake up / the noise)

4 그 식당은 많은 사람들에게 알려져 있다. (the restaurant / know / many)

5 그는 개에게 물렸니? (bite / a dog)

6 그 식탁은 천으로 덮여 있다. (cover / a cloth)

7 그 백화점은 쇼핑객들로 붐볐다. (the department store / crowded / shoppers)

8 나는 내 일에 싫증이 난다. (tired / job)

9 내 프린터는 지난 주에 수리되지 않았다. (fix)

10 그는 팝의 황제로 알려져 있다. (know / the King of Pop)

11 그는 너에게 도움을 받았니? (help)

12 나는 네 건강이 걱정된다. (worry / health)

1 밑줄 친 부분을 주어로 하여 수동태로 바꾸어 쓰시오.

(1) A lot of people love the actor.

→ _____

(2) The storm damaged the village.

→ _____

(3) The workers will move the furniture.

→ _____

2 주어진 단어를 이용하여 대회를 완성하시오.

A Minho, do you know who wrote this book?

B Sure, it _____ J.K. Rowling. (write)

3 우리말과 같은 뜻이 되도록 주어진 단어를 바르게 배열하시오.

신발은 그 가게에서 판매되지 않는다.
(store / sold / the / not / shoes / are / at)

→ _____

4 주어진 단어를 이용하여 우리말을 영작하시오. (단, 수동태 문장으로 쓸 것)

(1) 그 컵은 Tom이 깬 것이 아니다. (the cup, break)

→ _____

(2) 그 편지는 Smith 씨가 배달한 거니? (the letter, deliver)

→ _____

5 다음 빈칸에 공통으로 알맞은 전치사를 쓰시오.

· The box is filled _____ toys.
· I was satisfied _____ the test result.

6 우리말과 같은 뜻이 되도록 빈칸에 알맞은 말을 쓰시오.

(1) 너는 음악에 관심이 있니?

→ _____ you _____ _____ music?

(2) 그 식탁은 나무로 만들어졌다.

→ The table _____ _____ _____ wood.

(3) 그 사실은 모두에게 알려져 있다.

→ The fact _____ _____ _____ everyone.

7 다음 중 어법상 틀린 곳을 찾아 바르게 고쳐 쓰시오.

(1) Did the game canceled yesterday?
(2) Last week, we invited to the Jane's birthday party.
(3) The issue will discuss in the meeting.

(1) _____ → _____
(2) _____ → _____
(3) _____ → _____

UNIT
05

to부정사

to부정사의 명사적, 형용사적 용법

1 to부정사는 문장에서 명사처럼 **주어, 보어, 목적어**로 쓰일 수 있다. 이때 주어로 쓰인 to부정사구는 **가주어 it**으로 대신하고 문장 뒤로 보낼 수 있다.

주어 역할	~하는 것은	To eat breakfast *is* important. 아침을 먹는 것은 중요하다. → It is important to eat breakfast. 가주어　　　　　　　　　　진주어
보어 역할	~하는 것(이다)	My hobby *is* to play the drums. 내 취미는 드럼을 연주하는 것이다.
목적어 역할	~하는 것을, ~하기를	Mira *wants* to visit Australia someday. 미라는 언젠가 호주를 방문하기를 원한다. *to부정사를 목적어로 취하는 동사: want, need, hope, expect, decide, plan, 　　　　　　　　　　　　　　　promise, try, learn, forget, refuse 등

2 to부정사는 **형용사** 역할을 하여 **앞의 명사를 수식**하기도 한다. 형용사적 용법의 to부정사는 '~할, ~하는'으로 해석하고, 이때 to부정사의 동사가 자동사인 경우 뒤에 전치사를 빠뜨리지 않도록 주의해야 한다.

명사 + to부정사	I have a lot of homework to do today. 나는 오늘 해야 할 숙제가 많다.	
명사 + to부정사 + 전치사	a pen to write with 쓸 펜 some paper to write on 쓸 종이 a chair to sit on 앉을 의자	a house to live in 살 집 a friend to play with 함께 놀 친구 someone to talk to/with 이야기할 누군가

PLUS -thing/one/body으로 끝나는 부정대명사가 형용사와 to부정사의 수식을 함께 받을 경우, 「부정대명사 + 형용사 + to부정사」의 어순을 취한다.
e.g. Do you want *something cold to drink*? 차가운 마실 것 좀 줄까?

CHECK UP

● 밑줄 친 부분의 알맞은 뜻을 고르시오.

1 To study abroad is expensive. 　☐ 공부하는 것은 　☐ 공부하는 것을

2 His job is to teach foreigners Korean. 　☐ 가르칠 　☐ 가르치는 것(이다)

3 Jerry, I have a question to ask you. 　☐ 물어보는 것은 　☐ 물어볼

4 He promised to help his mother. 　☐ 돕는 것을 　☐ 돕는 것(이다)

5 The boy has no friends to play with. 　☐ 함께 놀 　☐ 함께 노는 것을

6 I want to buy a present for my friend. 　☐ 사기를 　☐ 사는 것(이다)

7 Ted's dream is to open his own café. 　☐ 여는 것을 　☐ 여는 것(이다)

8 It's time to go home. 　☐ 가야 할 　☐ 가는 것(이다)

9 It is important to come to class on time. 　☐ 오는 것은 　☐ 오는 것(이다)

box 안의 예문을 참고하여 우리말과 일치하도록 문장을 완성하시오.

WRITING POINT 1

- **It** is impossible **to live** without water. 불가능하다 / 사는 것은 / 물 없이
- My goal is **to read** five books a month. 내 목표는 / 읽는 것이다 / 책 다섯 권을 / 한 달에

1 그 강에서 수영하는 것은 위험하다.　　It is dangerous _____ in the river.

2 균형 잡힌 식사를 하는 것은 중요하다.　　It is important _____ a balanced diet.

3 누군가에게 조언하는 것은 쉽지 않다.　　It is not easy _____ advice to someone.

4 그녀의 꿈은 과학자가 되는 것이다.　　Her dream is _____ a scientist.

5 그의 바람은 좋은 직장을 찾는 것이다.　　His wish is _____ a good job.

WRITING POINT 2

- He wants **to buy** a new computer. 그는 / 원한다 / 사기를 / 새 컴퓨터를

1 나는 오늘 밤 공부할 필요가 있다.　　I need _____ tonight.

2 그녀는 그 시험에 합격하기를 희망한다.　　She hopes _____ the exam.

3 우리는 다른 도시로 이사 가기로 결정했다.　　We've decided _____ to another city.

4 그들은 6시까지 그 일을 끝내려고 노력했다.　　They tried _____ the work by six.

5 그는 제 시간에 오겠다고 약속했다.　　He promised _____ on time.

WRITING POINT 3

- I have a letter **to write**. 나는 / 있다 / 편지가 / 쓸
- I need a pen **to write with**. 나는 / 필요하다 / 펜이 / (가지고) 쓸

1 너에게 말해줄 좋은 소식이 있다.　　I have good news _____ you.

2 그는 마실 물을 좀 샀다.　　He bought some water _____.

3 너는 따뜻한 입을 것이 필요할 거야.　　You'll need something warm _____.

4 그녀는 함께 살 룸메이트를 원한다.　　She wants a roommate _____.

5 그는 이야기할 누군가가 필요하다.　　He needs someone _____.

우리말과 일치하도록 빈칸에 알맞은 말을 넣으시오.

• to부정사의 명사적 용법: 주어, 보어 •

1 좋은 친구들을 사귀는 것은 중요하다. (make)

→ It is important _____ _____ _____ _____ .

2 너의 안전을 위해 헬멧을 착용하는 것이 필요하다. (a helmet)

→ It is necessary _____ _____ _____ _____ for your safety.

3 그의 행복의 비밀은 남을 돕는 것이다. (others)

→ His secret to happiness is _____ _____ _____ .

4 그의 목표는 올림픽에서 금메달을 따는 것이다. (a gold medal)

→ His goal is _____ _____ _____ _____ at the Olympics.

• to부정사의 명사적 용법: 목적어 •

5 엄마는 내게 새 자전거를 사주기로 약속했다. (promise)

→ My mom _____ _____ _____ me a new bike.

6 그는 그의 차를 팔고 새것을 살 계획이다. (plan)

→ He _____ _____ _____ his car and _____ a new one.

7 나는 매일 일기를 쓰려고 노력한다. (keep a diary)

→ I _____ _____ _____ _____ _____ every day.

• to부정사의 형용사적 용법 •

8 외국어를 배우는 가장 좋은 방법은 무엇이니? (the best way)

→ What is _____ _____ _____ _____ _____ a foreign language?

9 그는 그의 가족과 같이 살 집을 샀다. (live in)

→ He bought _____ _____ _____ _____ _____ with his family.

10 그들은 그것을 할 용감한 누군가를 찾고 있다. (someone / brave)

→ They are looking for _____ _____ _____ _____ it.

( ) 안의 말을 이용하여 우리말을 영어로 옮기시오.

1   Mary는 오늘 오후에 쇼핑하러 가기를 원한다. (want / go shopping)

2   읽을 책 한 권 추천해주시겠어요? (can / recommend)

3   다른 나라들에 대해 배우는 것은 좋은 생각이다. (it / learn about / other countries)

4   그의 계획은 일주일에 5일 체육관에 가는 것이다. (the gym / five days)

5   그는 종종 불 끄는 것을 잊는다. (turn off / the lights)

6   낯선 사람을 따라가는 것은 안전하지 않다. (it / a stranger)

7   Philip은 이번 여름에 유럽에 갈 계획이다. (Europe)

8   나는 오늘 해야 할 일이 세 가지가 있다. (three things)

9   가장 중요한 것은 명확한 목표를 세우는 것이다. (set a clear goal)

10   우리는 묵을 호텔을 찾고 있다. (look for / stay at)

11   그의 글씨를 읽는 것은 불가능하다. (it / his handwriting)

12   이야기할 누군가가 필요할 때 나에게 전화해. (call / when)

LESSON 12
to부정사의 부사적 용법

to부정사는 **부사** 역할을 하여 **동사, 형용사, 다른 부사를 수식**하기도 한다. 부사적 용법의 to부정사는 문맥에 따라 **목적, 감정의 원인, 판단의 근거, 결과** 등의 의미를 나타낼 수 있다.

목적	~하기 위해, ~하러	I went for a walk to get some fresh air. 나는 신선한 공기를 쐬기 위해 산책하러 갔다. *목적을 나타내는 to부정사는 in order to로 바꾸어 쓸 수 있다.
감정의 원인	~해서	I'm *glad* to meet you again. 다시 만나서 반갑습니다. *함께 자주 쓰이는 표현: glad, happy, pleased, sorry, disappointed, surprised 등 감정을 나타내는 형용사
판단의 근거	~하다니, ~하는 것을 보니	He *must* be angry to say so. 그렇게 말하는 것을 보니 그는 화가 났음에 틀림없다. *함께 자주 쓰이는 표현: must(~임에 틀림없다), cannot(~일 리가 없다) 등
결과	~해서 …하다, 결국 ~하다 (only to)	Her son *grew up* to be a famous writer. 그녀의 아들은 자라서 유명한 작가가 되었다. I studied hard only to fail. 나는 열심히 공부했지만 결국 낙제했다. *함께 자주 쓰이는 표현: grow up, live, wake up, only to 등

CHECK UP

● 밑줄 친 to부정사의 의미로 알맞은 것을 고르시오.

1	He went to the cafeteria to have lunch.	☐ 목적	☐ (감정의) 원인
2	Jenny was surprised to see him there.	☐ 목적	☐ (감정의) 원인
3	What do you do to improve your English?	☐ 목적	☐ (감정의) 원인
4	I called Yumi to invite her for dinner.	☐ 목적	☐ (감정의) 원인
5	He was disappointed to miss his flight.	☐ 목적	☐ (감정의) 원인
6	His son grew up to be a doctor.	☐ 결과	☐ (판단의) 근거
7	She must be really smart to memorize all that.	☐ 결과	☐ (판단의) 근거
8	The man lived to be over 100 years old.	☐ 결과	☐ (판단의) 근거
9	He must be rich to buy that luxurious car.	☐ 결과	☐ (판단의) 근거
10	I hurried to the store only to find it closed.	☐ 결과	☐ (판단의) 근거

box 안의 예문을 참고하여 우리말과 일치하도록 문장을 완성하시오.

WRITING POINT ❶

- He left early **to avoid** traffic. 그는 / 일찍 떠났다 / 교통 체증을 피하기 위해
- We were happy **to hear** from him. 우리는 / 기뻤다 / 그의 소식을 들어서

1 나는 빵을 좀 사기 위해 빵집에 갔다. I went to the bakery _____ some bread.

2 그는 뉴스를 보기 위해 TV를 켰다. He turned on the TV _____ the news.

3 그녀는 주스를 만들기 위해 과일을 좀 샀다. She bought some fruit _____ juice.

4 살을 빼기 위해, 나는 매일 줄넘기를 한다. _____ weight, I jump rope every day.

5 너를 돕게 되어 기뻐. I am pleased _____ you.

6 슬픈 소식을 듣게 되어 유감입니다. I am sorry _____ the sad news.

7 사람들은 그녀의 나이를 알고 놀랐다. People were surprised _____ her age.

8 우리는 그 경기에 져서 실망했다. We were disappointed _____ the game.

WRITING POINT ❷

- He must be honest **to say** so. 그는 / 정직함에 틀림없다 / 그렇게 말하다니
- She grew up **to be** a famous novelist. 그녀는 / 자라서 되었다 / 유명한 소설가가

1 거기에 살다니 그는 부자임에 틀림없다. He must be rich _____ there.

2 그걸 믿다니 그는 바보임에 틀림없다. He must be a fool _____ that.

3 그렇게 하다니 그는 매우 용감함에 틀림없다. He must be very brave _____ so.

4 지금까지 자다니 그는 피곤함에 틀림없다. He must be tired _____ until now.

5 그 소녀는 자라서 변호사가 되었다. The girl grew up _____ a lawyer.

6 나의 할아버지는 98세까지 살았다. My grandfather lived _____ 98 years old.

7 그는 깨어나보니 자신이 유명해진 것을 발견했다. He woke up _____ himself famous.

8 우리는 최선을 다했지만 결국 실패했다. We did our best only _____.

우리말과 일치하도록 빈칸에 알맞은 말을 넣으시오.

• to부정사의 부사적 용법: 목적, 감정의 원인 •

1 나는 부산행 첫 기차를 타기 위해 일찍 일어났다. (catch)

→ I got up early ＿＿＿＿＿ ＿＿＿＿＿ ＿＿＿＿＿ ＿＿＿＿＿ ＿＿＿＿＿ to Busan.

2 Eric은 책을 몇 권 대출하기 위해 도서관에 갔다. (check out)

→ Eric went to the library ＿＿＿＿＿ ＿＿＿＿＿ ＿＿＿＿＿ ＿＿＿＿＿ ＿＿＿＿＿.

3 우리는 한국 역사에 대해 배우기 위해 그 박물관을 방문했다. (learn about)

→ We visited the museum ＿＿＿＿＿ ＿＿＿＿＿ ＿＿＿＿＿ ＿＿＿＿＿ ＿＿＿＿＿.

4 나는 너 같은 친구가 있어서 행복해. (happy / have)

→ I ＿＿＿＿＿ ＿＿＿＿＿ ＿＿＿＿＿ ＿＿＿＿＿ a friend like you.

5 그는 자신의 한국 팬들을 보고 흥분했다. (excited)

→ He ＿＿＿＿＿ ＿＿＿＿＿ ＿＿＿＿＿ ＿＿＿＿＿ his Korean fans.

• to부정사의 부사적 용법: 판단의 근거, 결과 •

6 그렇게 많이 먹는 걸 보니 그들은 배가 고픔에 틀림없다. (so much)

→ They must be hungry ＿＿＿＿＿ ＿＿＿＿＿ ＿＿＿＿＿ ＿＿＿＿＿.

7 하버드에 다니다니 그녀는 똑똑함에 틀림없다. (Harvard)

→ She must be smart ＿＿＿＿＿ ＿＿＿＿＿ ＿＿＿＿＿ ＿＿＿＿＿.

8 그는 자라서 세계 최고의 배우가 되었다. (grow up)

→ He ＿＿＿＿＿ ＿＿＿＿＿ ＿＿＿＿＿ ＿＿＿＿＿ the best actor in the world.

9 그는 깨어나보니 자신이 병원에 있는 것을 발견했다. (wake up)

→ He ＿＿＿＿＿ ＿＿＿＿＿ ＿＿＿＿＿ ＿＿＿＿＿ himself in hospital.

10 그들은 열심히 노력했지만 결국 그 경기에서 졌다. (only to)

→ They tried hard ＿＿＿＿＿ ＿＿＿＿＿ ＿＿＿＿＿ the game.

( ) 안의 말을 이용하여 우리말을 영어로 옮기시오.

1 Cathy는 패션 디자인을 공부하기 위해 파리에 갔다. (Paris / fashion design)

2 Sally는 그 생일 선물을 받고 행복했다. (get / present)

3 그런 짓을 하다니 그는 어리석음에 틀림없다. (foolish / such a thing)

4 나의 조부모님께서는 90세까지 사셨다. (live / be)

5 Steve는 그 축제에 참가하기 위해 드럼을 연습했다. (the drums / take part in)

6 그 소년은 자라서 훌륭한 음악가가 되었다. (grow up / be)

7 우리는 그들을 돕기 위해 뭔가를 해야 한다. (should / do something)

8 George는 그의 가족을 다시 보게 되어 행복했다. (happy / see)

9 그녀에게 매일 꽃을 주다니 그는 그녀를 좋아함에 틀림없다. (give her flowers)

10 우리는 서둘러 역에 갔지만 결국 그 기차를 놓쳤다. (hurry to / only to / miss)

11 그녀는 깨어나보니 자신이 혼자 있는 것을 발견했다. (wake up / find / alone)

12 매일 제시간에 오는 것을 보니 그는 부지런함에 틀림없다. (diligent / on time)

LESSON 13 to부정사 주요 구문

1 「too ~ to-v」는 '너무 ~해서 …할 수 없다', '…하기에는 너무 ~하다'란 의미로, 「so ~ that+주어+can't/couldn't」로 바꾸어 쓸 수 있다.

He is **too young to vote**. 그는 투표하기에는 너무 어리다.
= He is **so young that he can't vote**.

2 「~ enough to-v」는 '…할 만큼 (충분히) ~하다'란 의미로, 「so ~ that+주어+can/could」로 바꾸어 쓸 수 있다.

She is **tall enough to be** a model. 그녀는 모델이 될 만큼 충분히 키가 크다.
= She is **so tall that she can be** a model.

3 「의문사+to-v」는 문장에서 주어, 보어, 목적어 역할을 하고, 「의문사+주어+should+동사원형」으로 바꾸어 쓸 수 있다.

what to-v	무엇을 ~할지	where to-v	어디서 ~할지
when to-v	언제 ~할지	how to-v	어떻게 ~할지, ~하는 방법

I don't know **what to do** now. 나는 지금 무엇을 해야 할지 모르겠다.
= I don't know **what I should do** now.

● 빈칸에 알맞은 말을 고르시오.

1 The box is too _____ to lift. ☐ heavy ☐ light

2 This watch is too _____ to buy. ☐ cheap ☐ expensive

3 The question is too _____ to solve. ☐ easy ☐ difficult

4 The water is _____ enough to drink. ☐ clean ☐ dirty

5 He is _____ enough to move the sofa alone. ☐ weak ☐ strong

6 My pocket is _____ enough to hold my wallet. ☐ big ☐ small

7 Please tell me _____ to do next. ☐ when ☐ what

8 He told me _____ to stay in New York. ☐ what ☐ where

9 I don't really know _____ to call her. ☐ when ☐ what

10 I'll show you _____ to use this camera. ☐ how ☐ what

box 안의 예문을 참고하여 우리말과 일치하도록 문장을 완성하시오.

WRITING POINT ①

• I am **too busy to help** you right now. 나는 / 너무 바쁘다 / 너를 돕기에는 / 지금

1 나는 공부하기에는 너무 피곤하다. I am _____.

2 그는 차를 운전하기에는 너무 어리다. He is _____ a car.

3 그녀는 학교에 가기에는 너무 아팠다. She was _____ to school.

4 그 커피는 너무 뜨거워서 마실 수 없다. The coffee is _____.

5 이 책은 너무 어려워서 읽을 수 없다. This book is _____.

WRITING POINT ②

• She is **old enough to get** married. 그녀는 / 나이가 들었다 / 결혼을 할 만큼

1 나는 그 버스를 잡을 만큼 빨리 달렸다. I ran _____ the bus.

2 그는 그 바위를 들어 올릴 만큼 힘이 세다. He is _____ the rock.

3 그는 그 스포츠카를 살 만큼 부유하다. He is _____ the sports car.

4 그녀는 그 문제를 풀 만큼 똑똑하다. She is _____ the problem.

5 그녀는 가수가 될 만큼 노래를 잘한다. She sings _____ a singer.

WRITING POINT ③

• I don't know **what to say** to you. 나는 / 모르겠다 / 무슨 말을 해야 할지 / 너에게

1 나는 무엇을 입어야 할지 모르겠다. I don't know _____.

2 우리는 무엇을 해야 할지 몰랐다. We didn't know _____.

3 그는 나에게 언제 올지 말해주었다. He told me _____.

4 내일 어디서 만날지 정하자. Let's decide _____ tomorrow.

5 너는 이 노래 연주하는 법을 아니? Do you know _____ this song?

우리말과 일치하도록 빈칸에 알맞은 말을 넣으시오.

• too ~ to-v •

1 그 햄버거는 너무 두꺼워서 베어 물 수가 없다. (thick / bite)

→ The hamburger is _____ _____ _____ _____.

2 Jimmy는 키가 너무 작아서 그 롤러코스터를 탈 수 없다. (ride)

→ Jimmy is _____ _____ _____ _____ the roller coaster.

3 수영하러 가기에는 너무 춥다. (go swimming)

→ It is _____ _____ _____ _____ _____.

• ~ enough to-v •

4 그는 맨 위 선반에 닿을 만큼 키가 크다. (reach)

→ He is _____ _____ _____ _____ the top shelf.

5 그 남자는 혼자서 그 도둑을 잡을 만큼 충분히 용감했다. (catch)

→ The man was _____ _____ _____ _____ the thief alone.

6 그녀는 나에게 좋은 충고를 해줄 만큼 현명하다. (give)

→ She is _____ _____ _____ _____ me good advice.

• 의문사 + to부정사 •

7 엄마는 나에게 파스타 만드는 방법을 가르쳐주었다. (make)

→ My mom taught me _____ _____ _____ pasta.

8 너는 어디로 휴가 갈지 정했니? (go)

→ Have you decided _____ _____ _____ on your vacation?

9 나에게 파티에 무엇을 가져가야 할지 말해줘. (bring)

→ Please tell me _____ _____ _____ to the party.

10 나는 그에게 내 코트를 어디에 두어야 할지 물었다. (my coat)

→ I asked him _____ _____ _____ _____ _____.

( ) 안의 말을 이용하여 우리말을 영어로 옮기시오.

1 그는 그 셔츠를 입기에는 너무 크다. (big / the shirt)

2 그녀는 가난한 사람들을 도울 만큼 친절하다. (the poor)

3 나는 점심으로 무엇을 먹어야 할지 결정을 못하겠다. (decide / for lunch)

4 Jack은 그 어려운 수학 문제를 풀 만큼 똑똑하다. (smart)

5 나는 너무 피곤해서 오늘 아침에 조깅하러 갈 수 없었다. (go jogging)

6 지하철역에 어떻게 가야 하는지 말해주시겠어요? (can / get to)

7 그녀는 너무 어려서 그녀의 부모님을 이해할 수 없다. (understand)

8 날씨가 소풍을 갈 만큼 충분히 좋았다. (good / go on a picnic)

9 나는 이 화분을 어디에 두어야 할지 모르겠다. (put / this flowerpot)

10 그녀는 그 영화에서 Juliet 역을 맡을 만큼 충분히 아름답다. (play Juliet)

11 그는 마라톤을 뛰기에는 너무 약하다. (run a marathon)

12 나는 그녀의 생일 선물로 무엇을 사야 할지 모르겠다. (for her birthday)

1 우리말과 같은 뜻이 되도록 주어진 단어를 바르게 배열하시오.

(1) 영어로 편지를 쓰는 것은 쉽지 않다.
(easy / is / a letter / it / in / to / English / write / not)

→ _____

(2) 그의 직업은 동물원의 동물들에게 먹이를 주는 것이다.
(the animals / his job / in / feed / is / the zoo / to)

→ _____

(3) 이번 여름에 너는 무엇을 할 계획이니?
(planning / this summer / you / to / are / what / do)

→ _____

2 주어진 단어를 이용하여 우리말을 영작하시오.

(1) 나는 오늘 해야 할 일이 많다. (do, work)

→ I have a lot of _____ _____ _____ today.

(2) Sue는 앉을 의자가 필요하다. (sit, a chair)

→ Sue needs _____ _____ _____ _____ _____.

3 주어진 단어를 모두 포함하여 우리말을 영작하시오.

나는 책을 몇 권 사기 위해 서점에 갔다.
(some, order, in)

→ _____
_____

4 다음 두 문장을 한 문장으로 만들 때 빈칸에 알맞은 말을 쓰시오.

Jane passed the exam. + She was happy.

→ Jane was happy _____ _____ _____ _____.

5 두 문장이 같은 의미가 되도록 빈칸에 알맞은 말을 쓰시오.

(1) Greg is too fat to wear the pants.

→ Greg is _____ _____ that _____ _____ _____ the pants.

(2) We got up early enough to catch the first train.

→ We got up _____ _____ that _____ _____ _____ the first train.

6 그림을 보고 주어진 단어를 이용하여 문장을 완성하시오.

→ Minsu is _____ _____ _____ _____ the box.
(enough, carry)

7 주어진 단어를 이용하여 대화를 완성하시오.

A Sam, tomorrow is Mom's birthday.
B I know, but I don't know _____ _____ _____. (do)
A Why don't we cook for her? I learned _____ _____ _____ spaghetti. (make)
B That's a great idea. Let's do it.

UNIT
06

동명사와 분사

LESSON 14 동명사 vs. to부정사

1 동명사는 문장에서 명사처럼 **주어, 보어, 목적어** 역할을 하고, '~하는 것'으로 해석한다.

Riding a bike *is* fun. (주어) 자전거를 <u>타는 것은</u> 재미있다.
My hobby *is* **riding** a bike. (보어) 내 취미는 자전거 <u>타는 것</u>이다.
I *enjoy* **riding** a bike. (목적어) 나는 자전거 <u>타는 것을</u> 즐긴다.

2 동사에 따라 목적어로 **동명사**나 **to부정사**를 취할 수 있다.

동명사를 취하는 동사	enjoy, finish, mind, keep, practice, avoid, give up 등	I *practice* playing the piano every day. 나는 매일 피아노 치는 것을 연습한다.
to부정사를 취하는 동사	want, decide, hope, expect, try, need, plan, learn, promise 등	She *promised* to bring her camera. 그녀는 자신의 카메라를 가져오기로 약속했다.
동명사와 to부정사를 모두 취하는 동사	like, love, hate, start, begin 등	James *loves* cooking/to cook. James는 요리하는 것을 매우 좋아한다.

3 동명사 관용 표현

go -ing	~하러 가다	feel like -ing	~하고 싶다
be busy -ing	~하느라 바쁘다	be good at -ing	~을 잘하다
be worth -ing	~할 만한 가치가 있다	look forward to -ing	~하는 것을 고대하다
How/What about -ing	~하는 게 어때?	have difficulty/trouble -ing	~하는데 어려움을 겪다

CHECK UP

● 빈칸에 알맞은 말을 고르시오.

1 Mike enjoys _____ soccer. ☐ playing ☐ to play

2 Sara wants _____ a new cell phone. ☐ buying ☐ to buy

3 Let's go _____ after lunch. ☐ shopping ☐ to shop

4 Do you mind _____ for a minute? ☐ waiting ☐ to wait

5 I feel like _____ chicken for lunch. ☐ eating ☐ to eat

6 Jinsu decided _____ the basketball team. ☐ joining ☐ to join

7 Yumi finished _____ the dishes. ☐ washing ☐ to wash

8 How about _____ to the movies with me? ☐ going ☐ to go

9 What time do you expect _____ home tonight? ☐ being ☐ to be

box 안의 예문을 참고하여 우리말과 일치하도록 문장을 완성하시오.

WRITING POINT ①

· I enjoy **listening** to music. 나는 / 즐긴다 / 음악 듣는 것을

· Do you want **to go** for a walk? 너는 / 원하니 / 산책하러 가기를?

---

1 그는 강에서 낚시하는 것을 즐긴다. He enjoys _____ in the river.

2 나는 내 방 청소하는 것을 끝냈다. I finished _____ my room.

3 창문을 열어도 괜찮을까요? Do you mind _____ the window?

4 나는 전 세계를 여행하기를 희망한다. I hope _____ around the world.

5 그들은 소풍을 취소하기로 결정했다. They decided _____ the picnic.

6 우리는 다시 만나기로 약속했다. We promised _____ again.

7 그는 수영하는 것을 좋아하지 않는다. He doesn't like _____.

8 비가 내리기 시작했다. It started _____.

9 어떤 아이들은 학교에 가는 것을 싫어한다. Some children hate _____ to school.

WRITING POINT ②

· He **was busy doing** his homework. 그는 / 바빴다 / 그의 숙제를 하느라

---

1 그녀는 매일 아침 조깅을 하러 간다. She goes _____ every morning.

2 그 웨이터는 음식을 제공하느라 바쁘다. The waiter is busy _____ the food.

3 그 책은 읽을 만한 가치가 있다. The book is worth _____.

4 나랑 테니스 치는 게 어때? How about _____ tennis with me?

5 나는 매운 음식을 먹고 싶어. I feel like _____ spicy food.

6 Sam은 기타 연주를 잘한다. Sam is good at _____ the guitar.

7 나는 네 소식을 듣기를 고대하고 있다. I'm looking forward to _____ from you.

8 그는 이름들을 기억하는 데 어려움을 겪는다. He has difficulty _____ names.

우리말과 일치하도록 빈칸에 알맞은 말을 넣으시오.

• 동사 + 동명사/to부정사 •

1 나는 사람들을 웃게 하는 것을 즐긴다. (make)

→ I _____ _____ people laugh.

2 나는 너와 연락하고 지내길 희망한다. (hope / keep in touch)

→ I _____ _____ _____ _____ _____ with you.

3 그는 밤에 운전하는 것을 피한다. (avoid)

→ He _____ _____ at night.

4 너는 졸업 후에 무엇을 할 계획이니? (plan)

→ What do you _____ _____ _____ after graduation?

5 그는 계속해서 나에게 질문을 했다. (ask)

→ He _____ _____ me questions.

• 동명사 관용 표현 •

6 그녀는 아침을 준비하느라 바쁘다. (prepare)

→ She _____ _____ _____ breakfast.

7 나는 오늘 밤 나가고 싶지 않다. (feel like / go out)

→ I _____ _____ _____ _____ _____ tonight.

8 그 TV 프로그램은 볼만한 가치가 있니? (worth)

→ Is the TV program _____ _____?

9 우리는 그 상점을 찾는 데 어려움을 겪었다. (find)

→ We _____ _____ _____ the store.

10 그녀는 영어를 말하는 것을 잘한다. (good at)

→ She _____ _____ _____ _____ English.

( ) 안의 말을 이용하여 우리말을 영어로 옮기시오.

1 그 관광객들은 사진을 찍느라 바빴다. (the tourists / busy / take pictures)

2 나의 아버지는 중국 음식 요리하는 것을 잘하신다. (good at / Chinese food)

3 우리는 이번 주말에 여행 가는 것을 포기했다. (give up / go on a trip)

4 그들은 노숙자들을 돕기로 결심했다. (the homeless)

5 같이 컴퓨터 게임 하는 게 어때? (play computer games)

6 나는 시골에 사는 것을 꺼리지 않는다. (mind / in the countryside)

7 그는 그 시험에서 좋은 성적을 받기를 희망한다. (get a good grade / on the test)

8 나는 겨울에 스키 타러 가는 것을 좋아한다. (in winter)

9 그녀는 내 질문에 답하는 것을 피했다. (avoid / my question)

10 그의 충고는 따를 만한 가치가 있다. (worth / follow)

11 그녀는 그녀의 가족과 함께 시간 보내기를 고대하고 있다. (spend time)

12 나는 항상 점심 식사 후에 낮잠을 자고 싶다. (feel like / take a nap)

LESSON 15
현재분사, 과거분사

1 동사에 -ing나 -ed를 붙여 **형용사**처럼 쓰는 것을 분사라고 한다. 분사는 **현재분사**와 **과거분사**가 있으며, 형용사처럼 **명사를 수식**할 수 있다. 이때 분사가 구를 이루어 명사를 수식할 때는 명사 뒤에서 수식한다.

현재분사 (동사원형 + -ing)	~하는, ~하고 있는 (능동·진행)	Look at the sleeping *cat*. 잠자고 있는 고양이를 봐. Look at the *cat* sleeping under the table. 식탁 밑에서 잠자고 있는 고양이를 봐.
과거분사 (동사원형 + -ed)	~된, ~당한 (수동·완료)	He fixed the broken *window*. 그는 깨진 창문을 고쳤다. He fixed the *window* broken by the typhoon. 그는 태풍으로 깨진 창문을 고쳤다.

2 감정을 나타내는 타동사(interest, disappoint, surprise 등)가 현재분사로 쓰이면 그 감정을 유발하는 것을, 과거분사로 쓰이면 그 감정을 느끼는 것을 나타낸다.

현재분사	과거분사
The class is boring. 지루한	I am bored with the class. 지루함을 느끼는
She thinks that history is interesting. 흥미로운	She is interested in history. 흥미를 느끼는
The movie was disappointing. 실망스러운	I was disappointed with the movie. 실망한
The news was surprising. 놀라운	We were surprised at the news. 놀란
His job is tiring. 피곤한 (피곤함을 주는)	He's always tired after work. 피곤함을 느끼는
The road signs are confusing. 헷갈리는	People are confused by the road signs. 혼란스러워 하는

PLUS 그 외 excite(흥분시키다), shock(충격을 주다), satisfy(만족시키다), depress(우울하게 하다) 등도 현재분사와 과거분사로 쓰일 수 있다.

● 빈칸에 알맞은 말을 고르시오.

1 I like _____ potatoes. ☐ frying ☐ fried

2 It is a long, _____ story. ☐ boring ☐ bored

3 Who is the girl _____ water? ☐ drinking ☐ drunk

4 He lives in a house _____ in 1950. ☐ building ☐ built

5 The _____ glasses are mine. ☐ breaking ☐ broken

6 The boy _____ a bike is my brother. ☐ riding ☐ ridden

7 This is a sweater _____ by my mom. ☐ making ☐ made

8 Her new book is _____. ☐ interesting ☐ interested

9 What is the language _____ in the country? ☐ speaking ☐ spoken

box 안의 예문을 참고하여 우리말과 일치하도록 문장을 완성하시오.

WRITING POINT ❶

- Look at the boy **making** a snowman. 봐 / 저 소년을 / 만들고 있는 / 눈사람을
- She has a car **made** in Japan. 그녀는 / 가지고 있다 / 자동차를 / 만든 / 일본에서

---

1 너는 유성을 본 적이 있니?   Have you ever seen a _____ star?

2 거리에 낙엽들이 있다.   There are _____ leaves on the street.

3 국수를 끓는 물에 넣어라.   Put the noodles in _____ water.

4 나는 삶은 달걀 한 개를 먹었다.   I ate a _____ egg.

5 편지를 쓰고 있는 소녀는 누구니?   Who is the girl _____ a letter?

6 그녀는 영어로 쓰여진 편지를 읽고 있다.   She is reading a letter _____ in English.

7 사진을 찍고 있는 남자는 Peter이다.   The man _____ a picture is Peter.

8 이것은 Peter가 찍은 사진이다.   This is a picture _____ by Peter.

WRITING POINT ❷

- The news was **shocking**. 그 소식은 / 충격을 주었다
- People were **shocked** by the news. 사람들은 / 충격을 받았다 / 그 소식에 의해

---

1 그의 농담들은 지루하다.   His jokes are _____.

2 나는 지루할 때 음악을 듣는다.   I listen to music when I am _____.

3 그 여행은 신나는 경험이었다.   The trip was an _____ experience.

4 나는 그 여행으로 들떠 있었다.   I was _____ about the trip.

5 피곤한 하루였다.   It was a _____ day.

6 그는 집에 도착했을 때 피곤했다.   He was _____ when he got home.

7 그 시험 결과는 만족스러웠다.   The test result was _____.

8 나는 그 시험 결과에 만족했다.   I was _____ with the test result.

우리말과 일치하도록 빈칸에 알맞은 말을 넣으시오.

• 현재분사 / 과거분사 •

1 그의 별명은 걸어 다니는 사전이다. (dictionary)

→ His nickname is a _____ _____.

2 그는 한쪽 다리가 부러졌다. (break)

→ He has a _____ _____.

3 수영장에서 수영하는 아이들이 몇 명 있다. (in the pool)

→ There are some children _____ _____ _____ _____.

4 눈으로 뒤덮인 정원을 봐. (cover)

→ Look at the garden _____ with _____.

5 그는 Tiki라는 이름의 말하는 로봇을 가지고 있다. (talk / name)

→ He has a _____ robot _____ Tiki.

• 감정을 나타내는 분사 •

6 이 책에는 많은 감동적인 이야기들이 있다. (touch)

→ This book has many _____ _____.

7 그들은 나를 보고 놀랐다. (surprise)

→ They _____ _____ to see me.

8 오늘은 날씨가 우울하다. (depress)

→ The weather is _____ today.

9 이 지도는 나를 혼란스럽게 만들었다. (confuse)

→ This map made me _____.

10 그 경기장은 흥분한 축구팬들로 가득 차 있다. (excite / soccer fans)

→ The stadium is filled with _____ _____ _____.

( ) 안의 말을 이용하여 우리말을 영어로 옮기시오.

1 그 여자는 울고 있는 아기를 안고 있다. (hold)

2 이 수학 문제는 매우 헷갈린다. (so / confuse)

3 양복을 입고 있는 남자는 내 삼촌이다. (a suit)

4 그는 그의 도난당한 지갑을 찾았다. (steal / wallet)

5 이것은 내가 가장 좋아하는 가수가 쓴 곡이다. (the song / my favorite singer)

6 그는 벤치에 앉아 있는 그 소녀에게 말을 걸었다. (talk to / the bench)

7 한국어를 배우는 외국인들이 많이 있다. (there / many foreigners)

8 나는 내 직업에 만족한다. (satisfy / with my job)

9 시골에서 사는 것은 지루할 수 있다. (living in the country / can)

10 그녀는 궂은 날씨 때문에 우울했다. (depress / by the bad weather)

11 그 사고에서 부상당한 남자는 Brown 씨이다. (injure / in the accident)

12 영어는 전 세계에서 말해지는 언어이다. (the language / all over the world)

1 다음 문장에서 어법상 <u>틀린</u> 곳을 찾아 바르게 고쳐 쓰시오.

(1) Eating vegetables are good for your health.

(2) Is take pictures your hobby?

(1) _____ → _____
(2) _____ → _____

2 ( ) 안의 단어를 알맞게 고쳐 문장을 완성하시오.

(1) Boram enjoys _____ yoga. (do)

(2) Do you mind _____ off the light? (turn)

(3) Jiho tried _____ on time, but he missed the bus. (be)

3 주어진 단어를 바르게 배열하여 문장을 완성하시오.

(1) (piano / at / Jane / playing / good / is / the)

→ _____

(2) (the / difficulty / finding / we / restaurant / had)

→ _____

(3) (feel / I / eating / don't / lunch / like)

→ _____

4 주어진 단어를 이용하여 우리말을 영작하시오.

같이 하이킹하러 가는 게 어때? (hiking)

→ _____ _____ _____
_____ together?

5 그림을 보고 주어진 단어를 이용하여 아래 대화를 완성하시오.

A Do you know where Mina is?
B She's over there.
A I can't see her.
B She is the girl _____ _____
_____. (read)

6 빈칸에 들어갈 단어를 〈보기〉에서 골라 알맞은 형태로 고쳐 쓰시오.

보기	deliver / fly / paint

(1) Look at the bird _____ in the sky.

(2) This is the picture _____ by Van Gogh.

(3) There is a package _____ this morning.

7 주어진 단어를 이용하여 대화를 완성하시오.

A Hi, Minho. How was your weekend?
B I had a very _____ weekend because of the rain. (bore)

UNIT
07

명사와 대명사

LESSON 16 명사의 수량 표현

Ⅰ 일정한 모양과 크기가 없는 **물질명사(water, juice, bread, soap, sugar 등)**는 셀 수 없는 명사로 모양이나 담는 용기로 수를 표현한다.

수량 표현	명사	수량 표현	명사
a piece/slice of 한 조각 / (얇게 썬) 조각, 장	cake, bread, cheese, pizza	**a piece/sheet of** 한 장	paper
a cup of 한 잔	coffee, tea	**a loaf of** 한 덩어리	bread
a glass/bottle of 한 잔/병	water, juice, milk	**a can of** 한 캔	coke, soda, corn
a bowl of 한 그릇	rice, soup, salad	**a bar of** (막대 모양) 한 개	soap, chocolate

NOTE 물질명사는 셀 수 없는 명사이므로 복수형이 없으며, 단위명사를 복수형으로 써 준다.
e.g. *two cups* of coffee 차 두 잔 / *three loaves* of bread 빵 세 조각

2 **(a) few/(a) little**은 명사의 수나 양을 나타내는 형용사이다. **a few/a little**은 '조금의, 약간의'란 뜻이고, **few/little**은 '거의 없는'이란 부정적 의미로 사용한다. **(a) few** 뒤에는 셀 수 있는 명사가, **(a) little** 뒤에는 셀 수 없는 명사가 온다.

(a) few + 셀 수 있는 명사 (복수형)	John has a few *friends* at school. John은 학교에 친구들이 몇 명 있다. John has few *friends* at school. John은 학교에 친구들이 거의 없다.
(a) little + 셀 수 없는 명사	There is a little *water* in the bottle. 병에 물이 약간 있다. There is little *water* in the bottle. 병에 물이 거의 없다.

● 빈칸에 알맞은 말을 고르시오.

1 They left a _____ of cake.　　☐ loaf　　☐ piece

2 Can you bring me a _____ of paper?　　☐ sheet　　☐ slice

3 How many _____ of bread do you want?　　☐ bowls　　☐ loaves

4 Ann gave me a _____ of chocolate.　　☐ bar　　☐ can

5 The boy ate two _____ of rice.　　☐ cups　　☐ bowls

6 Jimmy has _____ money now.　　☐ few　　☐ little

7 _____ people understand him.　　☐ Few　　☐ Little

8 She wrote _____ words on the board.　　☐ a few　　☐ a little

9 We had _____ rain this summer.　　☐ a few　　☐ a little

box 안의 예문을 참고하여 우리말과 일치하도록 문장을 완성하시오.

WRITING POINT ①

• I drink **a glass of** milk every morning. 나는 / 마신다 / 우유 한 잔을 / 매일 아침

I 그는 하루에 커피 두 잔을 마신다. He drinks _____ coffee a day.

2 나는 종이 한 장이 필요하다. I need _____ paper.

3 그녀는 수프 한 그릇을 주문했다. She ordered _____ soup.

4 그는 우유 세 병을 샀다. He bought _____ milk.

5 나는 그에게 빵 한 덩어리를 주었다. I gave him _____ bread.

WRITING POINT ②

• There are **a few** books on the bookshelf. 책이 몇 권 있다 / 책장에
• There are **few** books on the bookshelf. 책이 거의 없다 / 책장에

I 그는 나에게 몇 가지 질문을 했다. He asked me _____ questions.

2 그는 나에게 거의 질문을 하지 않았다. He asked me _____ questions.

3 학생 몇 명이 그 시험에 합격했다. _____ students passed the test.

4 그 시험에 합격한 학생은 거의 없었다. _____ students passed the test.

WRITING POINT ③

• He had **a little** money in his pocket. 그는 / 돈이 조금 있었다 / 주머니에
• He had **little** money in his pocket. 그는 / 돈이 거의 없었다 / 주머니에

I 냉장고에 약간의 음식이 있다. There is _____ food in the fridge.

2 냉장고에 음식이 거의 없다. There is _____ food in the fridge.

3 그녀는 불어를 조금 할 수 있다. She can speak _____ French.

4 그녀는 불어를 거의 못한다. She can speak _____ French.

우리말과 일치하도록 빈칸에 알맞은 말을 넣으시오.

• 물질명사의 수량 표현 •

1 나는 치즈 두 장이 필요하다. (cheese)

→ I need _____ _____ _____ _____.

2 나의 가족은 한 달에 비누 한 개를 사용한다. (soap)

→ My family uses _____ _____ _____ _____ a month.

3 그는 점심으로 피자 두 조각을 먹었다. (pizza)

→ He had _____ _____ _____ _____ for lunch.

• a few / a little •

4 우리는 그 섬에서 며칠을 보냈다. (day)

→ We spent _____ _____ _____ on the island.

5 Susan은 친구 몇 명을 그녀의 집에 초대했다. (friend)

→ Susan invited _____ _____ _____ to her house.

6 그녀는 자신의 수프에 약간의 소금을 넣었다. (salt)

→ She put _____ _____ _____ in her soup.

7 나는 그곳에 몇 번 가본 적이 있다. (time)

→ I have been there _____ _____ _____.

• few / little •

8 그녀는 커피를 거의 마시지 않는다. (coffee)

→ She drinks _____ _____.

9 안타깝게도, 우리는 베니스에서는 거의 사진을 찍지 않았다. (picture)

→ Unfortunately, we took _____ _____ in Venice.

10 나는 스포츠에 거의 관심이 없다. (interest)

→ I have _____ _____ in sports.

( ) 안의 말을 이용하여 우리말을 영어로 옮기시오.

1   내가 물 한잔 마셔도 될까? (can / have)

2   Jessica는 몇 년 전에 독일에서 살았다. (Germany / ago)

3   우리에게는 지금 시간이 거의 없다. (have / time)

4   그녀는 후식으로 케이크 한 조각을 먹었다. (have / for dessert)

5   그는 카펫에 우유를 조금 엎질렀다. (spill / on the carpet)

6   나는 오늘 해야 할 숙제가 조금 있다. (to do)

7   바구니 안에 빵 세 덩어리가 있다. (there / in the basket)

8   병에 물이 조금 남아 있다. (there / left)

9   그 수학 문제를 푼 학생은 거의 없었다. (solve)

10   나는 초콜릿 바 한 개와 콜라 두 캔을 샀다. (chocolate / coke)

11   그는 그 시험에서 거의 실수를 하지 않았다. (mistake / on the test)

12   나는 보통 오후에 차 한잔을 마신다. (usually / have)

LESSON 17 재귀대명사

1 재귀대명사는 인칭대명사의 목적격이나 소유격에 **-self/selves**를 붙인 형태로 '~ 자신'을 의미한다. 재귀대명사는 동사나 전치사의 목적어가 주어와 같을 때 사용하는데, 이를 재귀대명사의 **재귀용법**이라고 한다.

단수		복수	
I	myself	**We**	ourselves
You	yourself	**You**	yourselves
He / She / It	himself / herself / itself	**They**	themselves

Sally loves **herself** very much. Sally는 그녀 자신을 매우 사랑한다.
He wrote a book about **himself**. 그는 자신에 관한 책을 썼다.

> **PLUS** 재귀대명사가 주어, 목적어를 강조하기 위해 쓰이는 강조용법의 경우에는 재귀대명사를 생략할 수 있다.
> e.g. I wrote this poem *myself*. 나는 이 시를 직접 썼다.
> The exam *itself* was easy. 그 시험 자체는 쉬웠다.

2 재귀대명사 관용 표현

enjoy oneself	즐거운 시간을 보내다	make oneself at home	편안히 있다
help oneself (to)	(~을) 마음껏 먹다	teach oneself	독학하다
by oneself	혼자서(alone), 혼자 힘으로(without help)	talk to oneself	혼잣말 하다
of itself	저절로	between ourselves	우리끼리만

CHECK UP

● 빈칸에 알맞은 말을 고르시오.

1 I hurt _____ in the gym yesterday. ☐ me ☐ myself

2 Mom bought _____ a pair of jeans. ☐ me ☐ myself

3 If you believe in _____, you will succeed. ☐ you ☐ yourself

4 I saw _____ at the theater. ☐ him ☐ himself

5 He can express _____ in English. ☐ him ☐ himself

6 Please help _____ to some food. ☐ you ☐ yourself

7 Let's keep this between _____. ☐ us ☐ ourselves

8 Sera, did you go there by _____? ☐ herself ☐ yourself

9 John and I enjoyed _____ at the party. ☐ myself ☐ ourselves

86

box 안의 예문을 참고하여 우리말과 일치하도록 문장을 완성하시오.

WRITING POINT ①

• She praised **herself**. 그녀는 / 칭찬했다 / 스스로를

1 나는 칼에 베었다.   I cut _____ with a knife.

2 자책하지 마세요.   Don't blame _____.

3 그는 우리에게 자신을 소개했다.   He introduced _____ to us.

4 그녀는 자신을 그렸다.   She drew a picture of _____.

5 우리는 우리 자신을 믿어야 한다.   We should believe in _____.

6 여러분, 몸조심하세요.   Everyone, take care of _____.

7 그들은 자신들을 자랑스러워했다.   They were proud of _____.

8 내 개는 다쳤다.   My dog hurt _____.

9 그녀는 자신에게 선물을 사주었다.   She bought a present for _____.

WRITING POINT ②

• I want you to **enjoy yourself**. 나는 / 원한다 / 네가 / 즐거운 시간을 보내기를

1 편안히 있으세요.   Please make _____ at home.

2 이 음식을 마음껏 드세요.   Help _____ to this food.

3 그는 큰 집에서 혼자 산다.   He lives by _____ in a big house.

4 나는 이 상자를 혼자서 옮길 수 없다.   I can't move this box by _____.

5 그 문은 저절로 닫혔다.   The door closed of _____.

6 그녀는 종종 혼잣말을 한다.   She often talks to _____.

7 그들은 축제에서 즐거운 시간을 보냈다.   They enjoyed _____ at the festival.

8 그는 수영하는 법을 혼자서 배웠다.   He taught _____ to swim.

9 이것은 우리끼리만 아는 얘기이다.   This is between _____.

우리말과 일치하도록 빈칸에 알맞은 말을 넣으시오.

• 재귀대명사 (재귀용법) •

1 여러분에게 제 소개를 할게요. (introduce)

→ Let me _____ _____ to you.

2 반 고흐는 37세의 나이로 자살했다. (kill)

→ Van Gogh _____ _____ at the age of 37.

3 내 여동생은 자기 자신만 생각한다. (think about)

→ My sister only _____ _____ _____.

4 우리는 그 실수에 대해 우리 자신을 탓했다. (blame)

→ We _____ _____ for the mistake.

5 아기들은 스스로를 돌볼 수 없다. (look after)

→ Babies cannot _____ _____ _____.

• 재귀대명사 관용 표현 •

6 그녀는 중국어를 독학했다. (teach)

→ She _____ _____ Chinese.

7 코트를 벗고 편안히 있으세요. (at home)

→ Take off your coat and _____ _____ _____ _____.

8 그 촛불은 저절로 꺼졌다.

→ The candle went out _____ _____.

9 그 아이들은 놀이터에서 즐거운 시간을 보냈다. (enjoy)

→ The children _____ _____ at the playground.

10 그들은 그들의 개를 혼자 집에 남겨두었다.

→ They left their dog at home _____ _____ .

( ) 안의 말을 이용하여 우리말을 영어로 옮기시오.

1 너 자신을 알라. (know)

2 나는 요리하다가 화상을 입었다. (burn / while cooking)

3 그녀는 자신의 사진을 찍었다. (take a picture of)

4 그 소년은 넘어져서 다쳤다. (fall down / hurt)

5 너는 왜 혼잣말을 하고 있니? (talk to)

6 그 고양이는 자신을 핥고 있다. (lick)

7 그들은 그 문제를 스스로 풀었다. (by)

8 그 여자는 세 자녀를 혼자 키운다. (raise / children / by)

9 너는 콘서트에서 즐거운 시간 보냈니? (enjoy / at the concert)

10 우리는 그 무료 음료를 마음껏 먹었다. (help / the free drinks)

11 그녀는 거울에 비친 자신을 보고 있다. (look at / in the mirror)

12 나는 기타 치는 것을 혼자서 배웠다. (teach / play)

1 그림을 보고 질문에 대한 답을 완성하시오.

Q What did you eat for breakfast?

A I ate a bowl of soup, _____

_____ _____ bread, and

_____ _____ _____

milk.

2 다음 문장에서 어법상 틀린 곳을 찾아 바르게 고쳐 쓰시오.

(1) We had three piece of cake for dessert.
(2) He drinks two cups of coffees a day.

(1) _____ → _____
(2) _____ → _____

3 (A)와 (B)에서 각각 한 표현씩을 사용하여 우리말을 영어로 옮기시오. (단, 필요하면 어법에 맞는 형태로 바꾸어 쓸 것)

(A)	(B)
cup, bowl, piece, sheet, can, bottle	salad, coke, pizza

(1) 샐러드 두 그릇 → _____
(2) 피자 세 조각 → _____
(3) 콜라 두 캔 → _____

4 〈보기〉에서 적절한 말을 골라 문장을 완성하시오.

보기   few / a few / little / a little

(1) There are _____ people on the bus.
It's almost empty.

(2) We still have _____ money. We can
buy some food.

(3) John had a traffic accident _____
days ago. He is in hospital now.

(4) Cathy eats _____ meat. She doesn't
like it.

5 빈칸에 알맞은 재귀대명사를 쓰시오.

(1) I am proud of _____.
(2) Can you introduce _____, please?
(3) Tim and Rita enjoyed _____ at the
zoo.

6 우리말과 같은 뜻이 되도록 주어진 단어를 바르게 배열하시오.

그는 거울에 비친 자신을 보았다.
(looked / mirror / at / the / himself / he / in)

→ _____

7 우리말과 같은 뜻이 되도록 빈칸에 알맞은 말을 쓰시오. (단, 재귀대명사를 사용할 것)

(1) 이 케이크를 마음껏 드세요.

→ _____ _____ to this cake.

(2) 그녀는 혼자 앉아 있다.

→ She is sitting _____ _____.

(3) 우리끼리 얘긴데, 나 거짓말했어.

→ _____ _____, I told a lie.

UNIT
08

비교

LESSON 18

as ~ as, 비교급

1 「as＋원급(형용사/부사)＋as」는 '~만큼 …한'이란 의미이다. 부정형은 「not as＋원급(형용사/부사)＋as」이며 '~만큼 …하지 않은'이라고 해석한다.

I think she is **as pretty as** an actress. 그녀는 여배우만큼 예쁜 것 같다.
My computer is **not as fast as** yours. 내 컴퓨터는 네 것만큼 빠르지 않다.

> **PLUS** 「as＋원급＋as possible」은 '가능한 ~한'이라는 뜻으로 「as＋원급＋as＋주어＋can/could」로 바꾸어 쓸 수 있다.
> e.g. I try to exercise *as often as possible*. 나는 가능한 자주 운동하려고 노력한다.
>   = I try to exercise *as often as I can*.

2 「비교급＋than」은 '~보다 더 …한'이란 의미이다. 비교급은 형용사와 부사 뒤에 **-er**을 붙이거나, 앞에 **more**을 붙여 만든다.

A horse is **bigger than** a donkey. 말은 당나귀보다 더 크다.
Tara drives **more carefully than** Alex. Tara는 Alex보다 더 조심해서 운전한다.

> **PLUS** 비교급을 강조할 때는 비교급 앞에 much, even, still, far, a lot을 붙이고 '훨씬 더 ~한'이라고 해석한다.
> e.g. This hotel is *much/even/still/far/a lot bottor* than I thought. 이 호텔은 내기 생각했던 것보다 훨씬 더 좋다.

3 「the＋비교급, the＋비교급」은 '~하면 할수록 더 …하다'란 의미이다.

If you study harder, your grades will be better.
→ **The harder** you study, **the better** your grades will be. 열심히 공부할수록 네 성적은 더 좋아질 것이다.

CHECK UP

• (   ) 안의 단어를 알맞은 형태로 빈칸에 써 넣으시오.

1 My hair is as ＿＿＿＿＿＿＿ as yours. (long)

2 Sandra's bag is ＿＿＿＿＿＿＿ than mine. (heavy)

3 Jane plays tennis much ＿＿＿＿＿＿＿ than me. (well)

4 Tom can jump as ＿＿＿＿＿＿＿ as Brad. (high)

5 You look ＿＿＿＿＿＿＿ than yesterday. (good)

6 Fishing is ＿＿＿＿＿＿＿ than hiking. (boring)

7 In the US, baseball is ＿＿＿＿＿＿＿ than soccer. (popular)

8 The sweater is ＿＿＿＿＿＿＿ than the pants. (cheap)

9 The ＿＿＿＿＿＿＿ it gets, the ＿＿＿＿＿＿＿ the stars shine. (dark / bright)

10 The ＿＿＿＿＿＿＿ money you spend, the ＿＿＿＿＿＿＿ you can save.
(little / much)

box 안의 예문을 참고하여 우리말과 일치하도록 문장을 완성하시오.

> **WRITING POINT ①**
> · Carol is **(not) as old as** Jane. Carol은 / 나이가 많다 (많지 않다) / Jane만큼

1. Sam은 Mark만큼 힘이 세다. Sam is _____ Mark.

2. Aron은 그의 형만큼 키가 크다. Aron is _____ his brother.

3. Harry는 Don만큼 기타를 잘 친다. Harry plays the guitar _____ Don.

4. Tim는 Jim만큼 열심히 공부하지 않는다. Tim doesn't study _____ Jim.

5. 그는 내가 생각했던 것만큼 어리지 않다. He is not _____ I thought.

> **WRITING POINT ②**
> · Bicycles are **slower than** cars. 자전거는 / 더 느리다 / 자동차보다
> · Skiing is **more dangerous than** swimming. 스키는 / 더 위험하다 / 수영보다

1. 멕시코는 캐나다보다 더 덥다. Mexico is _____ Canada.

2. 이 책은 저 책보다 더 두껍다. This book is _____ that book.

3. 과일은 초콜릿보다 건강에 더 좋다. Fruit is _____ chocolate.

4. Janet은 Daniel보다 더 인기가 있다. Janet is _____ Daniel.

5. 그의 차는 내 것보다 더 비싸다. His car is _____ mine.

> **WRITING POINT ③**
> · **The younger** you are, **the easier** it is to learn. 더 어릴수록 / 당신이 / 더 쉽다 / 배우기가

1. 더 많이 웃을수록 너는 더 좋아 보인다. _____ you smile, _____ you look.

2. 그를 적게 볼수록 나는 그가 더 그립다. _____ I see him, _____ I miss him.

3. 나이가 들수록 우리는 더 현명해진다. _____ we get, _____ we become.

4. 당신이 높이 오를수록 더 추워진다. _____ you climb, _____ it gets.

5. 오래 기다릴수록 나는 더 화가 났다. _____ I waited, _____ I got.

우리말과 일치하도록 빈칸에 알맞은 말을 넣으시오.

• as + 원급 + as •

1 그 시험은 지난번 것만큼 어려웠다. (difficult)

→ The exam _____ _____ _____ _____ the last one.

2 그의 신발은 그의 아버지 것만큼 크다. (big)

→ His shoes _____ _____ _____ _____ his father's.

3 나는 Peter만큼 많이 운동하지 않는다. (exercise)

→ I don't _____ _____ _____ _____ Peter.

4 그 강은 보이는 것만큼 깊지 않다. (deep)

→ The river _____ _____ _____ _____ _____ it looks.

• 비교급 + than •

5 그 식당은 평소보다 더 분주하다. (busy)

→ The restaurant _____ _____ _____ usual.

6 돌고래는 물고기보다 더 영리하다. (intelligent)

→ Dolphins _____ _____ _____ _____ fish.

7 Julian은 영어보다 불어를 훨씬 더 잘한다. (much / well)

→ Julian speaks French _____ _____ _____ English.

• the + 비교급, the + 비교급 •

8 더 열심히 공부할수록 너는 더 많이 배울 것이다. (hard / much)

→ _____ _____ you study, _____ _____ you will learn.

9 오래 잘수록 나는 더 피곤하다. (long / tired)

→ _____ _____ I sleep, _____ _____ _____ I am.

10 패스트푸드를 많이 먹을수록 너는 더 살찔 것이다. (much / fat)

→ _____ _____ fast food you eat, _____ _____ you will get.

( ) 안의 말을 이용하여 우리말을 영어로 옮기시오.

1 Jenny는 그녀의 언니만큼 날씬하다. (slim)

2 Robin은 Daniel만큼 부지런하다. (diligent)

3 내 영어는 네 영어만큼 좋지 않다. (good)

4 운동화는 하이힐보다 더 편하다. (sneakers / comfortable / high heels)

5 날이 화창할수록 나는 더 행복함을 느낀다. (sunny / it / happy)

6 그는 평소보다 더 일찍 잠자리에 들었다. (go to bed / early / usual)

7 오늘 날씨는 어제보다 훨씬 더 나쁘다. (today's weather / much / bad)

8 Jenny는 커피보다 차를 더 자주 마신다. (tea / often / coffee)

9 Michael은 그의 형만큼 참을성이 많지 않다. (as / patient)

10 일찍 시작할수록 너는 더 빨리 끝낼 것이다. (early / soon)

11 역사는 수학보다 더 흥미로운 것 같다. (I think / interesting)

12 더 많이 운동할수록 너는 더 튼튼해질 것이다. (exercise / get)

LESSON 19 최상급

1 「the+최상급(+in/of)」는 '(~ 중) 가장 …한'이란 의미이다. 최상급은 형용사와 부사 뒤에 **-est**를 붙이거나, 앞에 **most**를 붙여 만든다.

Mike is **the fastest** runner *of* the three. Mike는 셋 중에서 가장 빠른 주자이다.
Soccer is **the most popular** sports *in* Italy. 축구는 이탈리아에서 가장 인기 있는 스포츠이다.

PLUS 「one of the+최상급+복수명사」는 '가장 ~한 … 중 하나'란 뜻이다.
e.g. K2 is *one of the highest mountains* in the world. K2는 세계에서 가장 높은 산들 중 하나이다.

2 원급과 비교급을 이용한 최상급 표현

John is **the tallest** boy in the class. John은 그 반에서 가장 키가 큰 소년이다.
→ John is **taller than any other boy** in the class. 「비교급 + than any other+단수명사」
→ **No other boy** in the class **is taller than** John. 「No (other)+단수명사+동사+비교급+than」
→ **No other boy** in the class **is as tall as** John. 「No (other)+단수명사+동사+as+원급+as」

CHECK UP

- ( ) 안의 단어를 알맞은 형태로 빈칸에 써 넣으시오.

1 The blue pen is the _____ of all. (long)

2 The Vatican City is the _____ country in the world. (small)

3 Who is the _____ person in your family? (short)

4 Honesty is the _____ policy. (good)

5 He bought the _____ shirt in the shop. (expensive)

6 Tea is one of the _____ drinks in the world. (popular)

7 The Great Wall is the _____ structure in China. (famous)

- 각 문장의 의미가 모두 같도록 빈칸에 알맞은 말을 쓰시오.

8 The blue whale is the largest animal in the world.

= The blue whale is larger than _____ _____ _____ in the world.

= No _____ _____ in the world is _____ _____ the blue whale.

= No _____ _____ in the world is _____ _____ _____ the blue whale.

96

SENTENCE PRACTICE 1

box 안의 예문을 참고하여 우리말과 일치하도록 문장을 완성하시오.

> **WRITING POINT ①**
> • Cheetahs are **the fastest animal** in the world. 치타는 / 이다 / 가장 빠른 동물 / 세상에서

I   8월은 1년 중 가장 더운 달이다.   August is _____ of the year.

2   그녀는 내가 아는 가장 친절한 사람이다.   She is _____ I know.

3   그는 한국에서 가장 유명한 화가이다.   He is _____ in Korea.

4   가을은 독서하기에 가장 좋은 계절이다.   Fall is _____ for reading.

5   그것은 내 인생에서 최악의 실수였다.   It was _____ in my life.

> **WRITING POINT ②**
> • Cheetahs are **faster than** any other animal. 치타는 / 더 빠르다 / 다른 어떤 동물보다

I   목성은 다른 어떤 행성보다 더 크다.   Jupiter is _____ any other planet.

2   나일강은 다른 어떤 강보다 더 길다.   The Nile is _____ any other river.

3   파리는 다른 어떤 도시보다 더 아름답다.   Paris is _____ any other city.

4   망고는 다른 어떤 과일보다 더 달다.   Mango is _____ any other fruit.

5   여름은 다른 어떤 계절보다 더 좋다.   Summer is _____ any other season.

> **WRITING POINT ③**
> • No other animal is **faster than** Cheetahs. 다른 어떤 동물도 / 더 빠르지 않다 / 치타보다
> • No other animal is **as fast as** Cheetahs. 다른 어떤 동물도 / 빠르지 않다 / 치타만큼

I   다른 어떤 학생도 나보다 더 키가 크지 않다.   No other student is _____ me.

2   다른 어떤 소녀도 Julie보다 더 예쁘지 않다.   No other girl is _____ Julie.

3   다른 어떤 곳도 집보다 더 좋지 않다.   No other place is _____ home.

4   다른 어떤 학생도 Jim만큼 똑똑하지 않다.   No other student is _____ Jim.

5   다른 어떤 과목도 수학만큼 어렵지 않다.   No other subject is _____ math.

우리말과 일치하도록 빈칸에 알맞은 말을 넣으시오.

• the + 최상급 •

1 웃음은 가장 좋은 약이다. (good / medicine)

→ Laughter is _____ _____ _____.

2 2월은 1년 중 가장 짧은 달이다. (short)

→ February is _____ _____ _____ of the year.

3 그는 내가 아는 가장 지루한 사람이다. (boring)

→ He is _____ _____ _____ _____ I know.

4 당신 인생에서 가장 소중한 것은 무엇입니까? (precious)

→ What is _____ _____ _____ _____ in your life?

• 비교급 + than any other + 단수명사 •

5 겨울은 다른 어떤 계절보다 더 춥다. (cold)

→ Winter is _____ _____ _____ _____ _____.

6 그 교회는 그 마을에서 다른 어떤 건물보다 더 오래되었다. (old)

→ The church is _____ _____ _____ _____ _____ in the town.

7 에베레스트 산은 세계에서 다른 어떤 산보다 더 높다. (high)

→ Mt. Everest is _____ _____ _____ _____ _____ in the world.

• No (other) + 단수명사 + 동사 + 비교급 + than / No (other) + 단수명사 + 동사 + as + 원급 + as •

8 다른 어떤 스포츠도 축구보다 더 인기 있지 않다. (popular)

→ No other _____ _____ _____ _____ _____ soccer.

9 다른 어떤 동물도 개만큼 충직하지 않다. (faithful)

→ No other _____ _____ _____ _____ _____ the dog.

10 다른 어떤 음식도 엄마가 만든 파스타보다 더 맛있지 않다. (delicious)

→ No other _____ _____ _____ _____ _____ my mom's pasta.

( ) 안의 말을 이용하여 우리말을 영어로 옮기시오.

1   호주는 세계에서 가장 작은 대륙이다. (Australia / continent)

2   Eric은 그 팀에서 최고의 선수이다. (player / on the team)

3   누구도 Mark보다 더 힘이 세지 않다. (no one / strong)

4   브라질은 남미에서 다른 어떤 나라보다 더 크다. (Brazil / large / in South America)

5   그는 세상에서 가장 운이 좋은 사람이다. (lucky)

6   그날은 내 인생에서 가장 행복한 날이었다. (it / of my life)

7   그녀의 집은 그 마을에서 다른 어떤 집보다 더 아름답다. (beautiful / in the town)

8   다른 어떤 과목도 음악보다 더 흥미롭지 않다. (subject / interesting)

9   그는 내가 아는 가장 재미있는 사람이다. (funny / I know)

10   그것은 역사상 최악의 지진이었다. (earthquake / in history)

11   다른 어떤 시험도 수학 시험만큼 어렵지 않았다. (difficult / the math test)

12   에펠탑은 파리에서 다른 어떤 건물보다 더 높다. (the Eiffel Tower / in Paris)

1 다음 표를 보고 〈보기〉에서 적절한 말을 골라 문장을 완성하시오. (단, 필요하면 어법에 맞는 형태로 바꾸어 쓸 것)

보기	tall / old / heavy

	William	Brian	Chris
age	17	16	17
weight (kg)	51	72	69
height (cm)	163	175	180

(1) Chris is the _____ of the three.

(2) William is as _____ as Chris.

(3) Brian is _____ than Chris.

2 그림을 보고 주어진 단어를 이용하여 질문에 대한 답을 완성하시오.

Yesterday   Today

Q How is the weather today?

A It is _____ _____ _____ _____ _____.

(windy, as)

3 우리말과 같은 뜻이 되도록 빈칸에 알맞은 말을 쓰시오.

내 방은 내 형의 방보다 훨씬 더 깨끗하다.

→ My room is _____ _____ _____ my brother's room.

4 다음 문장에서 어법상 틀린 곳을 찾아 바르게 고쳐 쓰시오.

(1) Jack is smartest boy in his class.

(2) It is the most cheap bag in the store.

(3) We stayed in the badest hotel in the town.

(1) _____ → _____

(2) _____ → _____

(3) _____ → _____

5 주어진 단어를 이용하여 우리말을 영작하시오.

날씨가 따뜻할수록 나는 기분이 더 좋아진다. (warm, good)

→ _____ the weather is, _____ _____ I feel.

6 우리말과 같은 뜻이 되도록 주어진 단어를 바르게 배열하시오.

더 많은 종이를 재활용할수록, 우리는 더 적은 나무를 베어낸다.
(the / paper / fewer / recycle / trees / we / more / the / we / cut down)

→ _____
_____

7 주어진 문장과 같은 의미가 되도록 빈칸에 알맞은 말을 쓰시오. (단, 비교급 표현을 사용할 것)

Seoul is the largest city in Korea.

(1) Seoul is _____ _____ _____ _____ _____ in Korea.

(2) No other _____ _____ _____ _____ _____ _____ Seoul.

UNIT
09

관계사

주격 관계대명사

1 관계대명사는 접속사와 대명사 역할을 한다. 관계대명사는 **who, whom, which, that** 등이 있으며, 관계대명사가 이끄는 절은 **앞의 명사(선행사)를 수식하는 형용사절**이다.

2 주격 관계대명사는 관계사절에서 **주어**를 대신한다. 이때 선행사가 **사람**이면 **who**를, 선행사가 **사물/동물**이면 **which**를 쓴다. 관계대명사 **that**은 선행사의 종류에 상관없이 사용할 수 있다.

선행사가 사람일 때	선행사+who/that+동사	I know the girl. + She lives next door. 선행사 주어 → I know the girl who/that lives next door. 나는 옆집에 사는 그 소녀를 안다.
선행사가 사물/동물일 때	선행사+which/that+동사	The man has a parrot. + It can talk. 선행사 주어 → The man has a parrot which/that can talk. 그 남자는 말할 수 있는 앵무새를 가지고 있다.

3 관계대명사가 이끄는 절은 수식하는 **명사 바로 뒤**에 위치해야 한다.

The girl is my sister. + **She** has curly hair.
→ *The girl* **who** has curly hair is my sister. (O) 곱슬머리를 가진 그 소녀는 내 여동생이다.
 The girl is my sister **who** has curly hair. (X)

● 선행사에는 동그라미를 하고, 관계대명사절에는 밑줄을 치시오.

1 He told me a joke which is very funny.

2 A vet is a person who treats sick animals.

3 Jane lives in a house which has a beautiful garden.

4 The boy who broke the window ran away.

5 I don't like people who are always late.

6 Josh works for a company which makes cars.

7 They are my neighbors who live next doors.

8 This is wine which is made from grapes.

9 The bus which goes to the hotel runs every 30 minutes.

box 안의 예문을 참고하여 우리말과 일치하도록 문장을 완성하시오. (관계대명사 who, which를 사용할 것)

WRITING POINT ①

• I know a girl **who is** good at singing. 나는 / 안다 / 소녀를 / 노래를 잘하는

1	나는 캐나다에 사는 친구가 있다.	I have a friend _____ in Canada.
2	그는 유명한 배우인 아들이 있다.	He has a son _____ a famous actor.
3	안경을 쓰고 있는 저 소년은 Bill이다.	The boy _____ wearing glasses is Bill.
4	책을 읽고 있는 저 소녀는 Mary이다.	The girl _____ reading a book is Mary.
5	나를 도와준 그 남자는 매우 친절했다.	The man _____ me was very kind.
6	위층에 사는 그 남자는 변호사이다.	The man _____ upstairs is a lawyer.
7	나는 요리를 잘하는 남자가 좋다.	I like a man _____ good at cooking.
8	나는 거짓말하는 사람들이 싫다.	I don't like people _____ lies.
9	시험에 떨어진 그 소녀는 울었다.	The girl _____ the test cried.

WRITING POINT ②

• Tim is wearing a hat **which is** too big for him. Tim은 / 쓰고 있다 / 모자를 / 너무 큰 / 그에게

1	거미는 다리가 여덟 개인 동물이다.	A spider is an animal _____ eight legs.
2	펭귄은 날지 못하는 새이다.	A penguin is a bird _____ fly.
3	이것은 음식을 데우는 기계이다.	This is a machine _____ food.
4	이것은 커피를 만드는 기계이다.	This is a machine _____ coffee.
5	꼬리가 긴 저 개는 나의 것이다.	The dog _____ a long tail is mine.
6	그는 옷을 파는 상점에서 일한다.	He works in a shop _____ clothes.
7	그는 방이 네 개인 집을 샀다.	He bought a house _____ four rooms.
8	시내까지 가는 버스가 있나요?	Is there a bus _____ downtown?
9	책상 위에 있던 책은 어디 있니?	Where is the book _____ on the desk?

우리말과 일치하도록 빈칸에 알맞은 말을 넣으시오. (관계대명사 who, which를 사용할 것)

• 주격 관계대명사 who •

1 나는 유명한 음악가인 남자를 만났다. (a famous musician)

→ I met a man _____ _____ _____ _____ _____ .

2 소방관은 불을 끄는 사람이다. (put out)

→ A firefighter is a person _____ _____ _____ _____ .

3 어제 나에게 전화했던 그 남자는 나의 형이었다. (call)

→ The man _____ _____ _____ _____ was my brother.

4 세종대왕(King Sejong)은 한글(Hangeul)을 창제했던 사람이다. (create)

→ King Sejong is the person _____ _____ _____ .

5 그 축제에 간 사람들은 즐거운 시간을 보냈다. (the festival)

→ The people _____ _____ _____ _____ _____ enjoyed themselves.

• 주격 관계대명사 which •

6 이것은 대답하기 어려운 질문이다. (difficult)

→ This is a question _____ _____ _____ to answer.

7 당나귀는 작은 말처럼 생긴 동물이다. (look like)

→ A donkey is an animal _____ _____ _____ a small horse.

8 그 방은 호수가 내려다보이는 창문이 있다. (overlook)

→ The room has a window _____ _____ a lake.

9 Smith 씨는 그리스 음식을 제공하는 식당을 운영한다. (serve)

→ Mr. Smith runs a restaurant _____ _____ Greek food.

10 그들은 마당이 있는 집을 찾고 있다. (a yard)

→ They are looking for a house _____ _____ _____ _____ .

관계대명사와 (   ) 안의 말을 이용하여 우리말을 영어로 옮기시오.

1   나는 유머 감각이 뛰어난 사람들이 좋다. (a good sense of humor)

2   스포츠 용품을 파는 상점이 있나요? (there / a shop / sports goods)

3   캥거루는 호주에 사는 동물이다. (a kangaroo / in Australia)

4   바리스타는 커피를 만드는 사람이다. (a barista / a person)

5   나무에 앉아 있는 저 새를 봐. (sit on)

6   Tara는 아름다운 꽃들이 있는 정원을 가지고 있다. (a garden / have)

7   토머스 에디슨(Thomas Edison)은 전구를 발명한 사람이다. (the person / the light bulb)

8   경주에서 이긴 그 소년은 행복했다. (the race / happy)

9   축구를 하고 있는 저 소년들은 내 친구들이다. (those boys / soccer)

10   나에게 길을 알려준 그 남자는 친절했다. (give me directions)

11   나를 물었던 그 개는 내 이웃의 개였다. (bite / my neighbor's dog)

12   어젯밤에 일어난 그 사고는 끔찍했다. (the accident / happen / terrible)

목적격 관계대명사

1 목적격 관계대명사는 관계사절에서 **목적어**를 대신한다. 이때 선행사가 **사람**이면 **who(m)**을 쓰고, **사물/동물**이면 **which**를 쓴다. 관계대명사 **that**은 선행사의 성격에 상관없이 사용할 수 있다.

선행사가 사람일 때	선행사+who(m)/that +주어+동사	The girl was Jane. + I met her at the party. 선행사 목적어 → The girl who(m)/that I met at the party was Jane. 내가 파티에서 만난 소녀는 Jane이었다.
선행사가 사물/동물일 때	선행사+which/that +주어+동사	This is the book. + I lost it yesterday. 선행사 목적어 → This is the book which/that I lost yesterday. 이것은 내가 어제 잃어버린 책이다.

PLUS 관계대명사가 전치사의 목적어일 경우에는 관계대명사절 뒤에 전치사가 남는다.

e.g. What is the name of the song? + You are listening to the song.
→ What is the name of the song *which* you are listening *to*? 네가 듣고 있는 노래 제목이 뭐야?

2 목적격 관계대명사가 이끄는 절에서는 **목적어를 쓰지 않도록** 주의한다.

The movie was good. + We saw **it** last night.
→ *The movie* **which we saw last night** was good. (O) 우리가 어젯밤에 본 영화는 좋았다.
   The movie **which we saw it last night** was good. (X)

- 선행사에는 동그라미를 하고, 관계대명사절에는 밑줄을 치시오.

1 This is the camera which I want to buy.

2 Joanne Rowling is the writer whom I like most.

3 The e-mail which Bill sent to me hasn't arrived yet.

4 Do you remember the man whom we met in the park?

5 The shoes which you are wearing are nice.

6 Julie loves the students whom she teaches.

7 The sandwich which I ate for lunch wasn't good.

8 The bus which we were waiting for was 30 minutes late.

9 What's the name of the girl whom Steve is talking to?

box 안의 예문을 참고하여 우리말과 일치하도록 문장을 완성하시오. (관계대명사 whom, which를 사용할 것)

WRITING POINT ①

• Beyoncé is the singer **whom I like** the most. Beyoncé는 / 이다 / 가수 / 내가 가장 좋아하는

I 내가 본 그 남자는 Henry였다.   The man _____ was Henry.

2 나는 Sally가 좋아하는 남자를 안다.   I know the man _____.

3 Adel은 내가 만나고 싶은 가수이다.   Adel is the singer _____ to meet.

4 저 사람들은 내가 아는 사람들이다.   Those are people _____.

5 Daniel은 내가 믿을 수 있는 친구이다.   Daniel is a friend _____ trust.

6 Sam은 그가 만나는 모두에게 인사한다.   Sam greets everyone _____.

7 내가 초대한 그 소녀는 오지 않았다.   The girl _____ didn't come.

8 나와 이야기한 그 남자는 친절했다.   The man _____ was friendly.

9 나와 함께 춤춘 그 소녀는 Ann이다.   The girl _____ was Ann.

WRITING POINT ②

• I like the cookies **which my mom makes**. 나는 / 좋아한다 / 쿠키들을 / 엄마가 만드는

I 내가 산 그 식탁은 매우 크다.   The table _____ is very big.

2 우리가 먹었던 그 피자는 맛있었다.   The pizza _____ was delicious.

3 내가 예약한 그 항공편은 취소되었다.   The flight _____ was canceled.

4 우리가 본 그 시험은 쉽지 않았다.   The test _____ was not easy.

5 이것은 그가 쓴 책이다.   This is the book _____.

6 너는 네가 잃어버린 그 열쇠를 찾았니?   Have you found the key _____?

7 Jill은 내가 좋아하는 모자를 쓰고 있다.   Jill is wearing a hat _____.

8 이것이 Rick이 너에게 준 반지니?   Is this the ring _____ you?

9 이것이 네가 주문한 책이니?   Is this the book _____?

SENTENCE PRACTICE 2

우리말과 일치하도록 빈칸에 알맞은 말을 넣으시오. (관계대명사 whom, which를 사용할 것)

• 목적격 관계대명사 whom •

1 김 선생님은 내가 가장 좋아하는 선생님이다. (like)

→ Mr. Kim is the teacher _____ _____ _____ the most.

2 네가 어제 만났던 그 소녀는 누구니?

→ Who is the girl _____ _____ _____ yesterday?

3 그가 이야기하고 있는 저 여자는 그의 여동생이다. (talk to)

→ The woman _____ _____ _____ _____ _____ is his sister.

4 나는 너에게 소개시켜주고 싶은 친구가 있어. (want / introduce)

→ I have a friend _____ _____ _____ _____ _____ to you.

5 내가 저녁식사에 초대한 사람들은 늦었다. (to dinner)

→ The people _____ _____ _____ _____ _____ were late.

• 목적격 관계대명사 which •

6 나는 Jane이 나에게 빌려준 우산을 잃어버렸다. (lend)

→ I lost the umbrella _____ _____ _____ _____.

7 네가 쓰고 있는 선글라스는 멋지다. (wear)

→ The sunglasses _____ _____ _____ _____ are nice.

8 나는 네가 추천한 그 영화를 봤다. (recommend)

→ I watched the movie _____ _____ _____.

9 우리가 묵은 호텔은 해변 앞에 있었다. (stay at)

→ The hotel _____ _____ _____ _____ was in front of the beach.

10 이것이 네가 찾고 있는 책이니? (look for)

→ Is this the book _____ _____ _____ _____?

관계대명사와 ( ) 안의 말을 이용하여 우리말을 영어로 옮기시오.

1 우리가 방문했던 식당은 매우 분주했다. (the restaurant / busy)

2 나는 나와 함께 일하는 사람들이 좋다. (work with)

3 그는 마침내 그가 좋아하는 소녀에게 말을 걸었다. (finally / talk to)

4 그가 나에게 말한 이야기는 사실이다. (the story / tell / true)

5 Eddie는 그가 만나는 모두와 잘 지낸다. (get along with / everyone)

6 네가 가장 존경하는 사람은 누구니? (the person / respect)

7 내가 신고 있는 신발은 매우 편하다. (the shoes / wear / comfortable)

8 이것은 내가 아빠 생신 선물로 산 지갑이다. (the wallet / for my dad's birthday)

9 이것들은 나의 엄마가 나를 위해 만들어준 쿠키이다. (the cookies / for me)

10 나는 이탈리아에서 만난 사람들과 점심식사를 했다. (have lunch)

11 내가 샀던 그 재킷은 나에게 잘 맞지 않는다. (the jacket / fit / well)

12 올라프(Olaf)는 Anna와 Elsa가 함께 만든 눈사람이다. (the snowman / make)

관계대명사 what vs. that

관계대명사 **what**은 선행사를 포함하는 관계대명사로 '~하는 것(= the thing which)'의 의미이며, what이 이끄는 절은 명사절로 주어, 보어, 목적어 역할을 한다. 관계대명사 **that**은 선행사의 종류에 상관없이 **주격**이니 **목적격** 관계대명사 who, whom, which 대신 쓸 수 있다.

관계대명사 what	선행사 없음 (= the thing which)	What we need is time. (주어) 우리에게 필요한 것은 시간이다. This is what my sister drew. (보어) 이것은 내 여동생이 그린 것이다. Tell me what you want. (목적어) 네가 원하는 것을 나에게 말해줘.
관계대명사 that	선행사+that	He is the person that/who makes me smile. (주격) 그는 나를 웃게 만드는 사람이다. I like the poems that/which Andy wrote. (목적격) 나는 Andy가 쓴 시들이 좋다.

2 목적격 관계대명사와 「주격 관계대명사+be동사」는 생략이 가능하다.

The museum (**which/that**) we visited was closed. (목적격 관계대명사) 우리가 방문했던 박물관은 문을 닫았다.
The boy (**who is**) wearing a blue cap is Tom. (주격 관계대명사 + be동사) 파란 야구모자를 쓰고 있는 소년은 Tom이다.

CHECK UP

● 빈칸에 알맞은 말을 고르시오.

1 This is the song _____ I heard yesterday.　☐ that　☐ what

2 _____ I want now is a cup of tea.　☐ That　☐ What

3 Everything _____ he said is true.　☐ that　☐ what

4 The box _____ Harry is carrying is heavy.　☐ that　☐ what

5 Hiking is _____ I enjoy doing on the weekend.　☐ that　☐ what

6 We visited a castle _____ was built in 1280.　☐ that　☐ what

7 Sorry, I don't understand _____ you mean.　☐ that　☐ what

8 Show me _____ is in your pocket.　☐ that　☐ what

9 The man helped the boy _____ lost his mother.　☐ that　☐ what

10 I won't tell him _____ you said.　☐ that　☐ what

box 안의 예문을 참고하여 우리말과 일치하도록 문장을 완성하시오. (관계대명사 what, that을 사용할 것)

WRITING POINT ①

· He told me **what he saw** last night.　그는 / 나에게 말해주었다 / 그가 본 것을 / 어젯밤에

I　내가 원하는 것은 휴식이다.　　　　　　_____ is a break.

2　그들이 필요한 것은 물과 음식이다.　　_____ is water and food.

3　그가 말한 것은 사실이 아니다.　　　　_____ is not true.

4　네가 좋아하는 것을 나에게 말해줘.　　Tell me _____.

5　네가 아는 것을 나에게 말해줘.　　　　Tell me _____.

6　네가 들은 것을 나에게 말해줘.　　　　Tell me _____.

7　이것은 내가 기대했던 것이 아니다.　　This is not _____.

8　이것은 우리가 주문했던 것이 아니다.　This is not _____.

9　이것은 그가 한 것이 아니다.　　　　　This is not _____.

WRITING POINT ②

· He is the person **that wrote** this book.　그는 / 이다 / 사람 / 이 책을 쓴
· Summer is the season **that I like** the most.　여름은 / 이다 / 계절 / 내가 가장 좋아하는

I　나는 일본 출신인 친구가 있다.　　　I have a friend _____ Japan.

2　그는 결코 포기하지 않는 소년이다.　He is a boy _____.

3　그녀는 그가 사랑하는 여자이다.　　　She is the woman _____.

4　그녀가 요리한 음식은 맛있었다.　　　The food _____ was delicious.

5　네가 입고 있는 드레스는 예쁘다.　　　The dress _____ is pretty.

6　우리가 산 TV는 고장 났다.　　　　　The TV _____ is broken.

7　이곳은 나의 삼촌이 사시는 집이다.　This is the house _____.

8　우리가 갔던 파티는 재미있었다.　　　The party _____ was fun.

우리말과 일치하도록 빈칸에 알맞은 말을 넣으시오. (관계대명사 what, that을 사용할 것)

• 관계대명사 what •

1 그녀의 미소는 나를 행복하게 만드는 것이다. (make)

→ Her smile is _____ _____ _____ _____ .

2 내가 크리스마스에 원하는 것은 새 코트이다. (for Christmas)

→ _____ _____ _____ _____ _____ is a new coat.

3 Jane은 그녀가 쇼핑몰에서 산 것을 나에게 보여주었다. (buy)

→ Jane showed me _____ _____ _____ at the mall.

4 나는 Sarah로부터 들은 것을 믿을 수가 없다. (hear from)

→ I can't believe _____ _____ _____ _____ _____ .

5 민호(Minho)는 그가 수업시간에 배운 것을 복습했다. (in class)

→ Minho reviewed _____ _____ _____ _____ _____ .

• 관계대명사 that •

6 나는 정기적으로 만나는 몇몇 친구들이 있다. (regularly)

→ I have some friends _____ _____ _____ _____ .

7 나는 5개 국어를 할 수 있는 남자를 만났다. (can / languages)

→ I met a man _____ _____ _____ _____ _____ .

8 이곳은 나의 가족이 살던 집이다. (live in)

→ This is the house _____ _____ _____ _____ _____ .

9 나는 도서관에서 빌린 책을 반납해야 한다. (borrow)

→ I have to return the book _____ _____ _____ from the library.

10 나는 행복한 결말이 있는 영화들을 좋아한다. (happy endings)

→ I like movies _____ _____ _____ _____ .

( ) 안의 말을 이용하여 우리말을 영어로 옮기시오.

1 이 재킷은 내가 사고 싶은 것이다. (what / want to)

2 위층에 사는 아이들은 시끄럽다. (that / upstairs / noisy)

3 너는 그가 너에게 말한 것을 믿니? (what / tell)

4 이 샐러드는 내 여동생이 주문한 것이다. (what / order)

5 내가 내 생일에 원하는 것은 새 컴퓨터이다. (what / for my birthday)

6 이것들은 내가 런던에서 찍은 사진들이다. (pictures / that / take)

7 은행을 턴 그 남자는 도망쳤다. (that / rob / run away)

8 그에 대해서 네가 아는 것을 나에게 말해줘. (what / know about)

9 우리가 산 TV는 잘 작동하지 않는다. (that / work well)

10 그녀는 내가 학교를 함께 다녔던 소녀이다. (a girl / that / go to school with)

11 나는 선생님이 말씀하시고 있는 것을 이해하지 못하겠다. (what / the teacher / say)

12 에펠탑(the Eiffel Tower)은 내가 파리에서 방문하고 싶은 곳이다. (that / want to)

1 각 문장의 빈칸에 적절한 단어를 〈보기〉에서 한 번씩만 사용하여 문장을 완성하시오.

> 보기   who / whom / which

(1) He has two sons _____ are doctors.

(2) I gave the boy some food _____ I had.

(3) Do you know the girl _____ we met at the bookstore?

2 그림을 보고 주어진 단어와 관계대명사를 이용하여 질문에 대한 답을 완성하시오.

(1) Q Who is a bus driver?

    A A bus driver is _____
_____. (a person, a bus)

(2) Q What is a giraffe?

    A A giraffe is _____
_____. (an animal, a long neck)

3 다음 두 문장을 who나 which를 이용하여 한 문장으로 연결하시오.

(1) The boy is Nick. He is wearing shorts.

→ _____

(2) I found the backpack. I lost it yesterday.

→ _____

4 다음 두 문장을 한 문장으로 만들 때 빈칸에 알맞은 관계대명사를 쓰시오.

> Look at the man and the dog. They are running in the park.

→ Look at the man and the dog _____ are running in the park.

5 다음 중 어법상 틀린 문장 3개를 찾아 바르게 고쳐 쓰시오.

> (1) The boy is Bill who is riding a bike.
> (2) I have a friend whom I can trust.
> (3) There are many buses which goes downtown.
> (4) This is the apartment my uncle lives in.
> (5) The computer which I bought it was cheap.

_____

_____

_____

6 우리말과 같은 뜻이 되도록 주어진 단어를 바르게 배열하시오.

> 이 셔츠는 내가 사고 싶은 것이야.
> (want / buy / I / what / to)

→ This shirt is _____.

7 다음 두 문장을 what을 이용하여 한 문장으로 연결하시오.

> Susan showed me the thing. The thing was in her bag.

→ _____

UNIT
10

접속사

LESSON 23 시간, 조건의 접속사

I 시간을 나타내는 접속사

after / before	~ 한 후에 / ~ 하기 전에	Go to bed **after** you brush your teeth. **Before** you go to bed, brush your teeth.
when	~할 때	You should be careful **when** you cross the road.
while	~하는 동안	Bill hurt his ankle **while** he was riding a skateboard.
as soon as	~하자마자	**As soon as** he saw the deer, he stopped the car.
until	~할 때까지	She waited with me **until** the bus came.

2 조건을 나타내는 접속사

if	만약 ~한다면	**If** you study hard, you will pass the exam.
unless	만약 ~하지 않는다면	You will catch a cold **unless** you wear a coat. (= You will catch a cold if you don't wear a coat.)

3 시간과 조건의 **부사절**에서는 시제가 미래일지라도 반드시 **현재시제**를 써야 한다.

I will call you **as soon as** I get home. (will get: X) 집에 도착하자마자 너에게 전화할게.
If it **rains**, we will not go out. (will rain: X) 비가 온다면, 우리는 나가지 않을 것이다.

CHECK UP

● 빈칸에 알맞은 말을 고르시오.

I	Lisa got dressed _____ she left home.	☐ after	☐ before
2	I will call you _____ I get home.	☐ until	☐ as soon as
3	Emily had a car accident _____ she was 10.	☐ if	☐ when
4	They arrived _____ the game was over.	☐ after	☐ until
5	Don't open your eyes _____ I tell you to do so.	☐ until	☐ as soon as
6	I usually listen to music _____ I am studying.	☐ before	☐ while
7	Let's go for a walk _____ you are tired.	☐ if	☐ unless
8	We will arrive on time _____ we hurry.	☐ if	☐ unless
9	Let me know when you _____ California.	☐ visit	☐ will visit
10	You will be sick if you _____ stop smoking.	☐ won't	☐ don't

box 안의 예문을 참고하여 우리말과 일치하도록 문장을 완성하시오.

WRITING POINT ①

• I wanted to be a singer **when** I was young. 나는 / 원했다 / 가수가 되기를 / 내가 어렸을 때

---

1 외출하기 전에 불을 꺼라.　　　　Turn off the lights _____ you go out.

2 그는 샤워를 한 후에 자러 갔다.　　He went to bed _____ he took a shower.

3 영화가 끝날 때까지 조용히 하세요.　Please keep quiet _____ the movie ends.

4 그는 TV를 보는 동안 잠이 들었다.　He fell asleep _____ he was watching TV.

5 그녀가 올 때까지 여기서 기다리자.　Let's wait here _____ she comes.

6 우리는 해가 뜨자마자 떠날 것이다.　We will leave _____ the sun rises.

7 날씨가 화창할 때, 나는 산책하러 간다.　_____ it's sunny, I go for a walk.

8 그는 자명종이 울리자마자 일어났다.　He got up _____ the alarm clock rang.

9 운전 중에는 항상 조심해라.　　　　Always be careful _____ you are driving.

WRITING POINT ②

• I won't do it **if** you don't agree. 나는 / 하지 않을 것이다 / 그것을 / 네가 동의하지 않으면

• I won't do it **unless** you agree. 나는 / 하지 않을 것이다 / 그것을 / 네가 동의하지 않으면

---

1 우리는 서두르지 않으면 늦을 것이다.　We will be late _____ we hurry.

2 너는 원한다면 일찍 떠나도 좋다.　　You may leave early _____ you want to.

3 너는 표가 없으면 입장할 수 없다.　　You cannot enter _____ you have a ticket.

4 괜찮으시다면, 여기 앉을게요.　　　_____ you don't mind, I'll sit here.

5 비가 오지 않으면, 나는 외출할 것이다.　_____ it rains, I will go out.

6 내가 시간이 있으면, 너를 도와줄게.　_____ I have time, I will help you.

7 나는 춥지 않으면 조깅하러 갈 것이다.　I will go jogging _____ it is cold.

8 도움이 필요하면 이 버튼을 누르세요.　Press this button _____ you need help.

우리말과 일치하도록 빈칸에 알맞은 말을 넣으시오.

• 시간을 나타내는 접속사 •

1 Bill과 Jane은 저녁을 먹은 후에 산책하러 갔다. (have)

→ Bill and Jane went for a walk _____ _____ _____ _____.

2 우리는 너무 늦기 전에 무언가를 해야 한다. (it / too late)

→ We have to do something _____ _____ _____ _____ _____.

3 그는 네 살 때 읽고 쓸 수 있었다. (four)

→ He could read and write _____ _____ _____ _____.

4 그가 파스타를 요리하는 동안, 나는 샐러드를 준비했다. (cook)

→ _____ _____ _____ _____ pasta, I prepared the salad.

5 우리는 그가 올 때까지 기다려야 했다. (come)

→ We had to wait _____ _____ _____.

6 그는 운전면허를 따자마자 새 차를 샀다.

→ He bought a new car _____ _____ _____ he got his driver's license.

• 조건을 나타내는 접속사 •

7 질문이 있으면, 손을 들어주세요. (any questions)

→ _____ _____ _____ _____ _____, please raise your hand.

8 도움이 필요하면 나에게 알려만 줘. (help)

→ Just let me know _____ _____ _____.

9 나는 그가 나에게 사과하지 않는다면 그를 용서하지 않을 것이다. (apologize)

→ I won't forgive him _____ _____ _____ to me.

10 너는 그 시험에 통과하지 못하면 학교를 졸업할 수 없다.

→ You cannot graduate from school _____ _____ _____ the exam.

( ) 안의 말을 이용하여 우리말을 영어로 옮기시오.

1 그들은 영화가 시작하기 전에 팝콘을 좀 샀다. (some popcorn / start)

2 아침을 먹은 후에, 그는 보통 그의 개를 산책시킨다. (usually / walk one's dog)

3 기차가 정시에 온다면, 우리는 8시에 도착할 것이다. (be on time / at 8:00)

4 네가 나를 도와주지 않는다면, 나는 그것을 할 수 없다. (unless)

5 그가 그 소식을 들었을 때, 그의 얼굴은 창백해졌다. (turn pale)

6 네가 설거지를 하는 동안 나는 집을 청소할게. (will)

7 그 아이들은 어두워질 때까지 수영장에서 놀았다. (the swimming pool / it / get)

8 내가 일을 일찍 끝내면, 널 데리러 갈게. (work / pick you up)

9 너는 여권이 없으면 해외여행을 할 수 없다. (travel abroad / unless / a passport)

10 그는 학교를 마치자마자, 직장을 구했다 (finish school / get)

11 나는 뉴욕에 가면, 자유의 여신상(the Statue of Liberty)을 방문할 것이다. (go to / visit)

12 우산을 가져가지 않으면, 너는 젖게 될 것이다. (unless / get wet)

LESSON 24 이유, 결과, 양보의 접속사

1 because＋주어＋동사, because of＋명사(구): ~ 때문에

We couldn't go hiking **because** it rained heavily. 우리는 비가 많이 왔기 때문에 하이킹하러 갈 수 없었다.
We couldn't go hiking **because of** the heavy rain. 우리는 폭우 때문에 하이킹하러 갈 수 없었다.

2 so ~ that ···: 너무 ~해서 ···하다

The book was **so** interesting **that** I couldn't put it down. 그 책은 너무 재미있어서 나는 그것을 내려놓을 수 없었다.
The boy ran **so** fast **that** I couldn't catch him. 그 소년은 너무 빨리 달려서 나는 그를 붙잡을 수 없었다.

PLUS so that은 '~하기 위해'라는 목적의 의미이다.
e.g. He swims every day *so that* he can stay healthy. 그는 건강을 유지하기 위해 매일 수영한다.

3 although/though: 비록 ~이지만, ~임에도 불구하고

Although/Though he has a car, he never drives to work. 그는 차가 있지만, 결코 차로 출근하지 않는다.
Judy speaks French very well **although/though** she has never lived in France.
Judy는 프랑스에서 살아본 적이 없지만 불어를 매우 잘한다.

CHECK UP

● 다음 두 문장을 ( ) 안의 말을 이용하여 한 문장으로 바꾸시오.

1 I didn't like the concert. The band didn't play well. (because)

  → _____

2 The suitcase was too heavy. I couldn't carry it by myself. (so ~ that ···)

  → _____

3 The ring was expensive. He bought it for his girlfriend. (although)

  → _____

4 You'd better take an umbrella. It is going to rain. (because)

  → _____

5 The cat is too fat. It can't walk easily. (so ~ that ···)

  → _____

6 The class was not canceled. There were not enough students. (although)

  → _____

box 안의 예문을 참고하여 자연스러운 문장이 되도록 연결하시오.

WRITING POINT 1

• I was late **because** the traffic was heavy. 나는 / 늦었다 / 교통 체증이 심했기 때문에

• I was late **because of** the heavy traffic. 나는 / 늦었다 / 극심한 교통 체증 때문에

1	Jane doesn't eat meat •	• we took a taxi.
2	Tom didn't go to school •	• because of his job.
3	He had to move to Seoul •	• the school was closed.
4	Because of the heavy snow •	• because she is a vegetarian.
5	Because we missed the last bus, •	• because he had a bad cold.

WRITING POINT 2

• The book was **so** great **that** I read it twice. 그 책은 / 너무 훌륭해서 / 나는 / 읽었다 / 그것을 / 두 번

1	He is so smart •	• that we left early.
2	This pizza is so delicious •	• that I don't want to leave here.
3	The movie was so boring •	• that I can't stop eating it.
4	The weather was so cold •	• that he can solve any problems.
5	This island is so beautiful •	• that we canceled the trip.

WRITING POINT 3

• **Although** it was hot outside, he went jogging. 더웠지만 / 밖이 / 그는 / 조깅을 하러 갔다

1	I am sleepy •	• although the bus was late.
2	We arrived on time •	• although he was very tired.
3	He finished the work •	• although she didn't study hard.
4	She got a good grade •	• they could not win the game.
5	Although the team played well, •	• although it's only 7 p.m.

우리말과 일치하도록 빈칸에 알맞은 말을 넣으시오.

• because / because of •

1 그 음식이 짰기 때문에, 나는 물을 많이 마셨다. (salty)

→ _____ _____ _____ _____ _____, I drank a lot of water.

2 모든 항공편이 폭풍 때문에 취소되었다. (the storm)

→ All the flights were canceled _____ _____ _____ _____.

3 그는 그의 차가 고장 나서 버스를 타야 했다. (break down)

→ He had to take the bus _____ _____ _____ _____ _____.

4 그 선생님은 그의 무례한 행동 때문에 화가 났다. (rude behavior)

→ The teacher got angry _____ _____ _____.

• so ~ that ... •

5 너무 더워서 나는 아무것도 할 수가 없었다. (hot)

→ It was _____ _____ _____ _____ _____ do anything.

6 그 시험은 너무 어려워서 Tom은 잘 보지 못했다. (difficult)

→ The test was _____ _____ _____ _____ _____ do well.

7 나는 배가 너무 고파서 저녁으로 밥 두 공기를 먹었다. (hungry)

→ I was _____ _____ _____ _____ _____ two bowls of rice.

• although / though •

8 날씨가 나빴지만, 우리는 즐거운 시간을 보냈다. (the weather)

→ _____ _____ _____ _____ _____, we had a good time.

9 그는 프랑스에서 1년 동안 살았지만, 불어를 하지 못한다.

→ _____ _____ _____ in France for a year, he cannot speak French.

10 나의 할머니는 연세가 매우 많으시지만, 여전히 활동적이시다. (very old)

→ _____ _____ _____ _____ _____ _____, she is still active.

( ) 안의 말을 이용하여 우리말을 영어로 옮기시오.

1 따뜻하고 화창했기 때문에, 우리는 해변에 갔다. (it / warm / sunny)

2 나는 두통 때문에 공부를 할 수 없었다. (can / my headache)

3 그 가방은 너무 비싸서 나는 그것을 살 수 없었다. (expensive / that)

4 그 버스는 너무 붐벼서 나는 자리를 잡을 수 없었다. (crowded / that / get a seat)

5 그들은 바빴지만, 우리를 도와주었다. (busy / help)

6 그들은 서로 사랑했기 때문에, 결혼하기로 약속했다. (each other / get married)

7 나는 너무 늦게 일어나서 학교 버스를 놓쳤다. (get up / so late / that)

8 영어를 배우는 것은 어렵지만, 나는 그것을 즐긴다. (learning English / hard)

9 그는 눈이 나빠서 안경 없이는 읽을 수가 없다. (can / without glasses / his poor eyesight)

10 나는 너무 긴장해서 한마디도 할 수 없었다. (nervous / that / say a word)

11 그녀는 고소공포증이 있어서 비행기 타는 것을 싫어한다. (flying / be afraid of / heights)

12 Sally는 다이어트 중이었지만 후식으로 치즈 케이크를 먹었다. (for dessert / on a diet)

LESSON 25 상관접속사

1 상관접속사는 두 개가 짝으로 이루어진 접속사를 가리킨다. 상관접속사는 단어와 단어, 구와 구, 절과 절을 연결할 수 있다.

both A and B	A와 B 둘 다	I like **both** dogs **and** cats. 나는 개와 고양이 둘 다 좋아한다.
not only A but also B (=B as well as A)	A뿐만 아니라 B도	She is **not only** beautiful **but also** smart. (= She is smart as well as beautiful.) 그녀는 아름다울 뿐만 아니라 똑똑하다.
either A or B	A 또는 B 둘 중 하나	We will go on vacation **either** in June **or** in July. 우리는 6월이나 7월에 휴가를 갈 것이다.

2 상관접속사가 주어 자리에 놓일 경우 **동사의 수 일치**에 주의한다.

both A and B	복수 취급	Both *Nick* and *Jane* **were** late. Nick과 Jane 둘 다 늦었다.
not only A but also B	B에 일치	Not only Susan but also *I* **am** a student. Susan뿐만 아니라 나도 학생이다.
either A or B	B에 일치	Either you or *your friend* **is** a liar. 너와 네 친구 둘 중 하나는 거짓말쟁이다.

CHECK UP

● 빈칸에 알맞은 말을 고르시오.

1 He visited both Italy _____ Germany.　　☐ or　☐ and

2 This book is not only useful _____ interesting.　　☐ and　☐ but also

3 I'll drink either coke _____ orange juice.　　☐ or　☐ and

4 Tom enjoys _____ fishing but also skiing.　　☐ either　☐ not only

5 _____ ostriches and penguins cannot fly.　　☐ Both　☐ Not only

6 We can _____ walk or take the cable car to the hill.　　☐ both　☐ either

7 Both Tara and I _____ hiking.　　☐ enjoy　☐ enjoys

8 Not only Mr. Kim but also his students _____ happy.　　☐ was　☐ were

9 Either my parents or my sister _____ at home.　　☐ are　☐ is

10 You can either accept _____ refuse the offer.　　☐ or　☐ but also

box 안의 예문을 참고하여 우리말과 일치하도록 문장을 완성하시오.

WRITING POINT ①

• **Both Jane and Kate** are good students.   Jane과 Kate 둘 다 / 좋은 학생들이다

1 나는 닭고기와 소고기 둘 다 좋아한다.   I like _____.

2 우리는 시간과 돈 모두 필요하다.   We need _____.

3 그는 읽을 수도 쓸 수도 있다.   He can _____.

4 Judy와 Sally 둘 다 내 반 친구들이다.   _____ are my classmates.

5 서울과 런던은 둘 다 수도이다.   _____ are capital cities.

WRITING POINT ②

• The class was **not only difficult but also boring**.   그 수업은 / 어려웠을 뿐만 아니라 / 지루했다

1 나는 피곤했을 뿐만 아니라 졸렸다.   I was _____.

2 그는 부유할 뿐만 아니라 유명하다.   He is _____.

3 그는 테니스뿐만 아니라 골프도 친다.   He plays _____.

4 그뿐만 아니라 그의 가족도 여기 산다.   _____ live here.

5 그녀뿐만 아니라 나도 숙제가 있다.   _____ have homework.

WRITING POINT ③

• We will visit **either the museum or the zoo**.   우리는 / 방문할 것이다 / 박물관이나 동물원에

1 너는 차나 커피를 마실 수 있다.   You can have _____.

2 나는TV를 보거나 음악을 들을 것이다.   I will _____.

3 그녀는 중국이나 일본 출신이다.   She comes from _____.

4 David나 내가 너와 함께 갈 것이다.   _____ will go with you.

5 너와 네 친구 둘 중 하나는 틀렸다.   _____ is wrong.

우리말과 일치하도록 빈칸에 알맞은 말을 넣으시오.

• both A and B •

1 우리는 뉴욕(New York)과 보스턴(Boston)에 둘 다 갔다.

→ We went to _____ _____ _____ _____.

2 그녀는 생선과 고기를 둘 다 샀다.

→ She _____ _____ _____ _____ _____.

3 나의 부모님과 나 모두 그 시험 결과에 만족했다.

→ _____ my parents _____ I _____ satisfied with the test result.

4 나는 Jane과 Mike 둘 다 저녁식사에 초대했다.

→ I invited _____ _____ _____ _____ to dinner.

• not only A but also B •

5 그 음식은 맛있을 뿐만 아니라 건강에도 좋다. (delicious / healthy)

→ The food is _____ _____ _____ _____ _____ _____.

6 그녀는 노래를 잘할 뿐만 아니라 춤도 완벽하게 춘다.

→ She _____ _____ _____ well _____ _____ _____ perfectly.

7 나의 언니뿐만 아니라 내 사촌들도 부산에 산다. (my cousins)

→ _____ _____ my sister _____ _____ my cousins _____ in Busan.

• either A or B •

8 너는 밥이나 파스타를 선택할 수 있다.

→ You can choose _____ _____ _____ _____.

9 너는 그에게 물어보거나 인터넷을 검색할 수 있다. (search)

→ You can _____ _____ him _____ _____ on the Internet.

10 그는 보통 집에 있거나 학교에 있다. (at home / at school)

→ He is usually _____ _____ _____ _____ _____.

TRY WRITING

( ) 안의 말을 이용하여 우리말을 영어로 옮기시오.

1 그녀는 피자와 스파게티 둘 다 주문했다. (order / pizza / spaghetti)

2 나는 그 책과 그 영화 둘 다 좋았다. (like)

3 그는 낚시하는 것뿐만 아니라 스키 타는 것도 즐긴다. (fishing / skiing)

4 우리는 월요일이나 화요일에 만날 수 있다. (can)

5 베니스(Venice)와 로마(Rome)는 둘 다 아름다운 도시들이다. (beautiful)

6 너는 나에게 전화하거나 이메일을 보낼 수 있다. (send me an email)

7 구내식당과 카페 둘 다 사람들로 가득 차 있었다. (the cafeteria / the café / be full of)

8 나는 아침식사로 샌드위치나 베이글을 먹을 것이다. (have / a sandwich / a bagel)

9 그녀는 피아노뿐만 아니라 바이올린도 연주한다. (the piano / the violin)

10 나의 선생님뿐만 아니라 내 친구들도 나에 대해 걱정했다. (be worried about)

11 John이나 내가 내일 널 도울 것이다. (be going to)

12 경주하고 나서, 나는 목이 말랐을 뿐만 아니라 배도 고팠다. (after the race / thirsty)

1 각 문장의 빈칸에 적절한 단어를 〈보기〉에서 한 번씩만 사용하여 문장을 완성하시오.

보기   after / when / while / until

(1) He moved to Seoul _____ he was twelve.

(2) _____ I was watching TV, the phone rang.

(3) They didn't come _____ the game was over.

(4) _____ I turned off the light, I went to bed.

2 주어진 우리말을 참고하여 대화를 완성하시오.

A What is the first thing to do in the morning?
B I drink a glass of water _____
_____ _____ I get up.
(나는 일어나자마자 물 한잔을 마셔.)

3 주어진 단어를 이용하여 우리말을 영작하시오.

(1) 내일 비가 온다면, 나는 나가지 않을 것이다.
(will, go out)

→ If it _____ .

(2) 뛰지 않으면, 너는 늦을 거야. (run, will, late)

→ Unless you _____ .

4 두 문장이 같은 의미가 되도록 빈칸에 알맞은 말을 쓰시오.

I stayed home because the weather was bad.
= I stayed home _____ _____ the bad weather.

5 다음 두 문장을 so ~ that 구문을 이용하여 한 문장으로 연결하시오.

I was sick. + I couldn't go to school.

→ _____

6 다음 문장을 접속사 although를 사용하여 같은 의미의 문장으로 다시 쓰시오.

The man was poor, but he was happy.

→ Although _____ .

7 우리말과 같은 뜻이 되도록 빈칸에 알맞은 말을 쓰시오.

(1) 그 수업은 유익했을 뿐만 아니라 흥미로웠다.

→ The class was _____ _____ useful _____ _____ interesting.

(2) 나는 점심으로 스테이크나 파스타를 먹을 것이다.

→ I will have _____ steak _____ pasta for lunch.

(3) 아이들과 그들의 부모님 모두 그 연극을 좋아했다.

→ _____ the children _____ their parents liked the play.

UNIT
11

기타 구문

LESSON 26 간접의문문

1 간접의문문은 의문문이 다른 문장의 일부로 쓰인 의문문이다. 간접의문문은 명사절로, 일반적인 의문문과는 달리 「의문사＋주어＋동사」의 어순을 따른다.

Do you know? + Who is he? → Do you know **who he is**? 너는 그가 누구인지 아니?
I wonder. + Where does he live? → I wonder **where he lives**. 나는 그가 어디에서 사는지 궁금하다.

2 간접의문문은 의문사가 있는 경우 의문사가 접속사 역할을 한다. 의문사가 없는 의문문의 경우에는 **whether**나 **if**를 쓴다.

의문사가 있는 의문문	의문사＋주어＋동사	When does the bank close? → Do you know when the bank closes? 너는 은행이 언제 문을 닫는지 아니?
의문사가 없는 의문문	whether/if＋주어＋동사	Is Susan at home? → I am not sure whether/if Susan is at home. 나는 그녀가 집에 있는지 확실히 모르겠어.

3 의문사가 주어인 의문문의 경우, 간접의문문의 어순은 그대로 「의문사＋동사」이다.

의문사가 주어인 의문문	의문사＋동사	Who ate the cake? → Please tell me who ate the cake. 누가 그 케이크를 먹었는지 내게 말해줘.

CHECK UP

● 빈칸에 알맞은 말을 고르시오.

1 When _____ ? ☐ they leave ☐ do they leave

2 I don't know why _____ crying. ☐ she is ☐ is she

3 Do you know where _____ ? ☐ Tiffany is ☐ is Tiffany

4 Who _____ ? ☐ that girl is ☐ is that girl

5 Can you tell me why _____ him? ☐ you like ☐ do you like

6 Do you know how much _____ ? ☐ the scarf is ☐ is the scarf

7 _____ come today? ☐ They will ☐ Will they

8 I am not sure if _____ help her. ☐ I should ☐ should I

9 Tell me why _____ you last night. ☐ he called ☐ did he call

10 What _____ for lunch? ☐ you had ☐ did you have

box 안의 예문을 참고하여 주어진 문장을 간접의문문으로 바꾸어 쓰시오.

WRITING POINT ①

• **What does she like?** 그녀는 무엇을 좋아하니?

→ I don't know **what she likes.** 나는 모른다 / 그녀가 무엇을 좋아하는지

1 Who is he? → Do you know _____?

2 Where are they going? → I don't know _____.

3 How does he go to work? → Do you know _____?

4 When did they leave? → I don't know _____.

5 What did the teacher say? → Can I ask _____?

WRITING POINT ②

• **Can she come?** 그녀는 올 수 있니?

→ I wonder **whether/if she can come.** 나는 궁금하다 / 그녀가 올 수 있는지

1 Is the answer correct? → I'm not sure _____.

2 Does she have a pet? → I wonder _____.

3 Did he take an umbrella? → I don't know _____.

4 Can she speak Korean? → Do you know _____?

5 Will it rain tomorrow? → I wonder _____.

WRITING POINT ③

• **Who invented** the toothbrush? 누가 칫솔을 발명했니?

→ Do you know **who invented** the toothbrush? 너는 아니 / 누가 칫솔을 발명했는지?

1 Who wrote this book? → I don't know _____.

2 Who cooked dinner? → I asked him _____.

3 What happened to James? → I wonder _____.

4 What makes you happy? → Can you tell me _____?

우리말과 일치하도록 빈칸에 알맞은 말을 넣으시오.

• 의문사가 있는 간접의문문 •

1 너는 그 영화가 언제 시작하는지 아니? (start)

→ Do you know _____ _____ _____ _____?

2 너는 그가 방과 후에 무엇을 하는지 아니? (do)

→ Do you know _____ _____ _____ after school?

3 네 가장 친한 친구가 누구인지 물어봐도 돼? (your best friend)

→ Can I ask _____ _____ _____ _____ _____?

4 나는 그가 어떻게 그 문제를 풀었는지 궁금해. (solve)

→ I wonder _____ _____ _____ _____ _____.

• 의문사가 없는 간접의문문 •

5 나는 내가 그것을 할 수 있을지 모르겠어. (can / it)

→ I'm not sure _____ _____ _____ _____ _____.

6 그에게 이 버스가 시내에 가는지 물어보자. (downtown)

→ Let's ask him _____ _____ _____ _____ _____.

7 나는 그게 사실인지 궁금해. (it / true)

→ I wonder _____ _____ _____ _____.

• 의문사가 주어인 간접의문문 •

8 누가 내 안경을 깨뜨렸는지 말해줘. (my glasses)

→ Please tell me _____ _____ _____ _____.

9 너는 그 상자 안에 무엇이 들었는지 아니? (in the box)

→ Do you know _____ _____ _____ _____?

10 나는 무엇이 네 마음을 바꾸었는지 궁금해. (your mind)

→ I wonder _____ _____ _____ _____.

( ) 안의 말을 이용하여 우리말을 영어로 옮기시오.

1 몇 시인지 아세요? (it)

2 나는 그녀가 어디서 그 재킷을 샀는지 궁금해. (the jacket)

3 너는 저 소녀가 누구인지 아니? (that girl)

4 오늘 아침에 네가 왜 늦었는지 내게 말해줄 수 있니? (can / tell / late)

5 너는 몇 명이 그 파티에 있었는지 아니? (how many / there / at the party)

6 제가 이 책을 어디에서 찾을 수 있는지 아세요? (find)

7 나는 올해 누가 노벨 평화상을 탔는지 궁금해. (win / the Nobel Peace Prize)

8 Mike에게 무슨 일이 일어났는지 내게 말해줄 수 있니? (can / tell / happen to)

9 너는 무엇이 그녀를 화나게 했는지 아니? (make / angry)

10 나는 그가 그 시험에 합격할지 확실히 모르겠어. (sure / will / the exam)

11 그에게 저녁 식사가 준비되었는지 물어볼게. (ask / ready)

12 나는 내가 오늘 그 일을 끝낼 수 있을지 모르겠어. (know / can)

It ~ that 강조구문

▌ It ~ that 강조구문은 '…한 것은 바로 ~이다'라는 뜻으로, 강조하고자 하는 말을 It is/was와 that 사이에 넣어서 만든다. It ~ that 강조구문은 주로 **주어, 목적어, 부사(구)**를 강조할 때 사용한다.

<u>Judy</u> won <u>the first prize</u> <u>at the speech contest</u> <u>yesterday</u>.
　주어　　　　　　목적어　　　　　　부사구　　　　　　부사

→ **It was** *Judy* **that** won the first prize at the speech contest yesterday. (주어 강조)
→ **It was** *the first prize* **that** Judy won at the speech contest yesterday. (목적어 강조)
→ **It was** *at the speech contest* **that** Judy won the first prize yesterday. (부사구 강조)
→ **It was** *yesterday* **that** Judy won the first prize at the speech contest. (부사 강조)

PLUS　강조하는 하는 말이 사람, 사물인 경우 that 대신 who(m), which를 사용할 수 있다.
　　　e.g. It was <u>Judy</u> *who* won the first prize at the speech contest yesterday.
　　　　　It was <u>the first prize</u> *which* Judy won at the speech contest yesterday.

 CHECK UP

● 우리말과 일치하는 문장을 고르시오.

▌ 그 사진을 찍은 사람은 바로 내 여동생이었다.

☐ It was my sister that took the picture.

☐ It was the picture that my sister took.

2 그녀가 만나고 싶은 사람은 바로 버락 오바마이다.

☐ It is she that wants to meet Barack Obama.

☐ It is Barack Obama that she wants to meet.

3 James가 점심으로 원하는 것은 바로 피자이다.

☐ It is for lunch that James wants pizza.

☐ It is pizza that James wants for lunch.

4 우리가 처음 만난 것은 바로 1년 전 오늘이었다.

☐ It was for the first time that we met a year ago today.

☐ It was a year ago today that we met for the first time.

5 우리가 만날 곳은 바로 극장 앞이다.

☐ It is the theater that we are going to meet.

☐ It is in front of the theater that we are going to meet.

box 안의 예문을 참고하여 밑줄 친 부분을 강조하는 문장으로 바꾸어 쓰시오.

WRITING POINT ❶

· **Tom** called me yesterday. Tom은 / 나에게 전화했다 / 어제

→ **It was Tom that** called me yesterday. 바로 Tom이었다 / 나에게 전화한 사람은 / 어제

1 <u>Jake</u> gave me advice.　　　　　→ It was _____.

2 <u>My sister</u> lent me some money.　→ It was _____.

3 <u>My mom</u> made this cake.　　　　→ It was _____.

4 <u>Mr. Kim</u> teaches us math.　　　　→ It is _____.

5 <u>Nancy</u> is dancing on the stage.　→ It is _____.

WRITING POINT ❷

· He ordered <u>a hamburger and a coke</u>. 그는 / 주문했다 / 햄버거와 콜라를

→ **It was a hamburger and a coke that** he ordered. 바로 햄버거와 콜라였다 / 그가 주문한 것은

1 He visited <u>Italy</u> last summer.　　　→ It was _____.

2 I bought <u>this sweater</u> yesterday.　→ It was _____.

3 We played <u>baseball</u> after school.　→ It was _____.

4 Minho studies <u>English</u> every day.　→ It is _____.

5 Jessica is looking for <u>her glasses</u>.　→ It is _____.

WRITING POINT ❸

· Peter plays tennis <u>every Saturday</u>. Peter는 / 테니스를 친다 / 매주 토요일에

→ **It is every Saturday that** Peter plays tennis. 바로 매주 토요일이다 / Peter가 테니스를 치는 것은

1 She works <u>at a bookstore</u>.　　　　→ It is _____.

2 He left his bag <u>on the bus</u>.　　　　→ It was _____.

3 They arrived here <u>yesterday</u>.　　　→ It was _____.

4 The festival is held <u>in July</u>.　　　　→ It is _____.

SENTENCE PRACTICE 2

우리말과 일치하도록 빈칸에 알맞은 말을 넣으시오.

• It ~ that 강조구문: 주어 강조 •

1 나를 그 파티에 초대한 사람은 바로 Rick이었다.

→ It _____ _____ _____ invited me to the party.

2 내 숙제를 도와준 사람은 바로 내 형이었다.

→ It _____ _____ _____ _____ helped me with my homework.

3 내가 없는 동안 내 고양이를 돌봐준 사람은 바로 내 이웃이었다. (neighbor)

→ It _____ _____ _____ _____ took care of my cat.

• It ~ that 강조구문: 목적어 강조 •

4 내가 생일선물로 원하는 것은 바로 강아지이다. (a puppy)

→ It _____ _____ _____ _____ I want for my birthday.

5 그가 올림픽에서 딴 것은 바로 금메달이었다.

→ It _____ _____ _____ _____ _____ he won at the Olympics.

6 그가 그 영화에서 맡은 것은 바로 햄릿(Hamlet)이었다.

→ It _____ _____ _____ he played in the movie.

7 내가 내 자유시간에 즐기는 것은 바로 만화책을 읽는 것이다. (comic books)

→ It _____ _____ _____ _____ _____ I enjoy in my free time.

• It ~ that 강조구문: 부사(구) 강조 •

8 내가 그에게 이메일을 보낸 것은 바로 월요일이었다. (on Monday)

→ It _____ _____ _____ _____ I sent him an email.

9 그가 전자레인지를 발명한 것은 우연히였다. (by accident)

→ It _____ _____ _____ he invented the microwave.

10 그녀가 그녀의 여권을 잃어버린 곳은 바로 공항에서였다. (at the airport)

→ It _____ _____ _____ _____ she lost her passport.

( ) 안의 말을 이용하여 우리말을 영어로 옮기시오.

1 그녀에게 꽃을 준 사람은 바로 그녀의 남자친구였다. (flowers)

2 그녀가 슈퍼마켓에서 산 것은 바로 약간의 과일이었다. (some / at the supermarket)

3 내가 내 시계를 발견한 곳은 바로 내 가방 안이었다. (bag / watch)

4 오늘 아침에 그 소포를 받은 사람은 바로 나의 엄마였다. (receive / the package)

5 내가 내 친구에게 빌린 것은 바로 노트북이었다. (a laptop / borrow from)

6 한국 전쟁이 일어난 것은 바로 1950년이었다. (the Korean War / break out)

7 내가 어제 Sally를 만난 곳은 바로 이 식당이었다. (at this restaurant)

8 어제 공원에서 축구를 한 사람은 바로 내 친구와 나였다. (in the park)

9 그녀가 사랑에 빠진 사람은 바로 Bill이었다. (fall in love with)

10 그녀가 피아노 레슨을 받는 것은 바로 매주 수요일이다. (every / take piano lessons)

11 내가 차 사고가 난 것은 바로 어젯밤이었다. (have a car accident)

12 그 마술사가 그 모자에서 꺼낸 것은 바로 토끼였다. (the magician / pull / out of)

1 주어진 문장을 〈보기〉와 같이 바꿀 때 빈칸에 알맞은 말을 쓰시오.

보기   When is your birthday?
→ I want to know <u>when your birthday is.</u>

(1) Who is she?

→ Do you know _____?

(2) When did they leave?

→ I am not sure _____.

(3) What does she like to do in her free time?

→ I wonder _____
in her free time.

2 대화의 빈칸에 알맞은 말을 쓰시오.

A Can you tell me _____ _____
_____ _____?
B My name is Angela.

3 다음 두 문장을 한 문장으로 만들 때 빈칸에 알맞은 말을 쓰시오.

I don't know. + Does she like spicy food?

→ I don't know _____.

4 우리말과 같은 뜻이 되도록 주어진 단어를 바르게 배열하시오.

너는 Tom이 그녀를 위해 뭘 샀는지 아니?
(bought / know / you / her / Tom / for /
what / do)

→ _____

5 다음 문장에서 어법상 틀린 곳을 찾아 바르게 고쳐 쓰시오.

(1) May I ask what time is it?
(2) I don't remember when did I meet her.
(3) I'm not sure that she lives here.

(1) _____ → _____
(2) _____ → _____
(3) _____ → _____

6 그림을 보고 주어진 단어와 It ~ that 강조구문을 사용하여 질문에 대한 답을 완성하시오.

Q Did you leave your bag on the bus?
A No, it _____ _____
_____ _____ _____
_____ on the bus. (my camera)

7 다음 두 문장을 밑줄 친 부분을 강조하는 문장으로 다시 쓰시오.

(1) <u>Kevin</u> broke the window yesterday.

→ It _____.

(2) Sarah is making <u>a chocolate cake</u>.

→ It _____.

MEMO

MEMO

MEMO

MEMO

문장패턴이 보이고 **영작**이 쉬워진다! 　중학생을 위한 친절한 **영작문 시리즈**

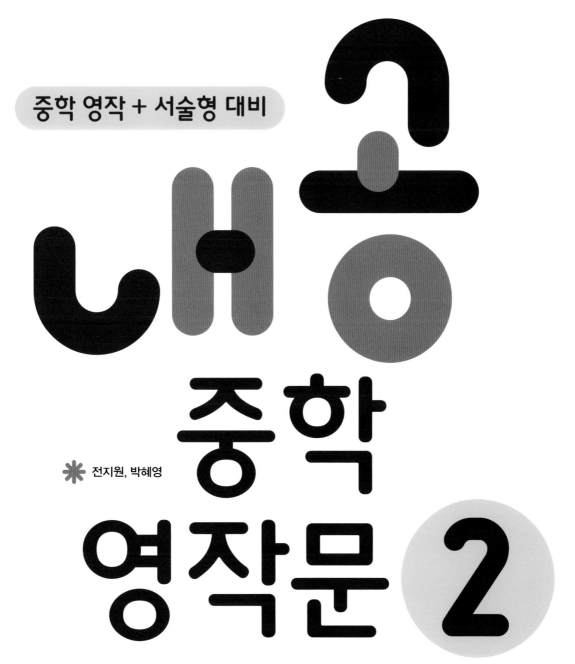

중학 영작 + 서술형 대비

내공

✳ 전지원, 박혜영

중학
영작문 2

문장 암기 Workbook

다락원

중학 영작 + 서술형 대비

내공

중학
영작문 2

문장 암기 Workbook

다락원

STEP 1 배운 문장을 쓰면서 외워보세요.

Score _____ / 15

	Korean	English
1	나는 방금 역에 도착했다.	I _____ _____ _____ at the station.
2	나는 아직 그 책을 읽지 않았다.	I _____ _____ the book _____.
3	나는 전에 그를 만난 적이 있다.	I _____ _____ him _____.
4	그는 뉴욕을 한 번 방문한 적이 있다.	He _____ _____ New York _____.
5	그는 학교에 지각한 적이 한 번도 없다.	He _____ _____ _____ _____ for school.
6	너는 유럽에 가본 적 있니?	_____ you _____ _____ _____ Europe?
7	우리는 무엇을 먹을지 결정하지 못했다.	We _____ _____ what to eat.
8	Susan은 아직 그 소포를 받지 못했다.	Susan _____ _____ the package yet.
9	나는 전에 말을 타본 적이 한 번도 없다.	I _____ _____ _____ a horse before.
10	그는 해외여행을 여러 번 해봤다.	He _____ _____ _____ many times.
11	너는 신데렐라(Cinderella)에 관한 이야기를 읽어본 적이 있니?	_____ _____ _____ _____ a story about Cinderella?
12	그는 이미 내 컴퓨터 고치는 것을 끝냈다.	He _____ _____ _____ fixing my computer.
13	Mary는 전에 스키를 타러 가본 적이 한 번도 없다.	Mary _____ _____ _____ _____ before.
14	너는 유명한 영화배우를 만나본 적이 있니?	_____ _____ _____ _____ a famous movie star?
15	올 겨울에는 아직 눈이 오지 않았다.	It _____ _____ _____ this winter.

STEP 2 배운 문장을 다시 한번 쓰면서 외워보세요.　　　　　Score ＿＿＿＿ / 15

	Korean	English
1	나는 방금 역에 도착했다.	I
2	나는 아직 그 책을 읽지 않았다.	I
3	나는 전에 그를 만난 적이 있다.	I
4	그는 뉴욕을 한 번 방문한 적이 있다.	He
5	그는 학교에 지각한 적이 한 번도 없다.	He
6	너는 유럽에 가본 적 있니?	Have
7	우리는 무엇을 먹을지 결정하지 못했다.	We
8	Susan은 아직 그 소포를 받지 못했다.	Susan
9	나는 전에 말을 타본 적이 한 번도 없다.	I
10	그는 해외여행을 여러 번 해봤다.	He
11	너는 신데렐라(Cinderella)에 관한 이야기를 읽어본 적이 있니?	Have
12	그는 이미 내 컴퓨터 고치는 것을 끝냈다.	He
13	Mary는 전에 스키를 타러 가본 적이 한 번도 없다.	Mary
14	너는 유명한 영화배우를 만나본 적이 있니?	Have
15	올 겨울에는 아직 눈이 오지 않았다.	It

STEP I   배운 문장을 쓰면서 외워보세요.   Score _____ / 15

	Korean	English
1	그는 10년 동안 영어를 가르쳐왔다.	He _____ _____ English _____ 10 years.
2	그들은 2014년부터 서로 알아왔다.	They _____ _____ each other _____ 2014.
3	그는 어렸을 때부터 안경을 써왔다.	He _____ _____ glasses _____ he was young.
4	나는 내 시계를 잃어버렸다.	I _____ _____ my watch.
5	그 기차는 역을 떠났다.	The train _____ _____ the station.
6	그 책은 내 인생을 바꿔놓았다.	The book _____ _____ my life.
7	그 집은 석 달째 비어있다.	The house _____ _____ empty _____ three months.
8	너는 이 아파트에 산지 얼마나 되었니?	_____ _____ you _____ in this apartment?
9	내 친구는 독일로 떠나버렸다.	My friend _____ _____ for Germany.
10	많이 컸구나!	You _____ _____ _____!
11	그는 5년 동안 수의사로 일했다.	He _____ _____ as a vet _____ 5 years.
12	우리는 그때부터 절친이었다.	We _____ _____ best friends _____ then.
13	영어를 공부한지 얼마나 되었니?	_____ _____ _____ you _____ English?
14	그들은 오늘 아침부터 아무것도 먹지 않았다.	They _____ _____ anything _____ this morning.
15	그는 살이 많이 빠졌다.	He _____ _____ a lot of weight.

STEP 2 배운 문장을 다시 한번 쓰면서 외워보세요. Score _____ / 15

	Korean	English
1	그는 10년 동안 영어를 가르쳐왔다.	He
2	그들은 2014년부터 서로 알아왔다.	They
3	그는 어렸을 때부터 안경을 써왔다.	He
4	나는 내 시계를 잃어버렸다.	I
5	그 기차는 역을 떠났다.	The train
6	그 책은 내 인생을 바꿔놓았다.	The book
7	그 집은 석 달째 비어있다.	The house
8	너는 이 아파트에 산지 얼마나 되었니?	How long
9	내 친구는 독일로 떠나버렸다.	My friend
10	많이 컸구나!	You
11	그는 5년 동안 수의사로 일했다.	He
12	우리는 그때부터 절친이었다.	We
13	영어를 공부한지 얼마나 되었니?	How long
14	그들은 오늘 아침부터 아무것도 먹지 않았다.	They haven't
15	그는 살이 많이 빠졌다.	He

동사 + 목적어 + 형용사/명사

월 ⬤ 일 ⬤

STEP I 배운 문장을 쓰면서 외워보세요.

Score _____ / 15

	Korean	English
1	그 소식은 우리를 슬프게 만들었다.	The news _____ _____ _____.
2	이 코트는 너를 따뜻하게 해줄 거야.	This coat will _____ _____ _____.
3	그들은 그 소녀를 혼자 두었다.	They _____ the girl _____.
4	나는 그 책이 흥미롭다는 것을 알게 되었다.	I _____ the book _____.
5	사람들은 그를 영웅이라고 부른다.	People _____ _____ a _____.
6	너는 이것을 비밀로 유지해야 한다.	You should _____ _____ a _____.
7	누가 그 문을 열어뒀니?	Who _____ the door _____?
8	너무 많은 커피를 마시는 것은 당신을 밤에 깨어있게 할 것이다.	Drinking too much coffee will _____ _____ _____ at night.
9	나는 그것이 유용한 도구인 것을 알게 되었다.	I _____ it _____ _____ _____.
10	그 부부는 그들의 딸을 Eva라고 이름 지었다.	The couple _____ _____ _____ _____.
11	그녀의 노력은 그녀를 훌륭한 피아니스트로 만들었다.	Her effort _____ _____ a _____ _____.
12	너는 그 상자를 안전하게 보관해야 한다.	You should _____ _____ _____ _____.
13	그 TV 쇼는 그를 스타로 만들었다.	The TV show _____ _____ a star.
14	그녀는 그 일이 매우 지루하다는 것을 알게 되었다.	She _____ _____ _____ very _____.
15	무엇이 그녀를 그렇게 화나게 만들었니?	What _____ _____ so _____?

STEP 2 배운 문장을 다시 한번 쓰면서 외워보세요.   Score _____ / 15

	Korean	English
1	그 소식은 우리를 슬프게 만들었다.	The news
2	이 코트는 너를 따뜻하게 해줄 거야.	This coat
3	그들은 그 소녀를 혼자 두었다.	They
4	나는 그 책이 흥미롭다는 것을 알게 되었다.	I
5	사람들은 그를 영웅이라고 부른다.	People
6	너는 이것을 비밀로 유지해야 한다.	You should
7	누가 그 문을 열어뒀니?	Who
8	너무 많은 커피를 마시는 것은 당신을 밤에 깨어있게 할 것이다.	Drinking too much coffee
9	나는 그것이 유용한 도구인 것을 알게 되었다.	I
10	그 부부는 그들의 딸을 Eva라고 이름 지었다.	The couple
11	그녀의 노력은 그녀를 훌륭한 피아니스트로 만들었다.	Her effort
12	너는 그 상자를 안전하게 보관해야 한다.	You should
13	그 TV 쇼는 그를 스타로 만들었다.	The TV show
14	그녀는 그 일이 매우 지루하다는 것을 알게 되었다.	She
15	무엇이 그녀를 그렇게 화나게 만들었니?	What

동사 + 목적어 + to부정사

STEP I 배운 문장을 쓰면서 외워보세요.

Score _____ / 15

	Korean	English
1	나는 네가 파티에 오길 원한다.	I _____ _____ _____ _____ to the party.
2	너는 내가 저녁을 요리하기를 원하니?	Do you _____ _____ _____ _____ dinner?
3	김 선생님은 우리에게 앉으라고 말했다.	Mr. Kim _____ _____ _____ _____ _____.
4	나는 그에게 창문을 열어달라고 부탁했다.	I _____ _____ _____ _____ the window.
5	나는 아버지가 세차하시는 것을 도왔다.	I _____ my father _____ his car.
6	나는 그에게 음악 소리를 줄여달라고 부탁했다.	I _____ _____ _____ _____ _____ the music.
7	그는 나에게 다음 정거장에서 내리라고 말했다.	He _____ _____ _____ _____ _____ at the next stop.
8	나는 나의 할머니가 건강하시길 원한다.	I _____ my grandmother _____ _____ _____.
9	우리는 네 꿈이 이뤄질 거라고 기대한다.	We _____ your dream _____ _____ _____.
10	선생님이 너에게 무엇을 하라고 조언하셨니?	What did the teacher _____ you _____ _____ ?
11	이 앱은 내가 영어 배우는 것을 돕는다.	This app _____ _____ _____ _____ _____.
12	요가를 하는 것은 당신이 긴장을 푸는데 도움이 될 수 있다.	Doing yoga can _____ _____ _____.
13	그 의사는 나에게 규칙적으로 운동하라고 조언했다.	The doctor _____ _____ _____ _____ regularly.
14	이 탁자 옮기는 것 좀 도와줄래?	Can you _____ _____ _____ this table?
15	그 소년은 그 노인이 길을 건너는 것을 돕고 있다.	The boy _____ _____ the old man _____ _____ _____.

STEP 2 배운 문장을 다시 한번 쓰면서 외워보세요.　　　　Score _____ / 15

	Korean	English
1	나는 네가 파티에 오길 원한다.	I want
2	너는 내가 저녁을 요리하기를 원하니?	Do you
3	김 선생님은 우리에게 앉으라고 말했다.	Mr. Kim
4	나는 그에게 창문을 열어달라고 부탁했다.	I
5	나는 아버지가 세차하시는 것을 도왔다.	I
6	나는 그에게 음악 소리를 줄여달라고 부탁했다.	I
7	그는 나에게 다음 정거장에서 내리라고 말했다.	He
8	나는 나의 할머니가 건강하시길 원한다.	I want
9	우리는 네 꿈이 이뤄질 거라고 기대한다.	We
10	선생님이 너에게 무엇을 하라고 조언하셨니?	What
11	이 앱은 내가 영어 배우는 것을 돕는다.	This app
12	요가를 하는 것은 당신이 긴장을 푸는데 도움이 될 수 있다.	Doing yoga
13	그 의사는 나에게 규칙적으로 운동하라고 조언했다.	The doctor
14	이 탁자 옮기는 것 좀 도와줄래?	Can you
15	그 소년은 그 노인이 길을 건너는 것을 돕고 있다.	The boy is

지각동사, 사역동사

STEP I 배운 문장을 쓰면서 외워보세요.

Score _____ / 15

	Korean	English
1	나는 한 소년이 무대에서 춤 추는 것을 보았다.	I _____ _____ _____ _____ on the stage.
2	나는 그들이 통화하는 것을 들었다.	I _____ _____ _____ _____ on the phone.
3	나는 누군가 나를 따라오는 것을 느꼈다.	I _____ _____ _____ _____ .
4	부엌에서 밥 짓는 냄새가 난다.	I can _____ the rice _____ _____ _____ _____ .
5	아빠는 내가 숙제를 끝내게 했다.	My dad made _____ _____ _____ _____ .
6	나는 그에게 호텔을 예약하라고 시켰다.	I had _____ _____ a _____ .
7	그녀는 내가 그녀의 책을 빌리게 해주었다.	She let _____ _____ _____ _____ .
8	나는 그가 내 이름 부르는 것을 들었다.	I _____ _____ _____ my name.
9	그녀는 누군가 자신의 어깨를 만지는 것을 느꼈다.	She _____ _____ _____ _____ her shoulder.
10	뭔가 타는 냄새 안나니?	Can you _____ _____ _____ _____ ?
11	그녀의 남자친구는 그녀를 웃게 하려고 애썼다.	Her boyfriend tried to _____ _____ _____ .
12	음악을 듣는 것은 나를 기분 좋게 만든다.	Listening to music _____ _____ _____ good.
13	우리 선생님은 우리에게 한 달에 책 두 권을 읽게 하신다.	Our teacher makes _____ _____ _____ _____ a month.
14	나는 그녀가 버스 정류장에서 버스를 기다리는 것을 보았다.	I _____ _____ _____ a bus at the bus stop.
15	나의 언니는 내가 그녀의 옷을 입지 못하게 한다.	My sister doesn't let _____ _____ _____ _____ .

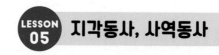

STEP 2 배운 문장을 다시 한번 쓰면서 외워보세요. Score _____ / 15

	Korean	English
1	나는 한 소년이 무대에서 춤 추는 것을 보았다.	I
2	나는 그들이 통화하는 것을 들었다.	I
3	나는 누군가 나를 따라오는 것을 느꼈다.	I
4	부엌에서 밥 짓는 냄새가 난다.	I can
5	아빠는 내가 숙제를 끝내게 했다.	My dad made
6	나는 그에게 호텔을 예약하라고 시켰다.	I had
7	그녀는 내가 그녀의 책을 빌리게 해주었다.	She let
8	나는 그가 내 이름 부르는 것을 들었다.	I
9	그녀는 누군가 자신의 어깨를 만지는 것을 느꼈다.	She
10	뭔가 타는 냄새 안나니?	Can you
11	그녀의 남자친구는 그녀를 웃게 하려고 애썼다.	Her boyfriend tried to
12	음악을 듣는 것은 나를 기분 좋게 만든다.	Listening to music
13	우리 선생님은 우리에게 한 달에 책 두 권을 읽게 하신다.	Our teacher makes
14	나는 그녀가 버스 정류장에서 버스를 기다리는 것을 보았다.	I
15	나의 언니는 내가 그녀의 옷을 입지 못하게 한다.	My sister doesn't

추측을 나타내는 조동사

월 ⃝ 일

STEP I 배운 문장을 쓰면서 외워보세요.

Score _____ / 15

	Korean	English
1	나의 부모님은 오늘 저녁에 외출하실지도 모른다.	My parents _____ _____ _____ this evening.
2	네 휴대전화는 차 안에 있을지도 모른다.	Your cell phone _____ _____ in the car.
3	이번 주말에는 비가 안 올지도 모른다.	It _____ _____ _____ this weekend.
4	화성에는 생명체가 있을지도 모른다.	_____ _____ _____ life on Mars.
5	그녀는 당신을 좋아하는 것이 틀림없다.	She _____ _____ _____.
6	그 소문은 사실일 리가 없다.	The rumor _____ _____ _____.
7	우리는 이번 여름에 태국에 갈지도 모른다.	We _____ _____ _____ Thailand this summer.
8	그는 의사일 리가 없다.	He _____ _____ a doctor.
9	그들은 틀림없이 매우 피곤할 것이다.	They _____ _____ very _____.
10	너는 이 영화를 좋아하지 않을지도 모른다.	You _____ _____ _____ this movie.
11	너희 부모님은 틀림없이 너를 자랑스러워하실 것이다.	Your parents _____ _____ _____ of you.
12	이번 크리스마스에는 눈이 올지도 모른다.	It _____ _____ this Christmas.
13	저기 있는 남자는 James임이 틀림없다.	The man over there _____ _____ _____.
14	이것은 실수임에 틀림없다.	This _____ _____ a mistake.
15	그 문제를 해결할 방법이 있을지도 모른다.	_____ _____ _____ a way to solve the problem.

STEP 2 배운 문장을 다시 한번 쓰면서 외워보세요. Score _____ / 15

Korean	English
1	나의 부모님은 오늘 저녁에 외출하실지도 모른다.	My parents
2	네 휴대전화는 차 안에 있을지도 모른다.	Your cell phone
3	이번 주말에는 비가 안 올지도 모른다.	It
4	화성에는 생명체가 있을지도 모른다.	There
5	그녀는 당신을 좋아하는 것이 틀림없다.	She
6	그 소문은 사실일 리가 없다.	The rumor
7	우리는 이번 여름에 태국에 갈지도 모른다.	We
8	그는 의사일 리가 없다.	He
9	그들은 틀림없이 매우 피곤할 것이다.	They
10	너는 이 영화를 좋아하지 않을지도 모른다.	You
11	너희 부모님은 틀림없이 너를 자랑스러워하실 것이다.	Your parents
12	이번 크리스마스에는 눈이 올지도 모른다.	It
13	저기 있는 남자는 James임이 틀림없다.	The man over there
14	이것은 실수임에 틀림없다.	This
15	그 문제를 해결할 방법이 있을지도 모른다.	There

STEP I 배운 문장을 쓰면서 외워보세요.

Score _____ / 15

	Korean	English
1	당신은 이 양식을 먼저 작성하셔야 합니다.	You _____ _____ _____ this form first.
2	방문객들은 동물원의 동물들에게 먹이를 주면 안 된다.	Visitors _____ _____ _____ the animals in the zoo.
3	나는 내 개를 수의사에게 데리고 가야 한다.	I _____ _____ _____ my dog _____ the vet.
4	Jane은 그의 남동생을 돌봐야 한다.	Jane _____ _____ take care of her little brother.
5	우리는 그를 30분 동안 기다려야 했다.	We _____ _____ _____ for him for 30 minutes.
6	그들은 토요일에 일해야 하니?	_____ _____ _____ _____ _____ on Saturday?
7	Tom은 정장을 입고 출근할 필요가 없다.	Tom _____ _____ _____ _____ a suit to work.
8	우리는 교통법규를 지켜야 한다.	We _____ _____ the traffic rules.
9	우리는 그 기차를 놓쳐서는 안 돼.	We _____ _____ _____ the train.
10	학생들은 시험에서 커닝하면 안 된다.	Students _____ _____ _____ on a test.
11	너는 수영장에서 수영모를 써야 한다.	You _____ _____ a swimming cap in the pool.
12	제가 얼마나 기다려야 하나요?	How long _____ _____ _____ _____ _____?
13	너는 모든 것을 외울 필요는 없다.	You _____ _____ _____ _____ everything.
14	나는 이 책을 도서관에 반납해야 한다.	I _____ _____ _____ this book _____ the library.
15	너는 반 친구들을 괴롭혀서는 안 된다.	You _____ _____ _____ your classmates.

STEP 2 배운 문장을 다시 한번 쓰면서 외워보세요.   Score _____ / 15

	Korean	English
1	당신은 이 양식을 먼저 작성하셔야 합니다.	You must
2	방문객들은 동물원의 동물들에게 먹이를 주면 안 된다.	Visitors must
3	나는 내 개를 수의사에게 데리고 가야 한다.	I have to
4	Jane은 그의 남동생을 돌봐야 한다.	Jane has to
5	우리는 그를 30분 동안 기다려야 했다.	We
6	그들은 토요일에 일해야 하니?	Do they
7	Tom은 정장을 입고 출근할 필요가 없다.	Tom
8	우리는 교통법규를 지켜야 한다.	We must
9	우리는 그 기차를 놓쳐서는 안 돼.	We must
10	학생들은 시험에서 커닝하면 안 된다.	Students must
11	너는 수영장에서 수영모를 써야 한다.	You must
12	제가 얼마나 기다려야 하나요?	How long
13	너는 모든 것을 외울 필요는 없다.	You
14	나는 이 책을 도서관에 반납해야 한다.	I have
15	너는 반 친구들을 괴롭혀서는 안 된다.	You must

조언, 권고를 나타내는 조동사

STEP I 배운 문장을 쓰면서 외워보세요.

Score _____ / 15

	Korean	English
1	너는 좀 더 조심해야 한다.	You _____ _____ more _____.
2	너는 Jane의 생일을 잊으면 안 돼.	You _____ _____ _____ Jane's birthday.
3	제 신발을 벗어야 하나요?	_____ _____ _____ _____ my shoes?
4	너는 집에 가서 누워 쉬는 게 낫다.	You _____ _____ home and _____ in bed.
5	너는 그 전선을 만지지 않는 게 낫다.	You _____ _____ _____ _____ the wire.
6	우리는 그 여행을 취소하는 게 나을 거 같아.	I think we _____ _____ _____ the trip.
7	그녀는 그의 조언을 받아들이는 게 낫다.	She _____ _____ take _____ _____.
8	우리는 어려움에 처한 사람들을 도와야 한다.	We _____ _____ _____ in need.
9	그녀는 옷에 너무 많은 돈을 쓰면 안 된다.	She _____ _____ _____ too much money _____ clothes.
10	제가 그에게 도움을 청해야 할까요?	_____ _____ _____ him for help?
11	내가 너를 몇 시에 데리러 갈까?	What time _____ _____ _____ you _____ ?
12	영어를 향상시키기 위해 제가 뭘 해야 할까요?	_____ _____ _____ _____ to improve my English?
13	그는 다시는 늦지 않는 게 낫다.	He _____ _____ _____ _____ _____ again.
14	우리는 눈이 얼어붙기 전에 치우는 게 낫다.	We _____ _____ _____ the snow before it _____ .
15	사람들은 그들의 애완동물들에 대해 책임을 져야 한다.	People _____ _____ _____ _____ their pets.

STEP 2 배운 문장을 다시 한번 쓰면서 외워보세요.   Score _____ / 15

	Korean	English
1	너는 좀 더 조심해야 한다.	You
2	너는 Jane의 생일을 잊으면 안 돼.	You
3	제 신발을 벗어야 하나요?	Should
4	너는 집에 가서 누워 쉬는 게 낫다.	You
5	너는 그 전선을 만지지 않는 게 낫다.	You
6	우리는 그 여행을 취소하는 게 나을 거 같아.	I think
7	그녀는 그의 조언을 받아들이는 게 낫다.	She
8	우리는 어려움에 처한 사람들을 도와야 한다.	We
9	그녀는 옷에 너무 많은 돈을 쓰면 안 된다.	She
10	제가 그에게 도움을 청해야 할까요?	Should
11	내가 너를 몇 시에 데리러 갈까?	What time
12	영어를 향상시키기 위해 제가 뭘 해야 할까요?	What
13	그는 다시는 늦지 않는 게 낫다.	He
14	우리는 눈이 얼어붙기 전에 치우는 게 낫다.	We
15	사람들은 그들의 애완동물들에 대해 책임을 져야 한다.	People

수동태의 시제

STEP I   배운 문장을 쓰면서 외워보세요.

Score _____ / 15

	Korean	English
1	그 영화는 아이들에게 사랑 받는다.	The movie _____ _____ _____ children.
2	멕시코에서는 스페인어를 말한다.	Spanish _____ _____ in Mexico.
3	그 시는 내 친구가 썼다.	The poem _____ _____ my friend.
4	이 사진들은 Tom이 찍었다.	These pictures _____ _____ Tom.
5	그 축제는 다음달에 열릴 것이다.	The festival _____ _____ _____ next month.
6	그 궁전은 많은 관광객들이 방문한다.	The palace _____ _____ _____ many tourists.
7	Robin 선생님은 그의 학생들에게 존경 받는다.	Mr. Robin _____ _____ _____ his students.
8	그 아이들은 자원봉사자들에 의해 도움을 받는다.	The children _____ _____ _____ volunteers.
9	내 자전거는 누군가에 의해 도난 당했다.	My bike _____ _____ _____ someone.
10	새로운 도서관이 그 회사에 의해 지어질 것이다.	A new library _____ _____ _____ _____ the company.
11	Frank는 그의 선생님께 칭찬을 받았다.	Frank _____ _____ _____ his teacher.
12	그 도둑은 한 젊은이에 의해 잡혔다.	The thief _____ _____ _____ a young man.
13	우천 시, 그 콘서트는 취소될 것이다.	In case of rain, the concert _____ _____ _____.
14	차와 커피가 식후에 제공될 것이다.	Tea and coffee _____ _____ _____ after the meal.
15	그 박물관은 유명 건축가가 설계했다.	The museum _____ _____ _____ a famous architect.

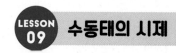

STEP 2 배운 문장을 다시 한번 쓰면서 외워보세요.　　　　　　　　　　　　　　Score _____ / 15

	Korean	English
1	그 영화는 아이들에게 사랑 받는다.	The movie
2	멕시코에서는 스페인어를 말한다.	Spanish
3	그 시는 내 친구가 썼다.	The poem
4	이 사진들은 Tom이 찍었다.	These pictures
5	그 축제는 다음달에 열릴 것이다.	The festival
6	그 궁전은 많은 관광객들이 방문한다.	The palace
7	Robin 선생님은 그의 학생들에게 존경 받는다.	Mr. Robin
8	그 아이들은 자원봉사자들에 의해 도움을 받는다.	The children
9	내 자전거는 누군가에 의해 도난 당했다.	My bike
10	새로운 도서관이 그 회사에 의해 지어질 것이다.	A new library
11	Frank는 그의 선생님께 칭찬을 받았다.	Frank
12	그 도둑은 한 젊은이에 의해 잡혔다.	The thief
13	우천 시, 그 콘서트는 취소될 것이다.	In case of rain,
14	차와 커피가 식후에 제공될 것이다.	Tea and coffee
15	그 박물관은 유명 건축가가 설계했다.	The museum

월 ○ 일 ○

STEP I 배운 문장을 쓰면서 외워보세요.

Score _____ / 15

Korean	English
1 그 책들은 수업에 쓰이니?	_____ the books _____ in class?
2 그 편지들은 James가 쓰지 않았다.	The letters _____ _____ _____ _____ James.
3 그 산은 눈으로 덮여 있다.	The mountain _____ _____ _____ snow.
4 그는 시험 결과에 만족했다.	He _____ _____ _____ the test result.
5 그 섬은 아름다운 경치로 유명하다.	The island _____ _____ _____ its beautiful scenery.
6 그 문은 잠겨 있지 않다.	The door _____ _____ _____ .
7 그 꽃들은 내가 심지 않았다.	The flowers _____ _____ _____ _____ me.
8 그들은 그 소식에 실망했다.	They _____ _____ _____ the news.
9 Carol은 유럽 역사에 관심이 있다.	Carol _____ _____ _____ European history.
10 사람들은 지구 온난화에 대해 걱정한다.	People _____ _____ _____ the global warming.
11 그 사무실은 매일 청소되는 않는다.	The office _____ _____ _____ every day.
12 그 다리는 강철로 만들어졌다.	The bridge _____ _____ _____ steel.
13 그 백화점은 쇼핑객들로 붐볐다.	The department store _____ _____ _____ shoppers.
14 나는 내 일에 싫증이 난다.	I _____ _____ _____ my job.
15 그는 너에게 도움을 받았니?	_____ _____ _____ _____ you?

STEP 2   배운 문장을 다시 한번 쓰면서 외워보세요.   Score _____ / 15

Korean	English
1 그 책들은 수업에 쓰이니?	Are
2 그 편지들은 James가 쓰지 않았다.	The letters
3 그 산은 눈으로 덮여 있다.	The mountain
4 그는 시험 결과에 만족했다.	He
5 그 섬은 아름다운 경치로 유명하다.	The island
6 그 문은 잠겨 있지 않다.	The door
7 그 꽃들은 내가 심지 않았다.	The flowers
8 그들은 그 소식에 실망했다.	They
9 Carol은 유럽 역사에 관심이 있다.	Carol
10 사람들은 지구 온난화에 대해 걱정한다.	People
11 그 사무실은 매일 청소되지는 않는다.	The office
12 그 다리는 강철로 만들어졌다.	The bridge
13 그 백화점은 쇼핑객들로 붐볐다.	The department store
14 나는 내 일에 싫증이 난다.	I
15 그는 너에게 도움을 받았니?	Was

STEP 1 배운 문장을 쓰면서 외워보세요.

Score _____ / 15

	Korean	English
1	그 강에서 수영하는 것은 위험하다.	It _____ _____ _____ _____ in the river.
2	그는 새 컴퓨터를 사기를 원한다.	He _____ _____ _____ a new computer.
3	그들은 6시까지 그 일을 끝내려고 노력했다.	They _____ _____ _____ the work by six.
4	그는 마실 물을 좀 샀다.	He bought some _____ _____ _____.
5	너는 따뜻한 입을 것이 필요할 거야.	You'll need _____ _____ _____ _____.
6	좋은 친구들을 사귀는 것은 중요하다.	It _____ _____ _____ _____ good friends.
7	너의 안전을 위해 헬멧을 착용하는 것이 필요하다.	It _____ _____ _____ a helmet for your safety.
8	그의 행복의 비밀은 남을 돕는 것이다.	His secret to happiness is _____ _____ _____.
9	그의 목표는 올림픽에서 금메달을 따는 것이다.	His goal is _____ _____ _____ _____ _____ at the Olympics.
10	엄마는 내게 새 자전거를 사주기로 약속했다.	My mom _____ _____ _____ _____ _____ a new bike.
11	외국어를 배우는 가장 좋은 방법은 무엇이니?	What is the best way _____ _____ _____ _____ ?
12	그는 그의 가족과 같이 살 집을 샀다.	He bought _____ _____ _____ _____ with his family.
13	읽을 책 한 권 추천해주시겠어요?	Can you recommend _____ _____ _____ ?
14	Philip은 이번 여름에 유럽에 갈 계획이다.	Philip _____ _____ _____ to Europe this summer.
15	나는 오늘 해야 할 일이 세 가지가 있다.	I have _____ _____ _____ _____ today.

STEP 2 배운 문장을 다시 한번 쓰면서 외워보세요.

Score _____ / 15

	Korean	English
1	그 강에서 수영하는 것은 위험하다.	It
2	그는 새 컴퓨터를 사기를 원한다.	He wants
3	그들은 6시까지 그 일을 끝내려고 노력했다.	They
4	그는 마실 물을 좀 샀다.	He
5	너는 따뜻한 입을 것이 필요할 거야.	You'll
6	좋은 친구들을 사귀는 것은 중요하다.	It
7	너의 안전을 위해 헬멧을 착용하는 것이 필요하다.	It
8	그의 행복의 비밀은 남을 돕는 것이다.	His secret
9	그의 목표는 올림픽에서 금메달을 따는 것이다.	His goal
10	엄마는 내게 새 자전거를 사주기로 약속했다.	My mom
11	외국어를 배우는 가장 좋은 방법은 무엇이니?	What
12	그는 그의 가족과 같이 살 집을 샀다.	He
13	읽을 책 한 권 추천해주시겠어요?	Can you
14	Philip은 이번 여름에 유럽에 갈 계획이다.	Philip
15	나는 오늘 해야 할 일이 세 가지가 있다.	I

to부정사의 부사적 용법

STEP I 배운 문장을 쓰면서 외워보세요.

Score _____ / 15

	Korean	English
1	그는 뉴스를 보기 위해 TV를 켰다.	He turned on the TV _____ _____ _____ _____.
2	우리는 그 경기에 져서 실망했다.	We _____ _____ _____ _____ the game.
3	그렇게 하다니 그는 용감함에 틀림없다.	He must be _____ _____ _____ so.
4	지금까지 자다니 그는 피곤함에 틀림없다.	He must be _____ _____ _____ until now.
5	그는 깨어나보니 자신이 유명해진 것을 발견했다.	He _____ _____ _____ himself famous.
6	우리는 최선을 다했지만 결국 실패했다.	We did our best _____ _____ _____.
7	Eric은 책을 몇 권을 대출하기 위해 도서관에 갔다.	Eric went to the library _____ _____ _____ _____ _____.
8	나는 너 같은 친구가 있어서 행복해.	I _____ _____ _____ _____ a friend like you.
9	그렇게 많이 먹는 걸 보니 그들은 배가 고픔에 틀림없다.	They must be _____ _____ _____ so much.
10	Cathy는 패션디자인을 공부하기 위해 파리에 갔다.	Cathy went to Paris _____ _____ _____ _____.
11	나의 조부모님께서는 90세까지 사셨다.	My grandparents _____ _____ _____ 90 years old.
12	Steve는 그 축제에 참가하기 위해 드럼을 연습했다.	Steve practiced the drums _____ _____ _____ _____ the festival.
13	그 소년은 자라서 훌륭한 음악가가 되었다.	The boy _____ _____ _____ a great musician.
14	George는 그의 가족을 다시 보게 되어 행복했다.	George _____ _____ _____ his family again.
15	매일 제시간에 오는 것을 보니 그는 부지런함에 틀림없다.	He must be _____ _____ _____ on time every day.

STEP 2 배운 문장을 다시 한번 쓰면서 외워보세요.　　　　　Score _____ / 15

	Korean	English
1	그는 뉴스를 보기 위해 TV를 켰다.	He
2	우리는 그 경기에 져서 실망했다.	We
3	그렇게 하다니 그는 용감함에 틀림없다.	He
4	지금까지 자다니 그는 피곤함에 틀림없다.	He
5	그는 깨어나보니 자신이 유명해진 것을 발견했다.	He
6	우리는 최선을 다했지만 결국 실패했다.	We
7	Eric은 책을 몇 권을 대출하기 위해 도서관에 갔다.	Eric
8	나는 너 같은 친구가 있어서 행복해.	I
9	그렇게 많이 먹는 걸 보니 그들은 배가 고픔에 틀림없다.	They
10	Cathy는 패션디자인을 공부하기 위해 파리에 갔다.	Cathy
11	나의 조부모님께서는 90세까지 사셨다.	My grandparents
12	Steve는 그 축제에 참가하기 위해 드럼을 연습했다.	Steve
13	그 소년은 자라서 훌륭한 음악가가 되었다.	The boy
14	George는 그의 가족을 다시 보게 되어 행복했다.	George
15	매일 제시간에 오는 것을 보니 그는 부지런함에 틀림없다.	He

to부정사 주요 구문

STEP 1   배운 문장을 쓰면서 외워보세요.

Score _____ / 15

	Korean	English
1	나는 공부하기에는 너무 피곤하다.	I am _____ _____ _____ _____.
2	그녀는 학교에 가기에는 너무 아팠다.	She _____ _____ _____ _____ _____ to school.
3	그는 그 바위를 들어 올릴 만큼 힘이 세다.	He is _____ _____ _____ _____ the rock.
4	나는 무엇을 입어야 할지 모르겠다.	I don't know _____ _____ _____.
5	내일 어디서 만날지 정하자.	Let's decide _____ _____ _____ tomorrow.
6	그 햄버거는 너무 두꺼워서 베어 물 수가 없다.	The hamburger is _____ _____ _____ _____.
7	수영하러 가기에는 너무 춥다.	It is _____ _____ _____ _____ swimming.
8	그는 맨 위 선반에 닿을 만큼 키가 크다.	He is _____ _____ _____ _____ the top shelf.
9	엄마는 나에게 파스타 만드는 방법을 가르쳐주셨다.	My mom _____ me _____ _____ _____ pasta.
10	나는 그에게 내 코트를 어디에 두어야 할지 물었다.	I _____ him _____ _____ _____ my coat.
11	Jack은 그 어려운 수학 문제를 풀 만큼 똑똑하다.	Jack is _____ _____ _____ _____ the difficult math problem.
12	날씨가 소풍을 갈 만큼 충분히 좋았다.	The weather was _____ _____ _____ _____ on a picnic.
13	그녀는 그 영화에서 Juliet 역을 맡을 만큼 충분히 아름답다.	She is _____ _____ _____ _____ Juliet in the movie.
14	그는 마라톤을 뛰기에는 너무 약하다.	He is _____ _____ _____ _____ a marathon.
15	나는 그녀의 생일 선물로 무엇을 사야 할지 모르겠다.	I don't know _____ _____ _____ for her birthday.

STEP 2 배운 문장을 다시 한번 쓰면서 외워보세요.　　　　　　　　　　　Score ＿＿＿＿＿ / 15

	Korean	English
1	나는 공부하기에는 너무 피곤하다.	I
2	그녀는 학교에 가기에는 너무 아팠다.	She
3	그는 그 바위를 들어 올릴 만큼 힘이 세다.	He
4	나는 무엇을 입어야 할지 모르겠다.	I
5	내일 어디서 만날지 정하자.	Let's
6	그 햄버거는 너무 두꺼워서 베어 물 수가 없다.	The hamburger
7	수영하러 가기에는 너무 춥다.	It
8	그는 맨 위 선반에 닿을 만큼 키가 크다.	He
9	엄마는 나에게 파스타 만드는 방법을 가르쳐주셨다.	My mom
10	나는 그에게 내 코트를 어디에 두어야 할지 물었다.	I
11	Jack은 그 어려운 수학 문제를 풀 만큼 똑똑하다.	Jack
12	날씨가 소풍을 갈 만큼 충분히 좋았다.	The weather
13	그녀는 그 영화에서 Juliet 역을 맡을 만큼 충분히 아름답다.	She
14	그는 마라톤을 뛰기에는 너무 약하다.	He
15	나는 그녀의 생일 선물로 무엇을 사야 할지 모르겠다.	I

STEP 1 배운 문장을 쓰면서 외워보세요.   Score _____ / 15

	Korean	English
1	너는 산책하러 가기를 원하니?	Do you _____ _____ _____ for a walk?
2	나는 내 방 청소하는 것을 끝냈다.	I _____ _____ my room.
3	그 책은 읽을만한 가치가 있다.	The book is _____ _____.
4	Sam은 기타 연주를 잘 한다.	Sam is _____ _____ _____ the guitar.
5	나는 네 소식을 듣기를 고대하고 있다.	I'm _____ _____ _____ _____ from you.
6	나는 사람들을 웃게 하는 것을 즐긴다.	I enjoy _____ _____ _____.
7	나는 너와 연락하고 지내길 희망한다.	I hope _____ _____ _____ _____ with you.
8	너는 졸업 후에 무엇을 할 계획이니?	What do you _____ _____ _____ after graduation?
9	나는 오늘 밤 나가고 싶지 않다.	I don't feel like _____ _____ _____.
10	우리는 그 상점을 찾는 데 어려움을 겪었다.	We _____ _____ _____ the store.
11	그 관광객들은 사진을 찍느라 바빴다.	The tourists _____ _____ _____ pictures.
12	그들은 노숙자들을 돕기로 결심했다.	They _____ _____ _____ the homeless.
13	같이 컴퓨터 게임 하는 게 어때?	_____ _____ _____ computer games together?
14	나는 시골에 사는 것을 꺼리지 않는다.	I _____ _____ _____ in the countryside.
15	그녀는 내 질문에 답하는 것을 피했다.	She avoided _____ _____ _____.

STEP 2 배운 문장을 다시 한번 쓰면서 외워보세요. Score _____ / 15

	Korean	English
1	너는 산책하러 가기를 원하니?	Do you
2	나는 내 방 청소하는 것을 끝냈다.	I
3	그 책은 읽을만한 가치가 있다.	The book
4	Sam은 기타 연주를 잘 한다.	Sam is
5	나는 네 소식을 듣기를 고대하고 있다.	I'm
6	나는 사람들을 웃게 하는 것을 즐긴다.	I
7	나는 너와 연락하고 지내길 희망한다.	I
8	너는 졸업 후에 무엇을 할 계획이니?	What do you
9	나는 오늘 밤 나가고 싶지 않다.	I don't feel like
10	우리는 그 상점을 찾는 데 어려움을 겪었다.	We had
11	그 관광객들은 사진을 찍느라 바빴다.	The tourists
12	그들은 노숙자들을 돕기로 결심했다.	They
13	같이 컴퓨터 게임 하는 게 어때?	How/What
14	나는 시골에 사는 것을 꺼리지 않는다.	I
15	그녀는 내 질문에 답하는 것을 피했다.	She

현재분사, 과거분사

월 일

STEP I 배운 문장을 쓰면서 외워보세요. Score _____ / 15

	Korean	English
1	그녀는 일본에서 만든 자동차를 가지고 있다.	She has a car _____ _____ _____.
2	사진을 찍고 있는 그 남자는 Peter이다.	The man _____ _____ _____ is Peter.
3	피곤한 하루였다.	It was _____ _____ _____.
4	수영장에서 수영하는 아이들이 몇 명 있다.	There are _____ _____ _____ in the pool.
5	눈으로 뒤덮인 정원을 봐.	Look at the garden _____ _____ _____.
6	그는 Tiki라는 이름의 말하는 로봇을 가지고 있다.	He has a _____ _____ _____ Tiki.
7	이 책에는 많은 감동적인 이야기들이 있다.	This book has many _____ _____.
8	그 경기장은 흥분한 축구팬들로 가득 차 있다.	The stadium is filled with _____ _____ _____.
9	그 여자는 울고 있는 아기를 안고 있다.	The woman is holding _____ _____ _____.
10	이 수학문제는 매우 헷갈린다.	This _____ _____ is so _____.
11	그는 그의 도난당한 지갑을 찾았다.	He found his _____ _____.
12	이것은 내가 가장 좋아하는 가수가 쓴 곡이다.	This is the song _____ _____ _____ _____ _____.
13	한국어를 배우는 외국인들이 많이 있다.	There are many _____ _____ _____.
14	시골에서 사는 것은 지루할 수 있다.	Living in the country _____ _____ _____.
15	그 사고에서 부상당한 남자는 Brown 씨이다.	_____ _____ _____ _____ in the accident is Mr. Brown.

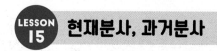

STEP 2 배운 문장을 다시 한번 쓰면서 외워보세요. Score _____ / 15

	Korean	English
1	그녀는 일본에서 만든 자동차를 가지고 있다.	She
2	사진을 찍고 있는 그 남자는 Peter이다.	The man
3	피곤한 하루였다.	It
4	수영장에서 수영하는 아이들이 몇 명 있다.	There
5	눈으로 뒤덮인 정원을 봐.	Look at
6	그는 Tiki라는 이름의 말하는 로봇을 가지고 있다.	He
7	이 책에는 많은 감동적인 이야기들이 있다.	This book
8	그 경기장은 흥분한 축구팬들로 가득 차 있다.	The stadium
9	그 여자는 울고 있는 아기를 안고 있다.	The woman
10	이 수학문제는 매우 헷갈린다.	This math problem
11	그는 그의 도난당한 지갑을 찾았다.	He
12	이것은 내가 가장 좋아하는 가수가 쓴 곡이다.	This is
13	한국어를 배우는 외국인들이 많이 있다.	There
14	시골에서 사는 것은 지루할 수 있다.	Living in the country
15	그 사고에서 부상당한 남자는 Brown 씨이다.	The man

명사의 수량 표현

STEP I 배운 문장을 쓰면서 외워보세요.

Score _____ / 15

Korean	English
1 그는 하루에 커피 두 잔을 마신다.	He drinks _____ _____ _____ _____ a day.
2 그녀는 수프 한 그릇을 주문했다.	She ordered _____ _____ _____ _____.
3 책장에 책이 몇 권 있다.	There are _____ _____ _____ on the bookshelf.
4 그는 주머니에 돈이 거의 없었다.	He had _____ _____ in his pocket.
5 나는 치즈 두 장이 필요하다.	I need _____ _____ _____ _____.
6 그는 점심으로 피자 두 조각을 먹었다.	He had _____ _____ _____ pizza for lunch.
7 우리는 그 섬에서 며칠을 보냈다.	We spent _____ _____ _____ on the island.
8 Susan은 친구 몇 명을 그녀의 집에 초대했다.	Susan invited _____ _____ _____ to her house.
9 그녀는 자신의 수프에 약간의 소금을 넣었다.	She put _____ _____ _____ in her soup.
10 나는 그곳에 몇 번 가본 적이 있다.	I have been there _____ _____ _____.
11 안타깝게도, 우리는 베니스에서는 거의 사진을 찍지 않았다.	Unfortunately, we _____ _____ _____ in Venice.
12 우리에게는 지금 시간이 거의 없다.	We _____ _____ _____ now.
13 나는 오늘 해야 할 숙제가 조금 있다.	I _____ _____ _____ _____ to do today.
14 바구니 안에 빵 세 덩어리가 있다.	There are _____ _____ _____ _____ in the basket.
15 그는 그 시험에서 거의 실수를 하지 않았다.	He _____ _____ _____ _____ on the test.

STEP 2 배운 문장을 다시 한번 쓰면서 외워보세요.

Score _____ / 15

	Korean	English
1	그는 하루에 커피 두 잔을 마신다.	He
2	그녀는 수프 한 그릇을 주문했다.	She
3	책장에 책이 몇 권 있다.	There
4	그는 주머니에 돈이 거의 없었다.	He
5	나는 치스 누 상이 필요하다.	I
6	그는 점심으로 피자 두 조각을 먹었다.	He
7	우리는 그 섬에서 며칠을 보냈다.	We
8	Susan은 친구 몇 명을 그녀의 집에 초대했다.	Susan
9	그녀는 자신의 수프에 약간의 소금을 넣었다.	She
10	나는 그곳에 몇 번 가본 적이 있다.	I
11	안타깝게도, 우리는 베니스에서는 거의 사진을 찍지 않았다.	Unfortunately,
12	우리에게는 지금 시간이 거의 없다.	We
13	나는 오늘 해야 할 숙제가 조금 있다.	I
14	바구니 안에 빵 세 덩어리가 있다.	There
15	그는 그 시험에서 거의 실수를 하지 않았다.	He

LESSON
17 재귀대명사

월 일

STEP 1 배운 문장을 쓰면서 외워보세요.

Score _____ / 15

Korean	English
1 나는 칼에 베었다.	I _____ _____ with a _____.
2 그녀는 자신을 그렸다.	She _____ a _____ of _____.
3 편안히 있으세요.	Please _____ _____ at _____.
4 나는 이 상자를 혼자서 옮길 수 없다.	I can't move this box _____ _____.
5 그 문은 저절로 닫혔다.	The door closed _____ _____.
6 그들은 축제에서 즐거운 시간을 보냈다.	They enjoyed _____ at the _____.
7 이것은 우리끼리만 아는 얘기이다.	This is _____ _____.
8 여러분에게 제 소개를 할게요.	Let me _____ _____ to _____.
9 우리는 그 실수에 대해 우리 자신을 탓했다.	We blamed _____ for _____ _____.
10 그녀는 중국어를 독학했다.	She _____ _____ Chinese.
11 그녀는 자신의 사진을 찍었다.	She _____ a _____ of _____.
12 그 소년은 넘어져서 다쳤다.	The boy _____ _____ and hurt _____.
13 너는 왜 혼잣말을 하고 있니?	Why are you _____ _____ _____?
14 그들은 그 문제를 스스로 풀었다.	They solved the problem _____ _____.
15 그녀는 거울에 비친 자신을 보고 있다.	She is _____ _____ _____ in the _____.

STEP 2 배운 문장을 다시 한번 쓰면서 외워보세요.   Score _____ / 15

	Korean	English
1	나는 칼에 베었다.	I
2	그녀는 자신을 그렸다.	She
3	편안히 있으세요.	Please
4	나는 이 상자를 혼자서 옮길 수 없다.	I can't
5	그 문은 저절로 닫혔다.	The door
6	그들은 축제에서 즐거운 시간을 보냈다.	They enjoyed
7	이것은 우리끼리만 아는 얘기이다.	This
8	여러분에게 제 소개를 할게요.	Let
9	우리는 그 실수에 대해 우리 자신을 탓했다.	We
10	그녀는 중국어를 독학했다.	She
11	그녀는 자신의 사진을 찍었다.	She
12	그 소년은 넘어져서 다쳤다.	The boy
13	너는 왜 혼잣말을 하고 있니?	Why
14	그들은 그 문제를 스스로 풀었다.	They
15	그녀는 거울에 비친 자신을 보고 있다.	She

STEP 1   배운 문장을 쓰면서 외워보세요.   Score _____ / 15

Korean	English
1 Aron은 그의 형만큼 키가 크다.	Aron is _____ _____ _____ his brother.
2 멕시코는 캐나다보다 더 덥다.	Mexico is _____ _____ Canada.
3 과일은 초콜릿보다 건강에 더 좋다.	Fruit is _____ _____ chocolate.
4 Janet은 Daniel보다 더 인기가 있다.	Janet is _____ _____ _____ Daniel.
5 그의 차는 내 것보다 더 비싸다.	His car is _____ _____ _____ mine.
6 더 많이 웃을수록 너는 더 좋아 보인다.	_____ _____ you smile, _____ _____ you look.
7 그를 적게 볼수록 나는 그가 더 그립다.	_____ _____ I see him, _____ _____ I miss him.
8 오래 기다릴수록 나는 더 화가 났다.	_____ _____ I waited, _____ _____ I got.
9 그의 신발은 그의 아버지 것만큼 크다.	His shoes are _____ _____ _____ his father's.
10 나는 Peter만큼 많이 운동하지 않는다.	I don't exercise _____ _____ _____ Peter.
11 열심히 공부할수록 너는 더 많이 배울 것이다.	_____ _____ you study, _____ _____ you will learn.
12 패스트푸드를 많이 먹을수록 너는 더 살찔 것이다.	_____ _____ _____ you eat, _____ _____ you will get.
13 날이 화창할수록 나는 더 행복함을 느낀다.	_____ _____ it is, _____ _____ I feel.
14 오늘 날씨는 어제보다 훨씬 더 나쁘다.	Today's weather is _____ _____ _____ yesterday's.
15 역사는 수학보다 더 흥미로운 것 같다.	I think that history is _____ _____ _____ math.

STEP 2 배운 문장을 다시 한번 쓰면서 외워보세요.   Score _____ / 15

	Korean	English
1	Aron은 그의 형만큼 키가 크다.	Aron
2	멕시코는 캐나다보다 더 덥다.	Mexico
3	과일은 초콜릿보다 건강에 더 좋다.	Fruit
4	Janet은 Daniel보다 더 인기가 있다.	Janet
5	그의 차는 내 것보다 더 비싸다.	His car
6	더 많이 웃을수록 너는 더 좋아 보인다.	The
7	그를 적게 볼수록 나는 그가 더 그립다.	The
8	오래 기다릴수록 나는 더 화가 났다.	The
9	그의 신발은 그의 아버지 것만큼 크다.	His shoes
10	나는 Peter만큼 많이 운동하지 않는다.	I
11	열심히 공부할수록 너는 더 많이 배울 것이다.	The
12	패스트푸드를 많이 먹을수록 너는 더 살찔 것이다.	The
13	날이 화창할수록 나는 더 행복함을 느낀다.	The
14	오늘 날씨는 어제보다 훨씬 더 나쁘다.	Today's weather
15	역사는 수학보다 더 흥미로운 것 같다.	I think that

STEP I 배운 문장을 쓰면서 외워보세요.

Score _____ / 15

	Korean	English
1	8월은 1년 중 가장 더운 달이다.	August is _____ _____ _____ of the year.
2	가을은 독서하기에 가장 좋은 계절이다.	Fall is _____ _____ _____ for _____.
3	나일강은 다른 어떤 강보다 더 길다.	The Nile is _____ _____ any other _____.
4	다른 어떤 소녀도 Julie보다 더 예쁘지 않다.	No _____ _____ is _____ _____ Julie.
5	웃음은 가장 좋은 약이다.	Laughter is _____ _____ _____.
6	그는 내가 아는 가장 지루한 사람이다.	He is _____ _____ _____ _____ I know.
7	당신 인생에서 가장 소중한 것은 무엇입니까?	What is _____ _____ _____ _____ in your life?
8	겨울은 다른 어떤 계절보다 더 춥다.	Winter is _____ _____ any other _____.
9	그 교회는 그 마을에서 다른 어떤 건물보다 더 오래되었다.	The church is _____ _____ any other _____ in the town.
10	에베레스트 산은 세계에서 다른 어떤 산보다 더 높다.	Mt. Everest is _____ _____ any other _____ in the world.
11	다른 어떤 스포츠도 축구보다 더 인기 있지 않다.	No _____ _____ is _____ _____ _____ soccer.
12	다른 어떤 동물도 개만큼 충직하지 않다.	No _____ _____ is _____ _____ _____ the dog.
13	누구도 Mark보다 더 힘이 세지 않다.	No one is _____ _____ Mark.
14	그날은 내 인생에서 가장 행복한 날이었다.	It was _____ _____ _____ of my life.
15	그것은 역사상 최악의 지진이었다.	It was _____ earthquake _____ _____.

STEP 2 배운 문장을 다시 한번 쓰면서 외워보세요.　　　　　　　　　Score _____ / 15

	Korean	English
1	8월은 1년 중 가장 더운 달이다.	August
2	가을은 독서하기에 가장 좋은 계절이다.	Fall
3	나일강은 다른 어떤 강보다 더 길다.	The Nile
4	다른 어떤 소녀도 Julie보다 더 예쁘지 않다.	No
5	웃음은 가장 좋은 약이다.	Laughter
6	그는 내가 아는 가장 지루한 사람이다.	He
7	당신 인생에서 가장 소중한 것은 무엇입니까?	What
8	겨울은 다른 어떤 계절보다 더 춥다.	Winter
9	그 교회는 그 마을에서 다른 어떤 건물보다 더 오래되었다.	The church
10	에베레스트 산은 세계에서 다른 어떤 산보다 더 높다.	Mt. Everest
11	다른 어떤 스포츠도 축구보다 더 인기 있지 않다.	No
12	다른 어떤 동물도 개만큼 충직하지 않다.	No
13	누구도 Mark보다 더 힘이 세지 않다.	No
14	그날은 내 인생에서 가장 행복한 날이었다.	It
15	그것은 역사상 최악의 지진이었다.	It

STEP I 배운 문장을 쓰면서 외워보세요.

Score _____ / 15

	Korean	English
1	나는 캐나다에 사는 친구가 있다.	I have a friend _____ _____ in Canada.
2	안경을 쓰고 있는 저 소년은 Bill이다.	The boy _____ _____ _____ _____ _____ Bill.
3	나를 도와준 그 남자는 매우 친절했다.	The man _____ _____ _____ _____ very kind.
4	그는 옷을 파는 상점에서 일한다.	He works in a shop _____ _____ _____.
5	시내까지 가는 버스가 있나요?	Is there a bus _____ _____ _____?
6	책상 위에 있던 책은 어디 있니?	Where is the book _____ _____ on the desk?
7	소방관은 불을 끄는 사람이다.	A fire fighter is a person _____ _____ _____ _____.
8	어제 나에게 전화했던 그 남자는 나의 형이었다.	The man _____ _____ _____ yesterday _____ my brother.
9	이것은 대답하기 어려운 질문이다.	This is a question _____ _____ _____ to answer.
10	당나귀는 작은 말처럼 생긴 동물이다.	A donkey is an animal _____ _____ _____ a small horse.
11	그 방은 호수가 내려다보이는 창문이 있다.	The room has a window _____ _____ a _____.
12	Smith 씨는 그리스 음식을 제공하는 식당을 운영한다.	Mr. Smith runs a restaurant _____ _____ Greek food.
13	나무에 앉아있는 저 새를 봐.	Look at the bird _____ _____ _____ on the tree.
14	경주에서 이긴 그 소년은 행복했다.	The boy _____ _____ _____ _____ happy.
15	나를 물었던 그 개는 내 이웃의 개였다.	The dog _____ _____ _____ my neighbor's dog.

STEP 2   배운 문장을 다시 한번 쓰면서 외워보세요.   Score _____ / 15

	Korean	English
1	나는 캐나다에 사는 친구가 있다.	I
2	안경을 쓰고 있는 저 소년은 Bill이다.	The boy
3	나를 도와준 그 남자는 매우 친절했다.	The man
4	그는 옷을 파는 상점에서 일한다.	He
5	시내까지 가는 버스가 있나요?	Is there
6	책상 위에 있던 책은 어디 있니?	Where
7	소방관은 불을 끄는 사람이다.	A fire fighter
8	어제 나에게 전화했던 그 남자는 나의 형이었다.	The man
9	이것은 대답하기 어려운 질문이다.	This
10	당나귀는 작은 말처럼 생긴 동물이다.	A donkey
11	그 방은 호수가 내려다보이는 창문이 있다.	The room
12	Smith 씨는 그리스 음식을 제공하는 식당을 운영한다.	Mr. Smith
13	나무에 앉아있는 저 새를 봐.	Look at
14	경주에서 이긴 그 소년은 행복했다.	The boy
15	나를 물었던 그 개는 내 이웃의 개였다.	The dog

STEP I 배운 문장을 쓰면서 외워보세요.

	Korean	English
1	내가 본 그 남자는 Henry였다.	The man _____ _____ _____ _____ Henry.
2	Daniel은 내가 믿을 수 있는 친구이다.	Daniel is a friend _____ _____ _____ _____.
3	나와 함께 춤춘 그 소녀는 Ann이다.	The girl _____ _____ _____ _____ _____ Ann.
4	내가 산 그 식탁은 매우 크다.	The table _____ _____ _____ _____ very big.
5	우리가 먹었던 그 피자는 맛있었다.	The pizza _____ _____ _____ _____ delicious.
6	Jill은 내가 좋아하는 모자를 쓰고 있다.	Jill is wearing a hat _____ _____ _____ _____.
7	이것이 Rick이 너에게 준 반지니?	Is this the ring _____ _____ _____ _____?
8	그가 이야기하고 있는 저 여자는 그의 여동생이다.	The woman _____ _____ _____ _____ _____ _____ his sister.
9	나는 너에게 소개시켜주고 싶은 친구가 있어.	I have a friend _____ _____ _____ _____ _____ to you.
10	나는 네가 추천한 그 영화를 봤다.	I watched the movie _____ _____ _____ _____.
11	이것이 네가 찾고 있는 책이니?	Is this the book _____ _____ _____ _____ _____?
12	우리가 방문했던 식당은 매우 분주했다.	The restaurant _____ _____ _____ _____ very busy.
13	그가 나에게 말한 이야기는 사실이다.	The story _____ _____ _____ _____ _____ true.
14	네가 가장 존경하는 사람은 누구니?	Who is the person _____ _____ _____ the most?
15	이것은 내가 아빠 생신 선물로 산 지갑이다.	This is the wallet _____ _____ _____ for my dad's birthday.

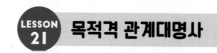
STEP 2 배운 문장을 다시 한번 쓰면서 외워보세요.   Score _____ / 15

	Korean	English
1	내가 본 그 남자는 Henry였다.	The man
2	Daniel은 내가 믿을 수 있는 친구이다.	Daniel
3	나와 함께 춤춘 그 소녀는 Ann이다.	The girl
4	내가 산 그 식탁은 매우 크다.	The table
5	우리가 먹었던 그 피자는 맛있었디.	The pizza
6	Jill은 내가 좋아하는 모자를 쓰고 있다.	Jill
7	이것이 Rick이 너에게 준 반지니?	Is this
8	그가 이야기하고 있는 저 여자는 그의 여동생이다.	The woman
9	나는 너에게 소개시켜주고 싶은 친구가 있어.	I
10	나는 네가 추천한 그 영화를 봤다.	I
11	이것이 네가 찾고 있는 책이니?	Is this
12	우리가 방문했던 식당은 매우 분주했다.	The restaurant
13	그가 나에게 말한 이야기는 사실이다.	The story
14	네가 가장 존경하는 사람은 누구니?	Who
15	이것은 내가 아빠 생신 선물로 산 지갑이다.	This

STEP I 　배운 문장을 쓰면서 외워보세요.　　　　　　　　　　Score _____ / 15

	Korean	English
1	그들이 필요한 것은 물과 음식이다.	_____ _____ _____ is water and food.
2	네가 좋아하는 것을 나에게 말해줘.	Tell me _____ _____ _____ .
3	이것은 내가 기대했던 것이 아니다.	This is not _____ _____ _____ .
4	그는 결코 포기하지 않는 소년이다.	He is a boy _____ never _____ _____ .
5	그녀가 요리한 음식은 맛있었다.	The food _____ _____ _____ was delicious.
6	이곳은 나의 삼촌이 사시는 집이다.	This is the house _____ my uncle _____ _____ .
7	그녀의 미소는 나를 행복하게 만드는 것이다.	Her smile is _____ _____ _____ _____ .
8	내가 크리스마스에 원하는 것은 새 코트이다.	_____ _____ _____ for _____ is a new coat.
9	민호(Minho)는 그가 수업시간에 배운 것을 복습했다.	Minho reviewed _____ _____ _____ in class.
10	나는 5개 국어를 할 수 있는 남자를 만났다.	I met a man _____ _____ _____ five _____ .
11	나는 도서관에서 빌린 책을 반납해야 한다.	I have to return the book _____ _____ from the library.
12	이 재킷은 내가 사고 싶은 것이다.	This jacket is _____ _____ to buy.
13	이 샐러드는 내 여동생이 주문한 것이다.	This salad is _____ _____ _____ _____ .
14	은행을 턴 그 남자는 도망쳤다.	The man _____ _____ _____ ran away.
15	나는 선생님이 말씀하시고 있는 것을 이해하지 못하겠다.	I don't understand _____ the teacher _____ _____ .

STEP 2 배운 문장을 다시 한번 쓰면서 외워보세요.　　　　　　　　　　　　　　　　Score _____ / 15

	Korean	English
1	그들이 필요한 것은 물과 음식이다.	What
2	네가 좋아하는 것을 나에게 말해줘.	Tell
3	이것은 내가 기대했던 것이 아니다.	This
4	그는 결코 포기하지 않는 소년이다.	He
5	그녀가 요리한 음식은 맛있었다.	The food
6	이곳은 나의 삼촌이 사시는 집이다.	This
7	그녀의 미소는 나를 행복하게 만드는 것이다.	Her smile
8	내가 크리스마스에 원하는 것은 새 코트이다.	What
9	민호(Minho)는 그가 수업시간에 배운 것을 복습했다.	Minho
10	나는 5개 국어를 할 수 있는 남자를 만났다.	I
11	나는 도서관에서 빌린 책을 반납해야 한다.	I have to
12	이 재킷은 내가 사고 싶은 것이다.	This jacket
13	이 샐러드는 내 여동생이 주문한 것이다.	This salad
14	은행을 턴 그 남자는 도망쳤다.	The man
15	나는 선생님이 말씀하시고 있는 것을 이해하지 못하겠다.	I

시간, 조건의 접속사

월 ○ 일

STEP I 배운 문장을 쓰면서 외워보세요.

Score _____ / 15

	Korean	English
1	외출하기 전에 불을 꺼라.	Turn off the lights _____ _____ _____ _____.
2	그는 샤워를 한 후에 자러 갔다.	He went to bed _____ _____ _____ _____ _____.
3	우리는 해가 뜨자마자 떠날 것이다.	We will leave _____ _____ _____ the sun _____.
4	운전 중에는 항상 조심해라.	Always be careful _____ _____ _____ _____.
5	비가 오지 않으면, 나는 외출할 것이다.	Unless _____ _____, I will go out.
6	Bill과 Jane은 저녁을 먹은 후에 산책하러 갔다.	Bill and Jane went for a walk _____ _____ had _____.
7	우리는 너무 늦기 전에 무언가를 해야 한다.	We have to do something _____ it is _____ _____.
8	그는 네 살 때 읽고 쓸 수 있었다.	He could read and write _____ _____ _____ _____.
9	그가 파스타를 요리하는 동안, 나는 샐러드를 준비했다.	_____ _____ _____ _____ _____ pasta, I prepared the salad.
10	우리는 그가 올 때까지 기다려야 했다.	We had to wait _____ _____ _____.
11	그는 운전면허를 따자마자 새 차를 샀다.	He bought a new car _____ _____ _____ _____ _____ his _____ _____.
12	질문이 있으면, 손을 들어주세요.	If _____ _____ any questions, please raise your hand.
13	네가 나를 도와주지 않는다면, 나는 그것을 할 수 없다.	Unless _____ _____ _____, I cannot do it.
14	그 아이들은 어두워질 때까지 수영장에서 놀았다.	The children played in the swimming pool _____ it _____ _____.
15	내가 일을 일찍 끝내면, 널 데리러 갈게.	If _____ _____ _____ early, I'll pick you up.

STEP 2   배운 문장을 다시 한번 쓰면서 외워보세요.   Score _____ / 15

	Korean	English
1	외출하기 전에 불을 꺼라.	Turn off
2	그는 샤워를 한 후에 자러 갔다.	He
3	우리는 해가 뜨자마자 떠날 것이다.	We
4	운전 중에는 항상 조심해라.	Always
5	비가 오지 않으면, 나는 외출할 것이다.	Unless
6	Bill과 Jane은 저녁을 먹은 후에 산책하러 갔다.	Bill and Jane
7	우리는 너무 늦기 전에 무언가를 해야 한다.	We
8	그는 네 살 때 읽고 쓸 수 있었다.	He
9	그가 파스타를 요리하는 동안, 나는 샐러드를 준비했다.	While
10	우리는 그가 올 때까지 기다려야 했다.	We
11	그는 운전면허를 따자마자 새 차를 샀다.	He
12	질문이 있으면, 손을 들어주세요.	If
13	네가 나를 도와주지 않는다면, 나는 그것을 할 수 없다.	Unless
14	그 아이들은 어두워질 때까지 수영장에서 놀았다.	The children
15	내가 일을 일찍 끝내면, 널 데리러 갈게.	If

STEP I 배운 문장을 쓰면서 외워보세요.   Score _____ / 15

	Korean	English
1	그 음식이 짰기 때문에, 나는 물을 많이 마셨다.	_____ _____ _____ _____ , I drank a lot of water.
2	모든 항공편이 폭풍 때문에 취소되었다.	All the flights were canceled _____ _____ _____ _____ .
3	그는 그의 차가 고장 나서 버스를 타야 했다.	He had to take the bus _____ _____ _____ _____ .
4	그 선생님은 그의 무례한 행동 때문에 화가 났다.	The teacher got angry _____ _____ _____ _____ .
5	너무 더워서 나는 아무것도 할 수가 없었다.	It was _____ _____ _____ I _____ _____ anything.
6	나는 배가 너무 고파서 저녁으로 밥 두 공기를 먹었다.	I was _____ _____ _____ I _____ two bowls of rice.
7	그는 프랑스에서 1년 동안 살았지만, 불어를 하지 못한다.	_____ _____ _____ _____ for a year, he cannot speak French.
8	나의 할머니는 연세가 매우 많으시지만, 여전히 활동적이시다.	_____ _____ _____ _____ very _____ , she is still active.
9	따뜻하고 화창했기 때문에, 우리는 해변에 갔다.	_____ it was _____ and _____ , we went to the beach.
10	나는 두통 때문에 공부를 할 수 없었다.	I couldn't study _____ _____ _____ .
11	그 가방은 너무 비싸서 나는 그것을 살 수 없었다.	The bag was _____ _____ I _____ _____ it.
12	그들은 바빴지만, 우리를 도와주었다.	_____ _____ _____ _____ , they helped us.
13	나는 너무 늦게 일어나서 학교 버스를 놓쳤다.	I got up _____ _____ I _____ the school bus.
14	나는 너무 긴장해서 한마디도 할 수 없었다.	I was _____ _____ _____ I _____ _____ a word.
15	그녀는 고소공포증이 있어서 비행기 타는 것을 싫어한다.	She hates flying _____ _____ _____ _____ heights.

STEP 2 배운 문장을 다시 한번 쓰면서 외워보세요.　　　　　　　　　Score _____ / 15

	Korean	English
1	그 음식이 짰기 때문에, 나는 물을 많이 마셨다.	Because
2	모든 항공편이 폭풍 때문에 취소되었다.	All the flights
3	그는 그의 차가 고장 나서 버스를 타야 했다.	He had to
4	그 선생님은 그의 무례한 행동 때문에 화가 났다.	The teacher
5	너무 더워서 나는 아무것도 할 수가 없었다.	It
6	나는 배가 너무 고파서 저녁으로 밥 두 공기를 먹었다.	I
7	그는 프랑스에서 1년 동안 살았지만, 불어를 하지 못한다.	Although/Though
8	나의 할머니는 연세가 매우 많으시지만, 여전히 활동적이시다.	Although/Though
9	따뜻하고 화창했기 때문에, 우리는 해변에 갔다.	Because
10	나는 두통 때문에 공부를 할 수 없었다.	I
11	그 가방은 너무 비싸서 나는 그것을 살 수 없었다.	The bag
12	그들은 바빴지만, 우리를 도와주었다.	Although/Though
13	나는 너무 늦게 일어나서 학교 버스를 놓쳤다.	I
14	나는 너무 긴장해서 한마디도 할 수 없었다.	I
15	그녀는 고소공포증이 있어서 비행기 타는 것을 싫어한다.	She

상관접속사

STEP I 배운 문장을 쓰면서 외워보세요.

Score _____ / 15

	Korean	English
1	Judy와 Sally 둘 다 내 반 친구들이다.	_____ _____ _____ _____ are my classmates.
2	서울과 런던은 둘 다 수도이다.	_____ _____ _____ _____ are capital cities.
3	그는 부유할 뿐만 아니라 유명하다.	He is _____ _____ _____ _____ _____ _____ .
4	그뿐만 아니라 그의 가족도 여기 산다.	_____ _____ _____ _____ _____ _____ live here.
5	나는TV를 보거나 음악을 들을 것이다.	I will _____ _____ _____ _____ or _____ _____ music.
6	너와 네 친구 둘 중 하나는 틀렸다.	_____ you _____ your friend _____ wrong.
7	그녀는 생선과 고기를 둘 다 샀다.	She bought _____ _____ _____ _____ .
8	나의 부모님과 나 모두 그 시험 결과에 만족했다.	_____ my parents _____ _____ satisfied with the test result.
9	나는 Jane과 Mike 둘 다 저녁식사에 초대했다.	I invited _____ _____ _____ _____ to dinner.
10	그 음식은 맛있을 뿐만 아니라 건강에도 좋다.	The food is _____ _____ _____ _____ _____ _____ .
11	그녀는 노래를 잘할 뿐만 아니라 춤도 완벽하게 춘다.	She _____ _____ _____ well _____ _____ _____ perfectly.
12	너는 그에게 물어보거나 인터넷을 검색할 수 있다.	You can _____ _____ _____ _____ _____ on the Internet.
13	우리는 월요일이나 화요일에 만날 수 있다.	We can meet _____ _____ _____ _____ .
14	그녀는 피아노뿐만 아니라 바이올린도 연주한다.	She plays _____ _____ _____ _____ _____ .
15	경주하고 나서, 나는 목이 말랐을 뿐만 아니라 배도 고팠다.	After the race, I was _____ _____ _____ _____ _____ _____ .

STEP 2 배운 문장을 다시 한번 쓰면서 외워보세요. Score _____ / 15

	Korean	English
1	Judy와 Sally 둘 다 내 반 친구들이다.	
2	서울과 런던은 둘 다 수도이다.	
3	그는 부유할 뿐만 아니라 유명하다.	He
4	그뿐만 아니라 그의 가족도 여기 산다.	
5	나는 TV를 보거나 음악을 들을 것이나.	I will
6	너와 네 친구 둘 중 하나는 틀렸다.	
7	그녀는 생선과 고기를 둘 다 샀다.	She
8	나의 부모님과 나 모두 그 시험 결과에 만족했다.	
9	나는 Jane과 Mike 둘 다 저녁식사에 초대했다.	I
10	그 음식은 맛있을 뿐만 아니라 건강에도 좋다.	The food
11	그녀는 노래를 잘할 뿐만 아니라 춤도 완벽하게 춘다.	She
12	너는 그에게 물어보거나 인터넷을 검색할 수 있다.	You can
13	우리는 월요일이나 화요일에 만날 수 있다.	We can
14	그녀는 피아노뿐만 아니라 바이올린도 연주한다.	She
15	경주하고 나서, 나는 목이 말랐을 뿐만 아니라 배도 고팠다.	After the race,

STEP I 배운 문장을 쓰면서 외워보세요.

Score _____ / 15

	Korean	English
1	너는 그 영화가 언제 시작하는지 아니?	Do you know _____ _____ _____ _____ ?
2	너는 그가 방과 후에 무엇을 하는지 아니?	Do you know _____ _____ _____ after school?
3	가장 친한 친구가 누구인지 물어봐도 돼?	Can I ask _____ _____ _____ _____ _____ ?
4	나는 그가 어떻게 그 문제를 풀었는지 궁금해.	I wonder _____ _____ _____ _____ .
5	그에게 이 버스가 시내에 가는지 물어보자.	Let's ask him _____ _____ _____ _____ .
6	나는 그게 사실인지 궁금해.	I wonder _____ _____ _____ _____ .
7	너는 그 상자 안에 무엇이 들었는지 아니?	Do you know _____ _____ _____ _____ ?
8	나는 무엇이 네 마음을 바꾸었는지 궁금해.	I wonder _____ _____ _____ _____ .
9	몇 시인지 아세요?	Do you know _____ _____ _____ ?
10	나는 그녀가 어디서 그 재킷을 샀는지 궁금해.	I wonder _____ _____ _____ _____ .
11	너는 저 소녀가 누구인지 아니?	Do you know _____ _____ _____ ?
12	너는 몇 명이 그 파티에 있었는지 아니?	Do you know _____ _____ _____ _____ at the party?
13	Mike에게 무슨 일이 일어났는지 내게 말해줄 수 있니?	Can you tell me _____ _____ _____ _____ ?
14	그에게 저녁 식사가 준비되었는지 물어볼게.	I will ask him _____ _____ _____ _____ ready.
15	나는 내가 오늘 그 일을 끝낼 수 있을지 모르겠어.	I don't know _____ _____ _____ _____ _____ today.

STEP 2 배운 문장을 다시 한번 쓰면서 외워보세요.   Score _____ / 15

	Korean	English
1	너는 그 영화가 언제 시작하는지 아니?	Do
2	너는 그가 방과 후에 무엇을 하는지 아니?	Do
3	가장 친한 친구가 누구인지 물어봐도 돼?	Can
4	나는 그가 어떻게 그 문제를 풀었는지 궁금해.	I
5	그에게 이 버스가 시내에 가는지 물어보자.	Let's
6	나는 그게 사실인지 궁금해.	I
7	너는 그 상자 안에 무엇이 들었는지 아니?	Do
8	나는 무엇이 네 마음을 바꾸었는지 궁금해.	I
9	몇 시인지 아세요?	Do
10	나는 그녀가 어디서 그 재킷을 샀는지 궁금해.	I
11	너는 저 소녀가 누구인지 아니?	Do
12	너는 몇 명이 그 파티에 있었는지 아니?	Do
13	Mike에게 무슨 일이 일어났는지 내게 말해줄 수 있니?	Can
14	그에게 저녁 식사가 준비되었는지 물어볼게.	I will
15	나는 내가 오늘 그 일을 끝낼 수 있을지 모르겠어.	I don't

It ~ that 강조구문

월   일

Score _____ / 15

	Korean	English
1	나를 그 파티에 초대한 사람은 바로 Rick이었다.	_____ _____ _____ _____ invited me to the party.
2	내 숙제를 도와준 사람은 바로 내 형이었다.	_____ _____ _____ _____ _____ helped me with my homework.
3	내가 생일선물로 원하는 것은 바로 강아지이다.	_____ _____ _____ _____ _____ I want for my birthday.
4	그가 올림픽에서 딴 것은 바로 금메달이었다.	_____ _____ he won at the Olympics.
5	내가 내 자유시간에 즐기는 것은 바로 만화책을 읽는 것이다.	_____ _____ I enjoy in my free time.
6	내가 그에게 이메일을 보낸 것은 바로 월요일이었다.	_____ _____ _____ I sent him an email.
7	그녀가 그녀의 여권을 잃어버린 곳은 바로 공항에서였다.	_____ _____ she lost her passport.
8	그녀에게 꽃을 준 사람은 바로 그녀의 남자친구였다.	_____ _____ gave her flowers.
9	그녀가 슈퍼마켓에서 산 것은 바로 약간의 과일이었다.	_____ _____ she bought at the supermarket.
10	내가 내 시계를 발견한 곳은 바로 내 가방 안이었다.	_____ _____ I found my watch.
11	내가 내 친구에게 빌린 것은 바로 노트북이었다.	_____ _____ _____ I borrowed from my friend.
12	한국 전쟁이 일어난 것은 바로 1950년이었다.	_____ _____ _____ the Korean War broke out.
13	어제 공원에서 축구를 한 사람은 바로 내 친구와 나였다.	_____ _____ _____ _____ played soccer in the park yesterday.
14	내가 차 사고가 난 것은 바로 어젯밤이었다.	_____ _____ _____ I had a car accident.
15	그 마술사가 그 모자에서 꺼낸 것은 바로 토끼였다.	_____ _____ the magician pulled out of the hat.

STEP 2 배운 문장을 다시 한번 쓰면서 외워보세요. Score _____ / 15

Korean	English
1 나를 그 파티에 초대한 사람은 바로 Rick이었다.	It
2 내 숙제를 도와준 사람은 바로 내 형이었다.	It
3 내가 생일선물로 원하는 것은 바로 강아지이다.	It
4 그가 올림픽에서 딴 것은 바로 금메달이었다.	It
5 내가 내 자유시간에 즐기는 것은 바로 만화책을 읽는 것이다.	It
6 내가 그에게 이메일을 보낸 것은 바로 월요일이었다.	It
7 그녀가 그녀의 여권을 잃어버린 곳은 바로 공항에서였다.	It
8 그녀에게 꽃을 준 사람은 바로 그녀의 남자친구였다.	It
9 그녀가 슈퍼마켓에서 산 것은 바로 약간의 과일이었다.	It
10 내가 내 시계를 발견한 곳은 바로 내 가방 안이었다.	It
11 내가 내 친구에게 빌린 것은 바로 노트북이었다.	It
12 한국 전쟁이 일어난 것은 바로 1950년이었다.	It
13 어제 공원에서 축구를 한 사람은 바로 내 친구와 나였다.	It
14 내가 차 사고가 난 것은 바로 어젯밤이었다.	It
15 그 마술사가 그 모자에서 꺼낸 것은 바로 토끼였다.	It

중학 영작 + 서술형 대비

내공

중학
영작문 **2**

문장 암기 Workbook

문장패턴이 보이고 **영작**이 쉬워진다!

중학생을 위한 친절한 **영작문 시리즈**

중학 영작 + 서술형 대비

내공

* 전지원, 박혜영

중학 영작문 **2**

정 답

다락원

중학 영작 + 서술형 대비

내공
중학
영작문 2

정답

다락원

UNIT 01

LESSON 01 현재완료의 완료, 경험

CHECK UP
p.010

1. 경험   **2.** 경험   **3.** 완료

4. 완료   **5.** 경험   **6.** 완료

7. 경험   **8.** 완료   **9.** 경험

10. 완료

SENTENCE PRACTICE 1
p.011

WRITING POINT ❶

1. I <u>have</u> just <u>arrived</u> at the station.
2. They <u>have</u> just <u>finished</u> their dinner.
3. She <u>has</u> just <u>found</u> a new job.
4. I <u>have</u> already <u>watched</u> the movie.
5. He <u>has</u> already <u>bought</u> the shirt.
6. They <u>have</u> already <u>gone</u> to bed.
7. I <u>haven't</u> <u>read</u> the book yet.
8. He <u>hasn't</u> <u>come</u> home yet.
9. The rain <u>hasn't</u> <u>stopped</u> yet.

WRITING POINT ❷

1. I <u>have</u> <u>met</u> him before.
2. I <u>have</u> <u>heard</u> the name before.
3. He <u>has</u> <u>visited</u> New York once.
4. She <u>has</u> <u>read</u> the book twice.
5. They <u>have</u> <u>won</u> the World Cup four times.
6. I <u>have</u> never <u>talked</u> to him.
7. He <u>has</u> never <u>been</u> late for school.
8. <u>Have</u> you ever <u>been</u> to Europe?
9. <u>Have</u> you ever <u>traveled</u> by ship?

SENTENCE PRACTICE 2
p.012

1. The concert <u>has</u> <u>just</u> <u>started</u>.
2. Jack and Paul <u>have</u> <u>already</u> <u>gone</u> <u>out</u>.
3. We <u>haven't</u> <u>decided</u> what to eat.
4. Susan <u>hasn't</u> <u>received</u> the package yet.
5. <u>Have</u> <u>you</u> <u>already</u> <u>finished</u> practicing the violin?
6. <u>Have</u> <u>you</u> <u>ever</u> <u>been</u> to Africa?
7. I <u>have</u> <u>gone</u> <u>fishing</u> with my father.
8. I <u>have</u> <u>never</u> <u>ridden</u> a horse before.

9. He <u>has</u> <u>traveled</u> <u>abroad</u> many times.
10. <u>Have</u> <u>you</u> <u>ever</u> <u>read</u> a story about Cinderella?

TRY WRITING ✓
p.013

1. Have you ever tried Greek food?
2. He has already finished fixing my computer.
3. Mary has never gone skiing before.
4. I have been to Busan once.
5. The movie has just come out.
6. I have already bought a present for Stella.
7. She has not[hasn't] decided what to do after college.
8. Have you ever met a famous movie star?
9. It has not[hasn't] snowed yet this winter.
10. I have lost my umbrella many times.
11. Have you ever fallen in love?
12. He has just found the information on the Internet.

LESSON 02 현재완료의 계속, 결과

CHECK UP
p.014

1. 계속   **2.** 결과   **3.** 결과

4. 계속   **5.** 계속   **6.** 결과

7. 계속   **8.** 계속   **9.** 결과

SENTENCE PRACTICE 1
p.015

WRITING POINT ❶

1. I <u>have</u> <u>been</u> sick for a week.
2. He <u>has</u> <u>studied</u> English for 10 years.
3. We <u>have</u> <u>lived</u> here for a long time.
4. They <u>have</u> <u>known</u> each other since 2014.
5. He <u>has</u> <u>stayed</u> at this hotel since Monday.
6. He <u>has</u> <u>worn</u> glasses since he was young.
7. How long <u>have</u> <u>you</u> <u>played</u> the piano?
8. How long <u>has</u> <u>he</u> <u>worked</u> here?
9. How long <u>has</u> <u>she</u> <u>had</u> a cold?

WRITING POINT ❷

1. I <u>have</u> <u>lost</u> my watch.
2. I <u>have</u> <u>forgotten</u> his name.
3. Someone <u>has</u> <u>broken</u> the window.

4. He <u>has</u> <u>gained</u> a lot of weight.

5. She <u>has</u> <u>gone</u> abroad.

6. The train <u>has</u> <u>left</u> the station.

7. The book <u>has</u> <u>changed</u> my life.

8. They <u>have</u> <u>found</u> the missing child.

9. Spring <u>has</u> <u>come</u>.

p.016

SENTENCE PRACTICE 2

1. I <u>have</u> <u>studied</u> French <u>since</u> January.

2. The house <u>has</u> <u>been</u> <u>empty</u> <u>for</u> three months.

3. My parents <u>have</u> <u>been</u> <u>married</u> <u>for</u> 20 years.

4. Greg <u>has</u> <u>had</u> his car <u>since</u> 2010.

5. <u>How</u> <u>long</u> <u>have</u> <u>you</u> <u>lived</u> in this apartment?

6. Mark <u>has</u> <u>gone</u> to the gym.

7. James <u>has</u> <u>broken</u> the copy machine.

8. My friend <u>has</u> <u>left</u> <u>for</u> Germany.

9. Adel <u>has</u> <u>become</u> a famous singer.

10. You <u>have</u> <u>grown</u> <u>up</u>!

TRY WRITING

p.017

1. He has worked as a vet for 5 years.

2. We have been best friends since then.

3. I have lost my house key.

4. He has played the piano since he was 5 years old.

5. How long have you studied English?

6. She has been in the hospital for a month.

7. Tim and Susan have gone shopping.

8. Amy has left her homework at home.

9. Angela has had her dog for a long time.

10. They have not[haven't] eaten anything since this morning.

11. How long have you had a headache?

12. He has lost a lot of weight.

미리 보는 서술형 SCHOOL TEST

p.018

1. I have just finished my homework.

2. The train hasn't left the station yet.

3. (1) He has never eaten Thai food.

　　(2) Have you ever seen a giraffe?

4. Have you been to / went to Australia

5. (1) I have lost my camera.

　　(2) Emily has gone to Paris.

6. (1) have learned / for

　　(2) has been / since

7. ③ Actually, I lived there 3 years ago.

　　⑥ How long have you lived there?

　　⑦ I've lived there since March.

UNIT 02

LESSON 03 동사+목적어+형용사/명사

CHECK UP

p.020

1. I found (her advice) helpful.

2. Please leave (me) alone.

3. Always keep (your desk) clean.

4. The game made (people) excited.

5. The noise kept (him) awake all night.

6. They left (the problem) unsolved.

7. The red dress made (her) lovely.

8. The girl calls (the doll) Barbie.

9. They kept (the party) a secret.

10. The movie made (him) a world-famous star.

SENTENCE PRACTICE 1

p.021

WRITING POINT ❶

1. The news made us <u>sad</u>.

2. The homework made him <u>busy</u>.

3. Don't make her <u>angry/upset</u>.

4. This coat will keep you <u>warm</u>.

5. He always keeps his room <u>dark</u>.

6. They left the girl <u>alone</u>.

7. Don't leave the refrigerator <u>open</u>.

8. I found the book <u>interesting</u>.

9. I found the exam <u>easy</u>.

WRITING POINT ❷

1. The coach made him <u>a great player</u>.

2. The song made him <u>a famous singer</u>.

3. People call him <u>a hero</u>.

4. His friends call him <u>a genius</u>.

5. They named her <u>Julie</u>.

6. My family named our dog <u>Roy</u>.

7. You should keep this <u>a secret</u>.

8. They found him <u>a doctor</u>.

9. He found it <u>a good exercise</u>.

SENTENCE PRACTICE 2   p.022

1. The movie <u>made</u> <u>me</u> sleepy.

2. The traffic jam <u>made</u> <u>him</u> late for work.

3. Who <u>left</u> <u>the</u> <u>door</u> open?

4. Drinking too much coffee will <u>keep</u> <u>you</u> <u>awake</u> at night.

5. The police <u>found</u> <u>the</u> <u>child</u> alive.

6. People <u>call</u> Bach "<u>the</u> <u>father</u> <u>of</u> <u>music</u>."

7. I <u>found</u> it <u>a</u> <u>useful</u> <u>tool</u>.

8. The couple <u>named</u> <u>their</u> <u>daughter</u> Eva.

9. Her effort <u>made</u> <u>her</u> <u>a</u> <u>great</u> <u>pianist</u>.

10. I'll keep <u>your</u> <u>decision</u> <u>a</u> <u>secret</u>.

TRY WRITING ✓   p.023

1. You should keep the box safe.

2. The TV show made him a star.

3. The curtains will keep your room dark.

4. She found the work very boring.

5. His performance made his fans excited.

6. They promised to keep it a secret.

7. Don't leave the door open.

8. We found it a good opportunity.

9. The air conditioner keeps the room cool.

10. Working too late will make you tired.

11. His classmates call him "Little Jiseong."

12. What made her so upset?

LESSON 04 동사＋목적어＋to부정사

CHECK UP   p.024

1. I want (the rain) to stop soon.

2. Do you want (me) to take you home?

3. The police officer told (the driver) to stop.

4. Cindy asked (me) to join her club.

5. I advised (Rick) to go to the dentist.

6. We expect (him) to arrive before dinner.

7. The boy is helping (the old woman) to carry her bag.

8. Can you help (me) to find this book?

9. I don't want (my parents) to know about it.

10. Please tell (him) to call me as soon as possible.

SENTENCE PRACTICE 1   p.025

WRITING POINT ❶

1. I want you <u>to stay</u> longer.

2. I want you <u>to come</u> to the party.

3. Do you want me <u>to cook</u> dinner?

4. Jin told me <u>to wait</u> for her.

5. Mr. Kim told us <u>to sit</u> down.

6. I asked him <u>to open</u> the window.

7. I asked him <u>to move</u> the chair.

8. He advised John <u>to stop/quit</u> smoking.

9. We expect him <u>to be/become</u> a singer.

WRITING POINT ❷

1. He helped me <u>(to) fix</u> my computer.

2. He helped me <u>(to) do</u> my homework.

3. I helped my father <u>(to) wash</u> his car.

4. I helped her <u>(to) clean</u> the house.

5. Can you help me <u>(to) plant</u> a tree?

6. Can you help me <u>(to) make</u> a cake?

7. This book helps me <u>(to) learn</u> English.

8. This tea helps you <u>(to) sleep</u> well.

9. This tool helps you <u>(to) work</u> fast.

SENTENCE PRACTICE 2   p.026

1. I <u>asked</u> <u>him</u> <u>to</u> <u>turn</u> <u>down</u> the music.

2. He <u>told</u> <u>me</u> <u>to</u> <u>get</u> <u>off</u> at the next stop.

3. I <u>want</u> my grandmother <u>to</u> <u>be</u> <u>healthy</u>.

4. We <u>expect</u> your dream <u>to</u> <u>come</u> true.

5. What did the teacher <u>advise</u> <u>you</u> <u>to</u> <u>do</u>?

6. This app <u>helps</u> <u>me</u> <u>learn</u> English.

7. They <u>helped</u> <u>her</u> <u>find</u> her family.

8. Can you <u>help</u> <u>me</u> <u>take</u> <u>out</u> the trash?

9. Doing yoga can <u>help</u> <u>you</u> <u>relax</u>.

10. I'm sorry, but I can't <u>help</u> <u>you</u> <u>wash</u> the dishes.

p.027

1. I want you to listen carefully.

2. My mom told me to make my bed.

3. The doctor advised me to exercise regularly.

4. Can you help me (to) move this table?

5. I asked him to speak louder.

6. I told you to be careful.

7. Dave helped me (to) solve the problem.

8. We expect him to do well on the exam.

9. Ms. Yoon told us to be on time.

10. I asked her to wake me up at 7.

11. The drama helps Mike (to) learn Korean.

12. The boy is helping the old man (to) cross the street.

LESSON 05 지각동사, 사역동사

CHECK UP
p.028

1. run
2. fix
3. feel
4. go
5. singing
6. licking
7. made
8. had
9. let
10. saw

SENTENCE PRACTICE 1
p.029

WRITING POINT ❶

1. I saw him cross/crossing the street.

2. I saw him leave/leaving the house.

3. I heard them laugh/laughing.

4. I heard them talk/talking on the phone.

5. I can smell the rice cook/cooking in the kitchen.

6. I can smell the bread bake/baking in the oven.

7. I felt someone look/looking at me.

8. I felt someone follow/following me.

WRITING POINT ❷

1. My dad made me finish my homework.

2. My mom made me practice the piano.

3. Our teacher made us stand in line.

4. I had him write a letter.

5. I had him book a hotel.

6. I had him answer the phone.

7. She let me eat the cake.

8. She let me borrow the book.

9. She let me go to the concert.

SENTENCE PRACTICE 2
p.030

1. We saw him sit/sitting on the bench.

2. I heard him call/calling my name.

3. She felt someone touch/touching her shoulder.

4. Can you smell something burn/burning

5. Can you hear people cheer/cheering loudly?

6. The movie made me cry.

7. I had him buy some milk at the supermarket.

8. Let me look at the menu.

9. Her boyfriend tried to make her laugh.

10. My mom won't let me stay overnight at my friend's house.

TRY WRITING
p.031

1. Listening to music makes me feel good.

2. He heard someone knock/knocking on the door.

3. Our teacher makes us read two books a month.

4. I saw her wait/waiting for a bus at the bus stop.

5. The man had me take a picture of him.

6. The coach let his team take a break.

7. Did you see me score/scoring a goal in the soccer game?

8. I felt someone pull/pulling my hair.

9. I heard someone snore/snoring in the next room.

10. Can you feel the spring come/coming?

11. Kate had her husband do the grocery shopping.

12. My sister does not[doesn't] let me wear her clothes.

I. (1) I found his speech very impressive.

(2) The chicken is keeping the eggs warm.

2. The news will make them happy.

3. left / open

4. Yuna to wash the dishes

5. (1) clean → to clean

(2) telling → to tell

6. let / play outside / makes / do / his homework

7. (1) I saw him enter/entering the building.

(2) He felt someone touch/touching his back.

UNIT 03

LESSON 06 추측을 나타내는 조동사

CHECK UP   p.034

I. may	**2.** must	**3.** cannot
4. may	**5.** must	**6.** cannot
7. may	**8.** may not	**9.** must
10. cannot		

SENTENCE PRACTICE 1   p.035

WRITING POINT ❶

I. He may come to the meeting.

2. He may not come to the meeting.

3. She may like the present.

4. She may not like the present.

5. It may rain tomorrow.

6. It may not rain tomorrow.

7. There may be another chance for you.

8. There may not be another chance for you.

WRITING POINT ❷

I. She must be sick today.

2. She cannot be sick today.

3. He must be older than you.

4. He cannot be older than you.

5. They must be sisters.

6. They cannot be sisters.

7. The baby must be hungry.

8. The baby cannot be hungry.

SENTENCE PRACTICE 2   p.036

I. My parents may go out this evening.

2. You may not believe it, but that's true.

3. Your cell phone may be in the car.

4. It may not rain this weekend.

5. There may be life on Mars.

6. She must like you.

7. The rumor cannot be true.

8. You must have the wrong number.

9. They cannot know each other.

10. Wow! You must be very excited.

TRY WRITING ✏️   p.037

I. We may go to Thailand this summer.

2. He cannot be a doctor.

3. They must be very tired.

4. You may not like this movie.

5. Your parents must be proud of you.

6. He may be a famous singer one day.

7. It may snow this Christmas.

8. He may not know my phone number.

9. The man over there must be James.

10. She must be angry with me.

II. This must be a mistake.

12. There may be a way to solve the problem.

LESSON 07 의무, 필요를 나타내는 조동사

CHECK UP   p.038

I. must	**2.** must not	**3.** have to
4. don't have to	**5.** must	**6.** have to
7. Do I have to	**8.** must not	**9.** has to
10. had to		

SENTENCE PRACTICE 1

p.039

WRITING POINT ❶

1. You <u>must leave</u> here.

2. You <u>must not leave</u> here.

3. She <u>must call</u> him now.

4. She <u>must not call</u> him now.

5. They <u>must bring</u> their food.

6. They <u>must not bring</u> their food.

7. I <u>must tell</u> him the secret.

8. I <u>must not tell</u> him the secret.

WRITING POINT ❷

1. He <u>has to go</u> there.

2. He <u>doesn't have to</u> go there.

3. <u>Does he have to go</u> there?

4. They <u>have to wear</u> school uniforms.

5. They <u>don't have to wear</u> school uniforms.

6. <u>Do they have to wear</u> school uniforms?

7. I <u>have to take</u> a test next week.

8. I <u>don't have to take</u> a test next week.

9. <u>Do I have to take</u> a test next week?

SENTENCE PRACTICE 2

p.040

1. You <u>must fill out</u> this form first.

2. You <u>must listen to</u> your parents.

3. Students <u>must not be late</u> for school.

4. Visitors <u>must not feed</u> the animals in the zoo.

5. You <u>must bring</u> your cup instead of using paper cups.

6. I <u>have to take</u> my dog to the vet.

7. Jane <u>has to take care of</u> her little brother.

8. We <u>had to wait</u> for him for 30 minutes.

9. <u>Do they have to work</u> on Saturday?

10. Tom <u>doesn't have to wear</u> a suit to work.

TRY WRITING

p.041

1. We must/have to follow the traffic rules.

2. We must not miss the train.

3. Students must not cheat on a test.

4. You must/have to wear a swimming cap in the pool.

5. How long do I have to wait?

6. You don't have to memorize everything.

7. I must/have to return this book to the library.

8. You must/have to pay attention in class.

9. I'm sorry, but I must/have to go now.

10. You must not bully your classmates.

11. She doesn't have to go on a diet.

12. You must/have to be 18 years old to get a driver's license.

LESSON 08 조언, 권고를 나타내는 조동사

CHECK UP

p.042

1. should not 2. should 3. should not

4. should 5. should not 6. had better

7. had better 8. had better not

9. had better not

SENTENCE PRACTICE 1

p.043

WRITING POINT ❶

1. We <u>should invite</u> him to the party.

2. We <u>should not invite</u> him to the party.

3. <u>Should we invite</u> him to the party?

4. I <u>should buy</u> the jacket.

5. I <u>should not buy</u> the jacket.

6. <u>Should I buy</u> the jacket?

7. Erin <u>should lose</u> weight.

8. Erin <u>should not lose</u> weight.

9. <u>Should Erin lose</u> weight?

WRITING POINT ❷

1. You <u>had better see</u> him again.

2. You <u>had better not see</u> him again.

3. We <u>had better stay</u> here.

4. We <u>had better not stay</u> here.

5. He <u>had better</u> drive there.

6. He <u>had better not drive</u> there.

7. They <u>had better change</u> the plan.

8. They <u>had better not change</u> the plan.

SENTENCE PRACTICE 2

p.044

1. We <u>should book</u> a <u>hotel</u> today.

2. You <u>should be</u> more <u>careful</u>.

3. You <u>should not forget</u> Jane's birthday.

4. <u>Should I take off</u> my shoes?

5. What should I wear to my sister's wedding?

6. You had better go home and stay in bed.

7. You had better not leave your bag here.

8. You had better not touch the wire.

9. I think we had better cancel the trip.

10. She had better take his advice.

p.045

TRY WRITING ✓

1. We should help people in need.

2. We had better rent a car at the airport.

3. She should not[shouldn't] spend too much money on clothes.

4. You had better not drink the milk.

5. Should I ask him for help?

6. What time should I pick you up?

7. You should not[shouldn't] forget to close the window before you go to bed.

8. You should save money for a rainy day.

9. What should I do to improve my English?

10. He had better not be late again.

11. We had better clear the snow before it freezes.

12. People should be responsible for their pets.

미리 보는 서술형 SCHOOL TEST

p.046

1. (1) may come   (2) must be   (3) cannot live

2. (1) The answer in this book may be wrong.
   (2) There must be a problem.

3. have to

4. You don't have to water the plant every day.

5. (1) should not use
   (2) should turn off

6. had better go to the dentist

7. (1) He had better take the subway.
   (2) You had better not touch the dog.

UNIT 04

LESSON 09 수동태의 시제

CHECK UP

p.048

1. is cleaned   2. planted   3. are loved

4. will buy   5. will be fixed   6. was written

7. finished invited   8. is held   9. will be

10. invented

SENTENCE PRACTICE 1

p.049

WRITING POINT ❶

1. The taxi is driven by my uncle.

2. Math is taught by Mr. Allen.

3. Spanish is spoken in Mexico.

4. My clothes are washed by my mom.

5. The cars are made by robots.

WRITING POINT ❷

1. The poem was written by my friend.

2. The vase was broken by my dog.

3. The worm was eaten by the bird.

4. These pictures were taken by Tom.

5. The trees were planted by my father.

WRITING POINT ❸

1. The car will be sold by Jack.

2. The festival will be held next month.

3. The house will be painted by Mike.

4. The music will be played by the band.

5. The question will be answered soon.

SENTENCE PRACTICE 2

p.050

1. The palace is visited by many tourists.

2. Mr. Robin is respected by his students.

3. The children are helped by volunteers.

4. My bike was stolen by someone.

5. A cat was hit by a car.

6. Papyrus was used in ancient Egypt.

7. The houses were damaged by the earthquake.

8. Dinner will be served at 7 o'clock.

9. The role will be played by Leonardo DiCaprio.

10. A new library will be built by the company.

1. The TV show is watched by many people.
2. Frank was praised by his teacher.
3. The wine was produced in France.
4. These pictures were painted by Picasso.
5. These days, Korean food is enjoyed by many people.
6. Hangeul was invented by King Sejong.
7. The thief was caught by a young man.
8. In case of rain, the concert will be canceled.
9. Tea and coffee will be served after the meal.
10. The people in the building will be rescued soon.
11. The museum was designed by a famous architect.
12. The dogs are taken care of at an animal shelter.

LESSON 10 주의해야 할 수동태

CHECK UP

p.052

1. isn't
2. didn't
3. wasn't
4. Did
5. was
6. of
7. in
8. with
9. of
10. for

SENTENCE PRACTICE 1

p.053

WRITING POINT 1

1. The festival is not held every year.
2. Is the festival held every year?
3. The books are not used in class.
4. Are the books used in class?
5. The ring was not found by Clair.
6. Was the ring found by Clair?
7. The letters were not written by James.
8. Were the letters written by James?

WRITING POINT 2

1. The room is filled with people.
2. The mountain is covered with snow.
3. He was satisfied with the test result.
4. He was disappointed with/at the test result.
5. The house is made of bricks.
6. The wine is made from grapes.

7. The island is known for its beautiful scenery.
8. The island is known to many tourists.
9. He was worried about the presentation.

SENTENCE PRACTICE 2

p.054

1. The door is not locked.
2. The package was not delivered in time.
3. The flowers were not planted by me.
4. Was the man caught by the police?
5. Were they taken to the hospital?
6. The drawer is covered with dust.
7. They were disappointed with/at the news.
8. Carol is interested in European history.
9. Hawaii is known as the best vacation spot.
10. People are worried about the global warming.

TRY WRITING

p.055

1. The office is not[isn't] cleaned every day.
2. The bridge is made of steel.
3. The baby was not[wasn't] woken up by the noise.
4. The restaurant is known to many people.
5. Was he bitten by a dog?
6. The table is covered with a cloth.
7. The department store was crowded with shoppers.
8. I am tired of my job.
9. My printer was not[wasn't] fixed last week.
10. He is known as the King of Pop.
11. Was he helped by you?
12. I am worried about your health.

SCHOOL TEST

p.056

1. (1) The actor is loved by a lot of people.
   (2) The village was damaged by the storm.
   (3) The furniture will be moved by the workers.
2. was written by
3. Shoes are not sold at the store.
4. (1) The cup was not broken by Tom.
   (2) Was the letter delivered by Mr. Smith?

정답 **9**

5. with
6. (1) Are / interested in
   (2) is made of
   (3) is known to
7. (1) Did → Was
   (2) invited → were invited
   (3) discuss → be discussed

UNIT 05

CHECK UP

1. 공부하는 것은
2. 가르치는 것(이다)
3. 물어볼
4. 돕는 것을
5. 함께 놀
6. 사는 것을
7. 여는 것(이다)
8. 가야 할
9. 오는 것은

SENTENCE PRACTICE 1

WRITING POINT ❶

1. It is dangerous to swim in the river.
2. It is important to have/eat a balanced diet.
3. It is not easy to give advice to someone.
4. Her dream is to be/become a scientist.
5. His wish is to find a good job.

WRITING POINT ❷

1. I need to study tonight.
2. She hopes to pass the exam.
3. We've decided to move to another city.
4. They tried to finish the work by six.
5. He promised to be on time.

WRITING POINT ❸

1. I have good news to tell you.
2. He bought some water to drink.
3. You'll need something warm to wear.
4. She wants a roommate to live with.
5. He needs someone to talk to/with.

SENTENCE PRACTICE 2

1. It is important to make good friends.
2. It is necessary to wear a helmet for your safety.
3. His secret to happiness is to help others.
4. His goal is to win a gold medal at the Olympics.
5. My mom promised to buy me a new bike.
6. He plans to sell his car and buy a new one.
7. I try to keep a diary every day.
8. What is the best way to learn a foreign language?
9. He bought a house to live in with his family.
10. They are looking for someone brave to do it.

TRY WRITING

1. Mary wants to go shopping this afternoon.
2. Can you recommend a book to read?
3. It is a good idea to learn about other countries.
4. His plan is to go to the gym five days a week.
5. He often forgets to turn off the lights.
6. It is not safe to follow a stranger.
7. Philip plans to go to Europe this summer.
8. I have three things to do today.
9. The most important thing is to set a clear goal.
10. We are looking for a hotel to stay at.
11. It is impossible to read his handwriting.
12. Call me when you need someone to talk to/with.

CHECK UP

1. 목적
2. (감정의) 원인
3. 목적
4. 목적
5. (감정의) 원인
6. 결과
7. (판단의) 근거
8. 결과
9. (판단의) 근거
10. 결과

p.063

WRITING POINT ❶

1. I went to the bakery <u>to buy</u> some bread.
2. He turned on the TV <u>to watch</u> the news.
3. She bought some fruit <u>to make</u> juice.
4. <u>To lose</u> weight, I jump rope every day.
5. I am pleased <u>to help</u> you.
6. I am sorry <u>to hear</u> the sad news.
7. People were surprised <u>to know</u> her age.
8. We were disappointed <u>to lose</u> the game.

WRITING POINT ❷

1. He must be rich <u>to live</u> there.
2. He must be a fool <u>to believe</u> that.
3. He must be very brave <u>to do</u> so.
4. He must be tired <u>to sleep</u> until now.
5. The girl grew up <u>to be</u> a lawyer.
6. My grandfather lived <u>to be</u> 98 years old.
7. He woke up <u>to find</u> himself famous.
8. We did our best only <u>to fail</u>.

SENTENCE PRACTICE **2**

p.064

1. I got up early <u>to catch</u> <u>the</u> <u>first</u> <u>train</u> to Busan.
2. Eric went to the library <u>to check out some books</u>.
3. We visited the museum <u>to learn about Korean history</u>.
4. I <u>am</u> <u>happy</u> <u>to have</u> a friend like you.
5. He <u>was</u> <u>excited</u> <u>to see</u> his Korean fans.
6. They must be hungry <u>to eat so much</u>.
7. She must be smart <u>to go to Harvard</u>.
8. He <u>grew up to be</u> the best actor in the world.
9. He <u>woke up to find</u> himself in hospital.
10. They tried hard <u>only to lose</u> the game.

TRY WRITING ✓

p.065

1. Cathy went to Paris to study fashion design.
2. Sally was happy to get the birthday present.
3. He must be foolish to do such a thing.
4. My grandparents lived to be 90 years old.
5. Steve practiced the drums to take part in the festival.
6. The boy grew up to be a great musician.

7. We should do something to help them.
8. George was happy to see his family again.
9. He must like her to give her flowers every day.
10. We hurried to the station only to miss the train.
11. She woke up to find herself alone.
12. He must be diligent to be on time every day.

LESSON 13 to부정사 주요 구문

CHECK UP

p.066

1. heavy
2. expensive
3. difficult
4. clean
5. strong
6. big
7. what
8. where
9. when
10. how

SENTENCE PRACTICE **1**

p.067

WRITING POINT ❶

1. I am <u>too tired to study</u>.
2. He is <u>too young to drive</u> a car.
3. She was <u>too sick to go</u> to school.
4. The coffee is <u>too hot to drink</u>.
5. This book is <u>too difficult to read</u>.

WRITING POINT ❷

1. I ran <u>fast enough to catch</u> the bus.
2. He is <u>strong enough to lift</u> the rock.
3. He is <u>rich enough to buy</u> the sports car.
4. She is <u>smart enough to solve</u> the problem.
5. She sings <u>well enough to be</u> a singer.

WRITING POINT ❸

1. I don't know <u>what to wear</u>.
2. We didn't know <u>what to do</u>.
3. He told me <u>when to come</u>.
4. Let's decide <u>where to meet</u> tomorrow.
5. Do you know <u>how to play</u> this song?

SENTENCE PRACTICE **2**

p.068

1. The hamburger is <u>too</u> <u>thick</u> <u>to bite</u>.
2. Jimmy is <u>too short to ride</u> the roller coaster.

3. It is <u>too</u> <u>cold</u> <u>to</u> <u>go</u> swimming.

4. He is <u>tall</u> enough <u>to</u> <u>reach</u> the top shelf.

5. The man was <u>brave</u> <u>enough</u> <u>to</u> <u>catch</u> the thief alone.

6. She is <u>wise</u> <u>enough</u> <u>to</u> <u>give</u> me good advice.

7. My mom taught me <u>how</u> <u>to</u> <u>make</u> pasta.

8. Have you decided <u>where</u> <u>to</u> <u>go</u> on your vacation?

9. Please tell me <u>what</u> <u>to</u> <u>bring</u> to the party.

10. I asked him <u>where</u> <u>to</u> <u>put</u> <u>my</u> <u>coat</u>.

TRY WRITING ✓

p.069

1. He is too big to wear the shirt.

2. She is kind enough to help the poor.

3. I can't decide what to eat for lunch.

4. Jack is smart enough to solve the difficult math problem.

5. I was too tired to go jogging this morning.

6. Can you tell me how to get to the subway station?

7. She is too young to understand her parents.

8. The weather was good enough to go on a picnic.

9. I don't know where to put this flowerpot.

10. She is beautiful enough to play Juliet in the movie.

11. He is too weak to run a marathon.

12. I don't know what to buy for her birthday.

미리 보는 서술형 SCHOOL TEST

p.070

1. (1) It is not easy to write a letter in English.

   (2) His job is to feed the animals in the zoo.

   (3) What are you planning to do this summer?

2. (1) work to do

   (2) a chair to sit on

3. (1) I went to the bookstore in order to buy some books.

4. to pass the exam

5. (1) so fat / he cannot[can't] wear.

   (2) so early / we could catch

6. strong enough to carry

7. what to do / how to make

   (2) My dad made dinner for us.

UNIT 06

LESSON 14 동명사 vs. to부정사

CHECK UP

p.072

1. playing
2. to buy
3. shopping
4. waiting
5. eating
6. to join
7. washing
8. going
9. to be

SENTENCE PRACTICE 1

p.073

WRITING POINT ❶

1. He enjoys <u>fishing</u> in the river.

2. I finished <u>cleaning</u> my room.

3. Do you mind <u>opening</u> the window?

4. I hope <u>to travel</u> around the world.

5. They decided <u>to cancel</u> the picnic.

6. We promised <u>to meet</u> again.

7. He doesn't like <u>swimming/to swim</u>.

8. It started <u>raining/to rain</u>.

9. Some children hate <u>to going/to go</u> to school.

WRITING POINT ❷

1. She goes <u>jogging</u> every morning.

2. The waiter is busy <u>serving</u> the food.

3. The book is worth <u>reading</u>.

4. How about <u>playing</u> tennis with me?

5. I feel like <u>eating</u> spicy food.

6. Sam is good at <u>playing</u> the guitar.

7. I'm looking forward to <u>hearing</u> from you.

8. He has difficulty <u>remembering</u> names.

SENTENCE PRACTICE 2

p.074

1. I <u>enjoy</u> <u>making</u> people laugh.

2. I <u>hope</u> <u>to</u> <u>keep</u> <u>in</u> <u>touch</u> with you.

3. He <u>avoids</u> <u>driving</u> at night.

4. What do you <u>plan</u> <u>to</u> <u>do</u> after graduation?

5. He <u>kept</u> <u>asking</u> me questions.

6. She <u>is</u> <u>busy</u> <u>preparing</u> breakfast.

7. I <u>don't</u> <u>feel</u> <u>like</u> <u>going</u> <u>out</u> tonight.

8. Is the TV program <u>worth</u> <u>watching</u>?

9. We <u>had</u> <u>difficulty/trouble</u> <u>finding</u> the store.

10. She <u>is</u> <u>good</u> <u>at</u> <u>speaking</u> English.

p.075

TRY WRITING ✔

1. The tourists were busy taking pictures.

2. My father is good at cooking Chinese food.

3. We gave up going on a trip this weekend.

4. They decided to help the homeless.

5. How/What about playing computer games together?

6. I don't mind living in the countryside.

7. He hopes to get a good grade on the test.

8. I like going/to go skiing in winter.

9. She avoided answering my question.

10. His advice is worth following.

11. She is looking forward to spending time with her family.

12. I always feel like taking a nap after lunch.

LESSON 15 현재분사, 과거분사

CHECK UP p.076

1. fried   2. boring   3. drinking

4. built   5. broken   6. riding

7. made   8. interesting   9. spoken

SENTENCE PRACTICE 1 p.077

WRITING POINT ❶

1. Have you ever seen a <u>falling</u> star?

2. There are <u>fallen</u> leaves on the street.

3. Put the noodles in <u>boiling</u> water.

4. I ate a <u>boiled</u> egg.

5. Who is the girl <u>writing</u> a letter?

6. She is reading a letter <u>written</u> in English.

7. The man <u>taking</u> a picture is Peter.

8. This is a picture <u>taken</u> by Peter.

WRITING POINT ❷

1. His jokes are <u>boring</u>.

2. I listen to music when I am <u>bored</u>.

3. The trip was an <u>exciting</u> experience.

4. I was <u>excited</u> about the trip.

5. It was a <u>tiring</u> day.

6. He was <u>tired</u> when he got home.

7. The test result was <u>satisfying</u>.

8. I was <u>satisfied</u> with the test result.

SENTENCE PRACTICE 2 p.078

1. His nickname is a <u>walking</u> <u>dictionary</u>.

2. He has a <u>broken</u> <u>leg</u>.

3. There are some children <u>swimming</u> <u>in</u> <u>the</u> <u>pool</u>.

4. Look at the garden <u>covered</u> with <u>snow</u>.

5. He has a <u>talking</u> robot <u>named</u> Tiki.

6. This book has many <u>touching</u> <u>stories</u>.

7. They <u>were</u> <u>surprised</u> to see me.

8. The weather is <u>depressing</u> today.

9. This map made me <u>confused</u>.

10. The stadium is filled with <u>excited</u> <u>soccer</u> <u>fans</u>.

TRY WRITING ✔ p.079

1. The woman is holding a crying baby.

2. This math problem is so confusing.

3. The man wearing a suit is my uncle.

4. He found his stolen wallet.

5. This is the song written by my favorite singer.

6. He talked to the girl sitting on the bench.

7. There are many foreigners learning Korean.

8. I am satisfied with my job.

9. Living in the country can be boring.

10. She was depressed by the bad weather.

11. The man injured in the accident is Mr. Brown.

12. English is the language spoken all over the world.

1. (1) are → is   (2) take → taking
2. (1) doing   (2) turning   (3) to be
3. (1) Jane is good at playing the piano.
   (2) We had difficulty finding the restaurant.
   (3) I don't feel like eating lunch.
4. How/What about going hiking
5. reading a book
6. (1) flying   (2) painted   (3) delivered
7. boring

UNIT 07

LESSON 16 명사의 수량 표현

CHECK UP

p.082

1. piece   2. sheet   3. loaves
4. bar   5. bowls   6. little
7. Few   8. a few   9. a little

SENTENCE PRACTICE 1

p.083

WRITING POINT ❶
1. He drinks two cups of coffee a day.
2. I need a piece/sheet of paper.
3. She ordered a bowl of soup.
4. He bought three bottles of milk.
5. I gave him a loaf of bread.

WRITING POINT ❷
1. He asked me a few questions.
2. He asked me few questions.
3. A few students passed the test.
4. Few students passed the test.

WRITING POINT ❸
1. There is a little food in the fridge.
2. There is little food in the fridge.
3. She can speak a little French.
4. She can speak little French.

SENTENCE PRACTICE 2

p.084

1. I need two slices of cheese.
2. My family uses a bar of soap a month.
3. He had two pieces/slices of pizza for lunch.
4. We spent a few days on the island.
5. Susan invited a few friends to her house.
6. She put a little salt in her soup.
7. I have been there a few times.
8. She drinks little coffee.
9. Unfortunately, we took few pictures in Venice.
10. I have little interest in sports.

TRY WRITING ✓

p.085

1. Can I have a glass of water?
2. Jessica lived in Germany a few years ago.
3. We have little time now.
4. She had a piece/slice of cake for dessert.
5. He spilt a little milk on the carpet.
6. I have a little homework to do today.
7. There are three loaves of bread in the basket.
8. There is a little water left in the bottle.
9. Few students solved the math problem.
10. I bought a bar of chocolate and two cans of coke.
11. He made few mistakes on the test.
12. I usually have a cup of tea in the afternoon.

LESSON 17 재귀대명사

CHECK UP

p.086

1. myself   2. me   3. yourself
4. him   5. himself   6. yourself
7. ourselves   8. yourself   9. ourselves

SENTENCE PRACTICE 1

p.087

WRITING POINT ❶
1. I cut myself with a knife.
2. Don't blame yourself.
3. He introduced himself to us.
4. She drew a picture of herself.

5. We should believe in <u>ourselves</u>.

6. Everyone, take care of <u>yourselves</u>.

7. They were proud of <u>themselves</u>.

8. My dog hurt <u>itself</u>.

9. She bought a present for <u>herself</u>.

WRITING POINT ❷

1. Please make <u>yourself</u> at home.

2. Help <u>yourself</u> to this food.

3. He lives by <u>himself</u> in a big house.

4. I can't move this box by <u>myself</u>.

5. The door closed of <u>itself</u>.

6. She often talks to <u>herself</u>.

7. They enjoyed <u>themselves</u> at the festival.

8. He taught <u>himself</u> to swim.

9. This is between <u>ourselves</u>.

SENTENCE PRACTICE 2　　　　　p.088

1. Let me <u>introduce</u> <u>myself</u> to you.

2. Van Gogh <u>killed</u> <u>himself</u> at the age of 37.

3. My sister only <u>thinks</u> <u>about</u> <u>herself</u>.

4. We <u>blamed</u> <u>ourselves</u> for the mistake.

5. Babies cannot <u>look</u> <u>after</u> <u>themselves</u>.

6. She <u>taught</u> <u>herself</u> Chinese.

7. Take off your coat and <u>make</u> <u>yourself</u> <u>at</u> <u>home</u>.

8. The candle went out <u>of</u> <u>itself</u>.

9. The children <u>enjoyed</u> <u>themselves</u> at the playground.

10. They left their dog at home <u>by</u> <u>itself</u>.

TRY WRITING　　　　　p.089

1. Know yourself.

2. I burnt/burned myself while cooking.

3. She took a picture of herself.

4. The boy fell down and hurt himself.

5. Why are you talking to yourself?

6. The cat is licking itself.

7. They solved the problem by themselves.

8. The woman raises three children by herself.

9. Did you enjoy yourself at the concert?

10. We helped ourselves to the free drinks.

11. She is looking at herself in the mirror.

12. I taught myself to play the guitar.

미리 보는 서술형 SCHOOL TEST　　　　　p.090

1. two loaves of / three glasses of

2. (1) piece → pieces
   (2) coffees → coffee

3. (1) two bowls of salad
   (2) three pieces of pizza
   (3) two cans of coke

4. (1) few　　(2) a little　　(3) a few
   (4) little

5. (1) myself　　(2) yourself
   (3) themselves

6. He looked at himself in the mirror.

7. (1) Help yourself
   (2) by herself
   (3) Between ourselves

UNIT 09

LESSON 18 as ～ as, 비교급

CHECK UP　　　　　p.092

1. long　　2. heavier　　3. better

4. high boring　　5. better　　6. more

7. more popular　8. cheaper

9. darker / brighter　　10. less / more

SENTENCE PRACTICE 1　　　　　p.093

WRITING POINT ❶

1. Sam is <u>as strong as</u> Mark.

2. Aron is <u>as tall as</u> his brother.

3. Harry plays the guitar <u>as well as</u> Don.

4. Tim doesn't study <u>as hard as</u> Jim.

5. He is not <u>as young as</u> I thought.

WRITING POINT ❷

1. Mexico is <u>hotter than</u> Canada.

2. This book is <u>thicker than</u> that book.

3. Fruit is <u>healthier than</u> chocolate.

4. Janet is <u>more popular than</u> Daniel.

5. His car is <u>more expensive than</u> mine.

WRITING POINT ❸

1. <u>The more</u> you smile, <u>the better</u> you look.
2. <u>The less</u> I see him, <u>the more</u> I miss him.
3. <u>The older</u> we get, <u>the wiser</u> we become.
4. <u>The higher</u> you climb, <u>the colder</u> it gets.
5. <u>The longer</u> I waited, <u>the angrier</u> I got.

SENTENCE PRACTICE 2

p.094

1. The exam <u>was</u> <u>as</u> <u>difficult</u> <u>as</u> the last one.
2. His shoes <u>are</u> <u>as</u> <u>big</u> <u>as</u> his father's.
3. I don't <u>exercise</u> <u>as</u> <u>much</u> <u>as</u> Peter.
4. The river <u>is</u> <u>not</u> <u>as</u> <u>deep</u> <u>as</u> it looks.
5. The restaurant <u>is</u> <u>busier</u> <u>than</u> usual.
6. Dolphins <u>are</u> <u>more</u> <u>intelligent</u> <u>than</u> fish.
7. Julian speaks French <u>much</u> <u>better</u> <u>than</u> English.
8. <u>The</u> <u>harder</u> you study, <u>the</u> <u>more</u> you will learn.
9. <u>The</u> <u>longer</u> I sleep, <u>the</u> <u>more</u> <u>tired</u> I am.
10. <u>The</u> <u>more</u> fast food you eat, <u>the</u> <u>fatter</u> you will get.

TRY WRITING

p.095

1. Jenny is as slim as her sister.
2. Robin is as diligent as Daniel.
3. My English is not as good as your English.
4. Sneakers are more comfortable than high heels.
5. The sunnier it is, the happier I feel.
6. He went to bed earlier than usual.
7. Today's weather is much worse than yesterday's.
8. Jenny drinks tea more often than coffee.
9. Michael is not as patient as his brother.
10. The earlier you start, the sooner you will finish.
11. I think (that) history is more interesting than math.
12. The more you exercise, the stronger you will get.

LESSON 19 최상급

CHECK UP

p.096

1. longest   2. smallest   3. shortest
4. best   5. most expensive
6. most popular 7. most famous
8. any other animal / other animal / larger than / other animal / as large as

SENTENCE PRACTICE 1

p.097

WRITING POINT ❶

1. August is <u>the hottest month</u> of the year.
2. She is <u>the kindest person</u> I know.
3. He is <u>the most famous painter</u> in Korea.
4. Fall is <u>the best season</u> for reading.
5. It was <u>the worst mistake</u> in my life.

WRITING POINT ❷

1. Jupiter is <u>bigger than</u> any other planet.
2. The Nile is <u>longer than</u> any other river.
3. Paris is <u>more beautiful than</u> any other city.
4. Mango is <u>sweeter than</u> any other fruit.
5. Summer is <u>better than</u> any other season.

WRITING POINT ❸

1. No other student is <u>taller than</u> me.
2. No other girl is <u>prettier than</u> Julie.
3. No other place is <u>better than</u> home.
4. No other student is <u>as smart as</u> Jim.
5. No other subject is <u>as difficult as</u> math.

SENTENCE PRACTICE 2

p.098

1. Laughter is <u>the</u> <u>best</u> <u>medicine</u>.
2. February is <u>the</u> <u>shortest</u> <u>month</u> of the year.
3. He is <u>the</u> <u>most</u> <u>boring</u> <u>person</u> I know.
4. What is <u>the</u> <u>most</u> <u>precious</u> <u>thing</u> in your life?
5. Winter is <u>colder</u> <u>than</u> <u>any</u> <u>other</u> <u>season</u>.
6. The church is <u>older</u> <u>than</u> <u>any</u> <u>other</u> <u>building</u> in the town.
7. Mt. Everest is <u>higher</u> <u>than</u> <u>any</u> <u>other</u> <u>mountain</u> in the world.
8. No other <u>sport</u> <u>is</u> <u>more</u> <u>popular</u> <u>than</u> soccer.
9. No other <u>animal</u> <u>is</u> <u>as</u> <u>faithful</u> <u>as</u> the dog.
10. No other <u>food</u> <u>is</u> <u>more</u> <u>delicious</u> <u>than</u> my mom's pasta.

p.099

1. Australia is the smallest continent in the world.
2. Eric is the best player on the team.
3. No one is stronger than Mark.
4. Brazil is larger than any other country in South America.
5. He is the luckiest person in the world.
6. It was the happiest day of my life.
7. Her house is more beautiful than any other house in the town.
8. No other subject is more interesting than music.
9. He is the funniest person I know.
10. It was the worst earthquake in history.
11. No other test was as difficult as the math test.
12. The Eiffel Tower is taller than any other building in Paris.

미리 보는 서술형 SCHOOL TEST

p.100

1. (1) tallest   (2) old   (3) heavier
2. not as windy as yesterday
3. much/even/still/far/a lot cleaner than
4. (1) smartest → the smartest
   (2) most cheap → cheapest
   (3) badest → worst
5. The warmer / the better
6. The more paper we recycle, the fewer trees we cut down.
7. (1) larger than any other city
   (2) city in Korea is larger than

UNIT 09

LESSON 20 주격 관계대명사

 CHECK UP

p.102

1. He told me a joke which is very funny.
2. A vet is a person who treats sick animals.

3. Jane lives in a house which has a beautiful garden.
4. The boy who broke the window ran away.
5. I don't like people who are always late.
6. Josh works for a company which makes cars.
7. They are my neighbors who live next doors.
8. This is wine which is made from grapes.
9. The bus which goes to the hotel runs every 30 minutes.

SENTENCE PRACTICE 1

p.103

WRITING POINT ❶

1. I have a friend who lives in Canada.
2. He has a son who is a famous actor.
3. The boy who is wearing glasses is Bill.
4. The girl who is reading a book is Mary.
5. The man who helped me was very kind.
6. The man who lives upstairs is a lawyer.
7. I like a man who is good at cooking.
8. I don't like people who tell lies.
9. The girl who failed the test cried.

WRITING POINT ❷

1. A spider is an animal which has eight legs.
2. A penguin is a bird which cannot fly.
3. This is a machine which heats food.
4. This is a machine which makes coffee.
5. The dog which has a long tail is mine.
6. He works in a shop which sells clothes.
7. He bought a house which has four rooms.
8. Is there a bus which goes downtown?
9. Where is the book which was on the desk?

SENTENCE PRACTICE 2

p.104

1. I met a man who is a famous musician.
2. A firefighter is a person who puts out fire.
3. The man who called me yesterday was my brother.
4. King Sejong is the person who created Hangeul.
5. The people who went to the festival enjoyed themselves.
6. This is a question which is difficult to answer.

7. A donkey is an animal <u>which</u> <u>looks</u> <u>like</u> a small horse.

8. The room has a window <u>which</u> <u>overlooks</u> a lake.

9. Mr. Smith runs a restaurant <u>which</u> <u>serves</u> Greek food.

10. They are looking for a house <u>which</u> <u>has</u> <u>a</u> <u>yard</u>.

TRY WRITING ✓
p.105

1. I like people who/that have a good sense of humor.

2. Is there a shop which/that sells sports goods?

3. A kangaroo is an animal which/that lives in Australia.

4. A barista is a person who/that makes coffee.

5. Look at the bird which/that is sitting on the tree.

6. Tara has a garden which/that has beautiful flowers.

7. Thomas Edison is the person who/that invented the light bulb.

8. The boy who/that won the race was happy.

9. Those boys who/that are playing soccer are my friends.

10. The man who/that gave me directions was kind.

11. The dog which/that bit me was my neighbor's dog.

12. The accident which/that happened last night was terrible.

LESSON 2 | 목적격 관계대명사

 CHECK UP
p.106

1. This is the camera <u>which I want to buy</u>.

2. Joanne Rowling is the writer <u>whom I like most</u>.

3. The e-mail <u>which Bill sent to me</u> hasn't arrived yet.

4. Do you remember the man <u>whom we met in the park</u>?

5. The shoes <u>which you are wearing</u> are nice.

6. Julie loves the students <u>whom she teaches</u>.

7. The sandwich <u>which I ate for lunch</u> wasn't good.

8. The bus <u>which we were waiting for</u> was 30 minutes late.

9. What's the name of the girl <u>whom Steve is talking to</u>?

SENTENCE PRACTICE 1
p.107

WRITING POINT ❶

1. The man <u>whom I saw</u> was Henry.

2. I know the man <u>whom Sally likes</u>.

3. Adel is the singer <u>whom I want</u> to meet.

4. Those are people <u>whom I know</u>.

5. Daniel is a friend <u>whom I can</u> trust.

6. Sam greets everyone <u>whom he meets</u>.

7. The girl <u>whom I invited</u> didn't come.

8. The man <u>whom I talked to/with</u> was friendly.

9. The girl <u>whom I danced with</u> was Ann.

WRITING POINT ❷

1. The table <u>which I bought</u> is very big.

2. The pizza <u>which we ate</u> was delicious.

3. The flight <u>which I booked</u> was canceled.

4. The test <u>which we took</u> was not easy.

5. This is the book <u>which he wrote</u>.

6. Have you found the key <u>which you lost</u>?

7. Jill is wearing a hat <u>which I like</u>.

8. Is this the ring <u>which Rick gave you</u>?

9. Is this the book <u>which you ordered</u>?

SENTENCE PRACTICE 2
p.108

1. Mr. Kim is the teacher <u>whom</u> I <u>like</u> the most.

2. Who is the girl <u>whom</u> <u>you</u> <u>met</u> yesterday?

3. The woman <u>whom</u> <u>he</u> <u>is</u> <u>talking</u> <u>to</u> is his sister.

4. I have a friend <u>whom</u> I <u>want</u> to <u>introduce</u> to you.

5. The people <u>whom</u> I <u>invited</u> to <u>dinner</u> were late.

6. I lost the umbrella <u>which</u> <u>Jane</u> <u>lent</u> <u>me</u>

7. The sunglasses <u>which</u> <u>you</u> <u>are</u> <u>wearing</u> are nice.

8. I watched the movie <u>which</u> <u>you</u> <u>recommended</u>.

9. The hotel <u>which</u> <u>we</u> <u>stayed</u> <u>at</u> was in front of the beach.

10. Is this the book <u>which</u> <u>you</u> <u>are</u> <u>looking</u> <u>for</u>?

p.109

1. The restaurant which/that we visited was very busy.

2. I like the people who(m)/that I work with.

3. He finally talked to the girl who(m)/that he likes.

4. The story which/that he told me is true.

5. Eddie gets along with everyone who(m)/that he meets.

6. Who is the person who(m)/that you respect (the) most?

7. The shoes which/that I am wearing are very comfortable.

8. This is the wallet which/that I bought for my dad's birthday.

9. These are the cookies which/that my mom made for me.

10. I had lunch with the people who(m)/that I met in Italy.

11. The jacket which/that I bought does not fit me well.

12. Olaf is the snowman which/that Anna and Elsa made together.

LESSON 22 관계대명사 what vs. that

CHECK UP p.110

1. that **2.** What **3.** that
4. that **5.** what **6.** that
7. what **8.** what **9.** that
10. what

SENTENCE PRACTICE 1 p.111

WRITING POINT ❶

1. <u>What I want</u> is a break.

2. <u>What they need</u> is water and food.

3. <u>What he said</u> is not true.

4. Tell me <u>what you like</u>.

5. Tell me <u>what you know</u>.

6. Tell me <u>what you heard</u>.

7. This is not <u>what I expected</u>.

8. This is not <u>what we ordered</u>.

9. This is not <u>what he did</u>.

WRITING POINT ❷

1. I have a friend <u>that comes from</u> Japan.

2. He is a boy <u>that never gives up</u>.

3. She is the woman <u>that he loves</u>.

4. The food <u>that she cooked</u> was delicious.

5. The dress <u>that you are wearing</u> is pretty.

6. The TV <u>that we bought</u> is broken.

7. This is the house <u>that my uncle lives in</u>.

8. The party <u>that we went to</u> was fun.

SENTENCE PRACTICE 2 p.112

1. Her smile is <u>what</u> <u>makes</u> <u>me</u> happy.

2. <u>What</u> <u>I</u> <u>want</u> for Christmas is a new coat.

3. Jane showed me <u>what</u> <u>she</u> <u>bought</u> at the mall.

4. I can't believe <u>what</u> <u>I</u> <u>heard</u> from Sarah.

5. Minho reviewed <u>what</u> <u>he</u> <u>learned</u> in class.

6. I have some friends <u>that</u> <u>I</u> <u>meet</u> regularly.

7. I met a man <u>that</u> <u>can</u> <u>speak</u> five languages.

8. This is the house <u>that</u> <u>my</u> <u>family</u> lived in.

9. I have to return the book <u>that</u> <u>I</u> <u>borrowed</u> from the library.

10. I like movies <u>that</u> <u>have</u> <u>happy</u> endings.

TRY WRITING p.113

1. This jacket is what I want to buy.

2. The children that live upstairs are noisy.

3. Do you believe what he told you?

4. This salad is what my sister ordered.

5. What I want for my birthday is a new computer.

6. These are pictures that I took in London.

7. The man that robbed the bank ran away.

8. Tell me what you know about him.

9. The TV that we bought does not[doesn't] work well.

10. She is a girl that I went to school with.

11. I do not[don't] understand what the teacher is saying.

12. The Eiffel Tower is the place that I want to visit in Paris.

p.114

I. (1) who (2) which (3) whom

2. (1) a person who/that drives a bus

  (2) an animal which/that has a long neck

3. (1) The boy who is wearing shorts is Nick.

  (2) I found the backpack which I lost yesterday.

4. that

5. (1) The boy who is riding a bike is Bill.

  (3) There are many buses which go downtown.

  (5) The computer which I bought was cheap.

6. what I want to buy

7. Susan showed me what was in her bag.

UNIT 10

LESSON 23 시간, 조건의 접속사

CHECK UP

p.116

I. before   **2.** as soon as   **3.** when

4. after   **5.** until   **6.** while

7. unless   **8.** if   **9.** visit

10. don't

SENTENCE PRACTICE 1

p.117

WRITING POINT ❶

I. Turn off the lights <u>before</u> you go out.

2. He went to bed <u>after</u> he took a shower.

3. Please keep quiet <u>until</u> the movie ends.

4. He fell asleep <u>while</u> he was watching TV.

5. Let's wait here <u>until</u> she comes.

6. We will leave <u>as soon as</u> the sun rises.

7. <u>When</u> it's sunny, I go for a walk.

8. He got up <u>as soon as</u> the alarm clock rang.

9. Always be careful <u>while</u> you are driving.

WRITING POINT ❷

I. We will be late <u>unless</u> we hurry.

2. You may leave early <u>if</u> you want to.

3. You cannot enter <u>unless</u> you have a ticket.

4. <u>If</u> you don't mind, I'll sit here.

5. <u>Unless</u> it rains, I will go out.

6. <u>If</u> I have time, I will help you.

7. I will go jogging <u>unless</u> it is cold.

8. Press this button <u>if</u> you need help.

SENTENCE PRACTICE 2

p.118

I. Bill and Jane went for a walk <u>after</u> <u>they</u> <u>had</u> <u>dinner</u>.

2. We have to do something <u>before</u> <u>it</u> <u>is</u> <u>too</u> <u>late</u>.

3. He could read and write <u>when</u> <u>he</u> <u>was</u> <u>four</u>.

4. <u>While</u> <u>he</u> <u>was</u> <u>cooking</u> pasta, I prepared the salad.

5. We had to wait <u>until</u> <u>he</u> <u>came</u>.

6. He bought a new car <u>as</u> <u>soon</u> <u>as</u> he got his driver's license.

7. <u>If</u> <u>you</u> <u>have</u> <u>any</u> <u>questions</u>, please raise your hand.

8. Just let me know <u>if</u> <u>you</u> <u>need</u> <u>help</u>.

9. I won't forgive him <u>unless</u> <u>he</u> <u>apologizes</u> to me.

10. You cannot graduate from school <u>unless</u> <u>you</u> <u>pass</u> the exam.

TRY WRITING

p.119

I. They bought some popcorn before the movie started.

2. After he has/eats breakfast, he usually walks his dog.

3. If the train is on time, we will arrive at 8:00.

4. Unless you help me, I cannot[can't] do it.

5. When he heard the news, his face turned pale.

6. I will clean the house while you wash the dishes.

7. The children played in the swimming pool until it got dark.

8. If I finish work early, I will pick you up.

9. You cannot[can't] travel abroad unless you have a passport.

10. As soon as he finished school, he got a job.

11. If I go to New York, I will visit the Statue of Liberty.

12. Unless you take an umbrella, you will get wet.

LESSON 24 이유, 결과, 양보의 접속사

CHECK UP p.120

1. I didn't like the concert because the band didn't play well.

2. The suitcase was so heavy that I couldn't carry it by myself.

3. Although the ring was expensive, he bought it for his girlfriend.

4. You'd better take an umbrella because it is going to rain.

5. The cat is so fat that it can't walk easily.

6. The class was not canceled although there were not enough students.

SENTENCE PRACTICE 1 p.121

WRITING POINT ❶

1. Jane doesn't eat meat because she is a vegetarian.

2. Tom didn't go to school because he had a bad cold.

3. He had to move to Seoul because of his job.

4. Because of the heavy snow the school was closed.

5. Because we missed the last bus, we took a taxi.

WRITING POINT ❷

1. He is so smart that he can solve any problems.

2. This pizza is so delicious that I can't stop eating it.

3. The movie was so boring that we left early.

4. The weather was so cold that we canceled the trip.

5. This island is so beautiful that I don't want to leave.

WRITING POINT ❸

1. I am sleepy although it's only seven o'clock.

2. We arrived on time although the bus was late.

3. He finished the work although he was very tired.

4. She got a good grade although she didn't study hard.

5. Although the team played well, they could not win the game.

SENTENCE PRACTICE 2 p.122

1. <u>Because</u> <u>the</u> <u>food</u> <u>was</u> <u>salty</u>, I drank a lot of water.

2. All the flights were canceled <u>because</u> <u>of</u> <u>the</u> <u>storm</u>.

3. He had to take the bus <u>because</u> <u>his</u> <u>car</u> <u>broke</u> <u>down</u>.

4. The teacher got angry <u>because</u> <u>of</u> <u>his</u> <u>rude</u> <u>behavior</u>.

5. It was <u>so</u> <u>hot</u> <u>that</u> <u>I</u> <u>couldn't</u> do anything.

6. The test was <u>so</u> <u>difficult</u> <u>that</u> <u>Tom</u> <u>didn't</u> do well.

7. I was <u>so</u> <u>hungry</u> <u>that</u> <u>I</u> <u>ate</u> two bowls of rice.

8. <u>Although/Though</u> <u>the</u> <u>weather</u> <u>was</u> <u>bad</u> , we had a good time.

9. <u>Although/Though</u> <u>he</u> <u>lived</u> in France for a year, he cannot speak French.

10. <u>Although/Though</u> <u>my</u> <u>grandmother</u> <u>is</u> <u>very</u> <u>old</u>, she is still active.

TRY WRITING p.123

1. Because it was warm and sunny, we went to the beach.

2. I couldn't study because of my headache.

3. The bag was so expensive that I couldn't buy it.

4. The bus was so crowded that I couldn't get a seat.

5. Although/Though they were busy, they helped us.

6. Because they loved each other, they promised to get married.

7. I got up so late that I missed the school bus.

8. Although/Though learning English is hard, I enjoy it.

9. He cannot[can't] read without glasses because of his poor eyesight.

10. I was so nervous that I couldn't say a word.

11. She hates flying because she is afraid of heights.

12. Sally ate cheesecake for dessert although/though she was on a diet.

LESSON **25** 상관접속사

CHECK UP

p.124

1. and
2. but also
3. or
4. not only
5. Both
6. either
7. enjoy
8. were
9. is
10. or

SENTENCE PRACTICE 1

p.125

WRITING POINT ❶

1. I like <u>both chicken and beef</u>.
2. We need <u>both time and money</u>.
3. He can <u>both read and write</u>.
4. <u>Both Judy and Sally</u> are my classmates.
5. <u>Both Seoul and London</u> are capital cities.

WRITING POINT ❷

1. I was <u>not only tired but also sleepy</u>.
2. He is <u>not only rich but also famous</u>.
3. He plays <u>not only tennis but also golf</u>.
4. <u>Not only he but also his family</u> live here.
5. <u>Not only she but also I</u> have homework.

WRITING POINT ❸

1. You can have <u>either tea or coffee</u>.
2. I will <u>either watch TV or listen to music</u>.
3. She comes from <u>either China or Japan</u>.
4. <u>Either David or I</u> will go with you.
5. <u>Either you or your friend</u> is wrong.

SENTENCE PRACTICE 2

p.126

1. We went to <u>both</u> <u>New York</u> <u>and</u> <u>Boston</u>.
2. She <u>bought</u> <u>both</u> <u>fish</u> <u>and</u> <u>meat</u>.
3. <u>Both</u> my parents <u>and</u> I <u>were</u> satisfied with the test result.

4. I invited <u>both</u> <u>Jane</u> <u>and</u> <u>Mike</u> to dinner.
5. The food is <u>not only</u> delicious <u>but</u> <u>also</u> <u>healthy</u>.
6. She <u>not</u> <u>only</u> sings well <u>but</u> <u>also</u> <u>dances</u> perfectly.
7. <u>Not</u> <u>only</u> my sister <u>but</u> <u>also</u> my cousins live in Busan.
8. You can choose <u>either</u> <u>rice</u> <u>or</u> <u>pasta</u>.
9. You can <u>either</u> <u>ask</u> him <u>or</u> <u>search</u> on the Internet.
10. He is usually <u>either</u> <u>at</u> <u>home</u> <u>or</u> <u>at</u> <u>school</u>.

TRY WRITING ✔

p.127

1. She ordered both pizza and spaghetti.
2. I liked both the book and the movie.
3. He enjoys not only fishing but also skiing.
4. We can meet either on Monday or on Tuesday.
5. Both Venice and Rome are beautiful cities.
6. You can either call me or send me an email.
7. Both the cafeteria and the cafe were full of people.
8. I will have either a sandwich or a bagel for breakfast.
9. She plays not only the piano but also the violin.
10. Not only my teacher but also my friends were worried about me.
11. Either John or I am going to help you tomorrow.
12. After the race, I was not only thirsty but also hungry.

미리 보는 서술형 SCHOOL TEST

p.128

1. (1) when   (2) While   (3) until
   (4) After
2. as soon as
3. (1) rains tomorrow, I will not go out
   (2) run, you will be late
4. because of
5. I was so sick that I couldn't go to school.
6. the man was poor, he was happy
7. (1) not only / but also
   (2) either / or
   (3) Both / and

UNIT 11

LESSON 26 간접의문문

p.130

CHECK UP

1. do they leave 2. she is 3. Tiffany is
4. is that girl 5. you like 6. the scarf is
7. Will they 8. I should 9. he called
10. did you have

SENTENCE PRACTICE 1

p.131

WRITING POINT ❶

1. Do you know who he is?
2. I don't know where they are going.
3. Do you know how he goes to work?
4. I don't know when they left.
5. Can I ask what the teacher said?

WRITING POINT ❷

1. I'm not sure whether/if the answer is correct.
2. I wonder whether/if she has a pet.
3. I don't know whether/if he took an umbrella.
4. Do you know whether/if she can speak Korean?
6. I wonder whether/if it will rain tomorrow.

WRITING POINT ❸

1. I don't know who wrote this book.
2. I asked him who cooked dinner.
3. I wonder what happened to James.
4. Can you tell me what makes you happy?

SENTENCE PRACTICE 2

p.132

1. Do you know when the movie starts?
2. Do you know what he does after school?
3. Can I ask who your best friend is?
4. I wonder how he solved the problem.
5. I'm not sure whether/if I can do it.
6. Let's ask him whether/if this bus goes downtown.
7. I wonder whether/if it is true.
8. Please tell me who broke my glasses.
9. Do you know what is in the box?
10. I wonder what changed your mind.

TRY WRITING ✓

p.133

1. Do you know what time it is?
2. I wonder where she bought the jacket.
3. Do you know who that girl is?
4. Can you tell me why you were late this morning?
5. Do you know how many people there were at the party?
6. Do you know where I can find this book?
7. I wonder who won the Nobel Peace Prize this year.
8. Can you tell me what happened to Mike?
9. Do you know what made her angry?
10. I am not sure whether/if he will pass the exam.
11. I will ask him whether/if the dinner is ready.
12. I don't know whether/if I can finish the work today.

LESSON 27 It ~ that 강조구문

CHECK UP

p.134

1. It was my sister that took the picture.
2. It is Barack Obama that she wants to meet.
3. It is pizza that James wants for lunch.
4. It was a year ago today that we met for the first time.
5. It is in front of the theater that we are going to meet.

SENTENCE PRACTICE 1

WRITING POINT ❶

p.135

1. It was Jake that gave me advice.
2. It was my sister that lent me some money.
3. It was my mom that made this cake.
4. It is Mr. Kim that teaches us math.
5. It is Nancy that is dancing on the stage.

WRITING POINT ❷

1. It was Italy that he visited last summer.
2. It was this sweater that I bought yesterday.
3. It was baseball that we played after school.
4. It is English that Minho studies every day.
5. It is her glasses that Jessica is looking for.

WRITING POINT ③

1. It is <u>at a bookstore that she works</u>.
2. It was <u>on the bus that he left his bag</u>.
3. It was <u>yesterday that they arrived here.</u>
4. It is <u>in July that the festival is held</u>.

SENTENCE PRACTICE 2
p.136

1. It <u>was</u> <u>Rick</u> <u>that</u> invited me to the party.
2. It <u>was</u> <u>my</u> <u>brother</u> <u>that</u> helped me with my homework.
3. It <u>was</u> <u>my</u> <u>neighbor</u> <u>that</u> took care of my cat.
4. It <u>is</u> <u>a puppy</u> <u>that</u> I want for my birthday.
5. It <u>was</u> <u>a gold</u> <u>medal</u> <u>that</u> he won at the Olympics.
6. It <u>was</u> <u>Hamlet</u> <u>that</u> he played in the movie.
7. It <u>is</u> <u>reading</u> <u>comic</u> <u>books</u> <u>that</u> I enjoy in my free time.
8. It <u>was</u> <u>on</u> <u>Monday</u> <u>that</u> I sent him an email.
9. It <u>was</u> <u>by</u> <u>accident</u> <u>that</u> he invented the microwave.
10. It <u>was</u> <u>at</u> <u>the</u> <u>airport</u> <u>that</u> she lost her passport.

TRY WRITING
p.137

1. It was her boyfriend that gave her flowers.
2. It was some fruit that she bought at the supermarket.
3. It was in my bag that I found my watch.
4. It was my mom that received the package this morning.
5. It was a laptop that I borrowed from my friend.
6. It was in 1950 that the Korean War broke out.
7. It was at this restaurant that I met Sally yesterday.
8. It was my friend and I that played basketball in the park yesterday.
9. It was Bill that she fell in love with.
10. It is every Wednesday that she takes piano lessons.
11. It was last night that I had a car accident.
12. It was a rabbit that the magician pulled out of the hat.

SCHOOL TEST
p.138

1. (1) who she is
   (2) when they left
   (3) what she likes to do
2. what your name is
3. whether/if she likes spicy food
4. Do you know what Tom bought for her?
5. (1) is it → it is
   (2) did I meet → I met
   (3) that → whether/if
6. was my camera that I left
7. (1) was Kevin that broke the window yesterday
   (2) is a chocolate cake that Sarah is making

WORKBOOK

LESSON 01 현재완료의 완료, 경험

p.003

1. I have just arrived at the station.
2. I haven't read the book yet.
3. I have met him before.
4. He has visited New York once.
5. He has never been late for school.
6. Have you ever been to Europe?
7. We haven't decided what to eat.
8. Susan hasn't received the package yet.
9. I have never ridden a horse before.
10. He has traveled abroad many times.
11. Have you ever read a story about Cinderella?
12. He has already finished fixing my computer.
13. Mary has never gone skiing before.
14. Have you ever met a famous movie star?
15. It hasn't snowed yet this winter.

LESSON 02 현재완료의 계속, 결과

p.005

1. He has taught English for 10 years.
2. They have known each other since 2014.
3. He has worn glasses since he was young.
4. I have lost my watch.
5. The train has left the station.
6. The book has changed my life.
7. The house has been empty for three months.
8. How long have you lived in this apartment?
9. My friend has left for Germany.
10. You have grown up!
11. He has worked as a vet for 5 years.
12. We have been best friends since then.
13. How long have you studied English?
14. They haven't eaten anything since this morning.
15. He has lost a lot of weight.

LESSON 03 동사＋목적어＋형용사/명사

p.007

1. The news made us sad.
2. This coat will keep you warm.
3. They left the girl alone.
4. I found the book interesting.
5. People call him a hero.
6. You should keep this a secret.
7. Who left the door open?
8. Drinking too much coffee will keep you awake at night.
9. I found it a useful tool.
10. The couple named their daughter Eva.
11. Her effort made her a great pianist.
12. You should keep the box safe.
13. The TV show made him a star.
14. She found the work very boring.
15. What made her so upset?

LESSON 04 동사＋목적어＋to부정사

p.009

1. I want you to come to the party.
2. Do you want me to cook dinner?
3. Mr. Kim told us to sit down.
4. I asked him to open the window.
5. I helped my father wash his car.
6. I asked him to turn down the music.
7. He told me to get off at the next stop.
8. I want my grandmother to be healthy.
9. We expect your dream to come true.
10. What did the teacher advise you to do?
11. This app helps me learn English.
12. Doing yoga can help you relax.
13. The doctor advised me to exercise regularly.
14. Can you help me move this table?
15. The boy is helping the old man cross the street.

LESSON 05 지각동사, 사역동사

p.010

1. I saw a boy dance/dancing on the stage.
2. I heard them talk/talking on the phone.

3. I felt someone follow/following me.

4. I can smell the rice cook/cooking in the kitchen.

5. My dad made me finish my homework.

6. I had him book a hotel.

7. She let me borrow the book.

8. I heard him call/calling my name.

9. She felt someone touch/touching her shoulder.

10. Can you smell something burn/burning?

11. Her boyfriend tried to make her laugh.

12. Listening to music makes me feel good.

13. Our teacher makes us read two books a month.

14. I saw her wait/waiting for a bus at the bus stop.

15. My sister doesn't let me wear her clothes.

LESSON 06 추측을 나타내는 조동사

p.013

1. My parents may go out this evening.

2. Your cell phone may be in the car.

3. It may not rain this weekend.

4. There may be life on Mars.

5. She must like you.

6. The rumor cannot be true.

7. We may go to Thailand this summer.

8. He cannot be a doctor.

9. They must be very tired.

10. You may not like this movie.

11. Your parents must be proud of you.

12. It may snow this Christmas.

13. The man over there must be James.

14. This must be a mistake.

15. There may be a way to solve the problem.

LESSON 07 의무, 필요를 나타내는 조동사

p.015

1. You must fill out this form first.

2. Visitors must not feed the animals in the zoo.

3. I have to take my dog to the vet.

4. Jane has to take care of her little brother.

5. We had to wait for him for 30 minutes.

6. Do they have to work on Saturday?

7. Tom doesn't have to wear a suit to work.

8. We must follow the traffic rules.

9. We must not miss the train.

10. Students must not cheat on a test.

11. You must wear a swimming cap in the pool.

12. How long do I have to wait?

13. You don't have to memorize everything.

14. I have to return this book to the library.

15. You must not bully your classmates.

LESSON 08 조언, 권고를 나타내는 조동사

p.017

1. You should be more careful.

2. You should not forget Jane's birthday.

3. Should I take off my shoes?

4. You had better go home and stay in bed.

5. You had better not touch the wire.

6. I think we had better cancel the trip.

7. She had better take his advice.

8. We should help people in need.

9. She should not spend too much money on clothes.

10. Should I ask him for help?

11. What time should I pick you up?

12. What should I do to improve my English?

13. He had better not be late again.

14. We had better clear the snow before it freezes.

15. People should be responsible for their pets.

LESSON 09 수동태의 시제

p.019

1. The movie is loved by children.

2. Spanish is spoken in Mexico.

3. The poem was written by my friend.

4. These pictures were taken by Tom.

5. The festival will be held next month.

6. The palace is visited by many tourists.

7. Mr. Robin is respected by his students.

8. The children are helped by volunteers.

9. My bike was stolen by someone.

10. A new library will be built by the company.

11. Frank was praised by his teacher.

12. The thief was caught by a young man.

13. In case of rain, the concert will be canceled.

14. Tea and coffee will be served after the meal.

15. The museum was designed by a famous architect.

p.021

LESSON 10 주의해야 할 수동태

1. Are the books used in class?

2. The letters were not written by James.

3. The mountain is covered with snow.

4. He was satisfied with the test result.

5. The island is known for its beautiful scenery.

6. The door is not locked.

7. The flowers were not planted by me.

8. They were disappointed with/at the news.

9. Carol is interested in European history.

10. People are worried about the global warming.

11. The office is not cleaned every day.

12. The bridge is made of steel.

13. The department store was crowded with shoppers.

14. I am tired of my job.

15. Was he helped by you?

LESSON 11 to부정사의 명사적, 형용사적 용법

p.023

1. It is dangerous to swim in the river.

2. He wants to buy a new computer.

3. They tried to finish the work by six.

4. He bought some water to drink.

5. You'll need something warm to wear.

6. It is important to make good friends.

7. It is necessary to wear a helmet for your safety.

8. His secret to happiness is to help others.

9. His goal is to win a gold medal at the Olympics.

10. My mom promised to buy me a new bike.

11. What is the best way to learn a foreign language?

12. He bought a house to live in with his family.

13. Can you recommend a book to read?

14. Philip plans to go to Europe this summer.

15. I have three things to do today.

LESSON 12 to부정사의 부사적 용법

p.025

1. He turned on the TV to watch the news.

2. We were disappointed to lose the game.

3. He must be brave to do so.

4. He must be tired to sleep until now.

5. He woke up to find himself famous.

6. We did our best only to fail.

7. Eric went to the library to check out some books.

8. I am happy to have a friend like you.

9. They must be hungry to eat so much.

10. Cathy went to Paris to study fashion design.

11. My grandparents lived to be 90 years old.

12. Steve practiced the drums to take part in the festival.

13. The boy grew up to be a great musician.

14. George was happy to see his family again.

15. He must be diligent to be on time every day.

LESSON 13 to부정사 주요 구문

p.027

1. I am too tired to study.

2. She was too sick to go to school.

3. He is strong enough to lift the rock.

4. I don't know what to wear.

5. Let's decide where to meet tomorrow.

6. The hamburger is too thick to bite.

7. It is too cold to go swimming.

8. He is tall enough to reach the top shelf.

9. My mom taught me how to make pasta.

10. I asked him where to put my coat.

11. Jack is smart enough to solve the difficult math problem.

12. The weather was good enough to go on a picnic.

13. She is beautiful enough to play Juliet in the movie.

14. He is too weak to run a marathon.

15. I don't know what to buy for her birthday.

LESSON 14 동명사 vs. to부정사

p.029

1. Do you want to go for a walk?

2. I finished cleaning my room.

3. The book is worth reading.

4. Sam is good at playing the guitar.

5. I'm looking forward to hearing from you.

6. I enjoy making people laugh.

7. I hope to keep in touch with you.

8. What do you plan to do after graduation?

9. I don't feel like going out tonight.

10. We had difficulty/trouble finding the store.

11. The tourists were busy taking pictures.

12. They decided to help the homeless.

13. How/What about playing computer games together?

14. I don't mind living in the countryside.

15. She avoided answering my question.

LESSON 15 현재분사, 과거분사

p.031

1. She has a car made in Japan.

2. The man taking a picture is Peter.

3. It was a tiring day.

4. There are some children swimming in the pool.

5. Look at the garden covered with snow.

6. He has a talking robot named Tiki.

7. This book has many touching stories.

8. The stadium is filled with excited soccer fans.

9. The woman is holding a crying baby.

10. This math problem is so confusing.

11. He found his stolen wallet.

12. This is the song written by my favorite singer.

13. There are many foreigners learning Korean.

14. Living in the country can be boring.

15. The man injured in the accident is Mr. Brown.

LESSON 16 명사의 수량 표현

p.033

1. He drinks two cups of coffee a day.

2. She ordered a bowl of soup.

3. There are a few books on the bookshelf.

4. He had little money in his pocket.

5. I need two slices of cheese.

6. He had two pieces/slices of pizza for lunch.

7. We spent a few days on the island.

8. Susan invited a few friends to her house.

9. She put a little salt in her soup.

10. I have been there a few times.

11. Unfortunately, we took few pictures in Venice.

12. We have little time now.

13. I have a little homework to do today.

14. There are three loaves of bread in the basket.

15. He made few mistakes on the test.

LESSON 17 재귀대명사

p.035

1. I cut myself with a knife.

2. She drew a picture of herself.

3. Please make yourself at home.

4. I can't move this box by myself.

5. The door closed of itself.

6. They enjoyed themselves at the festival.

7. This is between ourselves.

8. Let me introduce myself to you.

9. We blamed ourselves for the mistake.

10. She taught herself Chinese.

11. She took a picture of herself.

12. The boy fell down and hurt himself.

13. Why are you talking to yourself?

14. They solved the problem by themselves.

15. She is looking at herself in the mirror.

p.037

1. Aron is as tall as his brother.
2. Mexico is hotter than Canada.
3. Fruit is healthier than chocolate.
4. Janet is more popular than Daniel.
5. His car is more expensive than mine.
6. The more you smile, the better you look.
7. The less I see him, the more I miss him.
8. The longer I waited, the angrier I got.
9. His shoes are as big as his father's.
10. I don't exercise as much as Peter.
11. The harder you study, the more you will learn.
12. The more fast food you eat, the fatter you will get.
13. The sunnier it is, the happier I feel.
14. Today's weather is much worse than yesterday's.
15. I think that history is more interesting than math.

p.039

1. August is the hottest month of the year.
2. Fall is the best season for reading.
3. The Nile is longer than any other river.
4. No other girl is prettier than Julie.
5. Laughter is the best medicine.
6. He is the most boring person I know.
7. What is the most precious thing in your life?
8. Winter is colder than any other season.
9. The church is older than any other building in the town.
10. Mt. Everest is higher than any other mountain in the world.
11. No other sport is more popular than soccer.
12. No other animal is as faithful as the dog.
13. No one is stronger than Mark.
14. It was the happiest day of my life.
15. It was the worst earthquake in history.

p.041

1. I have a friend who/that lives in Canada.
2. The boy who/that is wearing glasses is Bill.
3. The man who/that helped me was very kind.
4. He works in a shop which/that sells clothes.
5. Is there a bus which/that goes downtown?
6. Where is the book which/that was on the desk?
7. A fire fighter is a person who/that puts out fire.
8. The man who/that called me yesterday was my brother.
9. This is a question which/that is difficult to answer.
10. A donkey is an animal which/that looks like a small horse.
11. The room has a window which/that overlooks a lake.
12. Mr. Smith runs a restaurant which/that serves Greek food.
13. Look at the bird which/that is sitting on the tree.
14. The boy who/that won the race was happy.
15. The dog which/that bit me was my neighbor's dog.

p.043

1. The man who(m)/that I saw was Henry.
2. Daniel is a friend who(m)/that I can trust.
3. The girl who(m)/that I danced with was Ann.
4. The table which/that I bought is very big.
5. The pizza which/that we ate was delicious.
6. Jill is wearing a hat which/that I like.
7. Is this the ring which/that Rick gave you?
8. The woman who(m)/that he is talking to is his sister.
9. I have a friend who(m)/that I want to introduce to you.
10. I watched the movie which/that you recommended.
11. Is this the book which/that you are looking for?
12. The restaurant which/that we visited was very busy.

13. The story which/that he told me is true.

14. Who is the person who(m)/that you respect the most?

15. This is the wallet which/that I bought for my dad's birthday.

LESSON 22 관계대명사 what vs. that

p.045

1. What they need is water and food.

2. Tell me what you like.

3. This is not what I expected.

4. He is a boy that never gives up.

5. The food that she cooked was delicious.

6. This is the house that my uncle lives in.

7. Her smile is what makes me happy.

8. What I want for Christmas is a new coat.

9. Minho reviewed what he learned in class.

10. I met a man that can speak five languages.

11. I have to return the book that I borrowed from the library.

12. This jacket is what I want to buy.

13. This salad is what my sister ordered.

14. The man that robbed the bank ran away.

15. I don't understand what the teacher is saying.

LESSON 23 시간, 조건의 접속사

p.047

1. Turn off the lights before you go out.

2. He went to bed after he took a shower.

3. We will leave as soon as the sun rises.

4. Always be careful while you are driving.

5. Unless it rains, I will go out.

6. Bill and Jane went for a walk after they had dinner.

7. We have to do something before it is too late.

8. He could read and write when he was four.

9. While he was cooking pasta, I prepared the salad.

10. We had to wait until he came.

11. He bought a new car as soon as he got his driver's license.

12. If you have any questions, please raise your hand.

13. Unless you help me, I cannot[can't] do it.

14. If I finish work early, I'll pick you up.

15. The children played in the swimming pool until it got dark.

LESSON 24 이유, 결과, 양보의 접속사

p.049

1. Because the food was salty, I drank a lot of water.

2. All the flights were canceled because of the storm.

3. He had to take the bus because his car broke down.

4. The teacher got angry because of his rude behavior.

5. It was so hot that I couldn't do anything.

6. I was so hungry that I ate two bowls of rice.

7. Although/Though he lived in France for a year, he cannot speak French.

8. Although/Though my grandmother is very old, she is still active.

9. Because it was warm and sunny, we went to the beach.

10. I couldn't study because of my headache.

11. The bag was so expensive that I couldn't buy it.

12. Although/Though they were busy, they helped us.

13. I got up so late that I missed the school bus.

14. I was so nervous that I couldn't say a word.

15. She hates flying because she is afraid of heights.

LESSON 25 상관접속사

p.051

1. Both Judy and Sally are my classmates.

2. Both Seoul and London are capital cities.

3. He is not only rich but also famous.

4. Not only he but also his family live here.

5. I will either watch TV or listen to music.

6. Either you or your friend is wrong.

7. She bought both fish and meat.

---

8. Both my parents and I were satisfied with the test result.

9. I invited both Jane and Mike to dinner.

10. The food is not only delicious but also healthy.

11. She not only sings well but also dances perfectly.

12. You can either ask him or search on the Internet.

13. We can meet either on Monday or on Tuesday.

14. She plays not only the piano but also the violin.

15. After the race, I was not only thirsty but also hungry.

LESSON 26 간접의문문

p.053

1. Do you know when the movie starts?

2. Do you know what he does after school?

3. Can I ask who your best friend is?

4. I wonder how he solved the problem.

5. Let's ask him whether/if this bus goes downtown.

6. I wonder whether/if it is true.

7. Do you know what is in the box?

8. I wonder what changed your mind.

9. Do you know what time it is?

10. I wonder where she bought the jacket.

11. Do you know who that girl is?

12. Do you know how many people there were at the party?

13. Can you tell me what happened to Mike?

14. I will ask him whether/if the dinner is ready.

15. I don't know whether/if I can finish the work today.

LESSON 27 It ~ that 강조구문

p.055

1. It was Rick that invited me to the party.

2. It was my brother that helped me with my homework.

3. It is a puppy that I want for my birthday.

4. It was a gold medal that he won at the Olympics.

5. It is reading comic books that I enjoy in my free time.

6. It was on Monday that I sent him an email.

7. It was at the airport that she lost her passport.

8. It was her boyfriend that gave her flowers.

9. It was some fruit that she bought at the supermarket.

10. It was in my bag that I found my watch.

11. It was a laptop that I borrowed from my friend.

12. It was in 1950 that the Korean War broke out.

13. It was my friend and I that played soccer in the park yesterday.

14. It was last night that I had a car accident.

15. It was a rabbit that the magician pulled out of the hat.